The Intellectual Hero

ALSO BY VICTOR BROMBERT

The Criticism of T. S. Eliot

Stendhal et la Voie Oblique

The Intellectual Hero

STUDIES IN THE FRENCH NOVEL

1880-1955

BY *Victor Brombert*

J. B. LIPPINCOTT COMPANY · *Philadelphia & New York*

To Beth

To Lise and Raymond Giraud

Foreword

A quick glance at the table of contents will show the reader that this book, though covering a span of over fifty years, is not a "survey." Convinced that trends, issues and problems are far too complex for one individual to expose completely, I preferred to concentrate on a number of key works, and attempted to strike a balance between the critical and the historical methods. Close analyses of given novels thus alternate with chapters that raise larger issues and present broader panoramas. The emergence of a new type of hero is the subject of my book. Its purpose is to define an intellectual climate and cast light on literary trends that are of specific relevance to our times. But although I have tried to situate the intellectual hero in a broad context, I have remained concerned, in each case, with the unique literary quality of the works discussed.

A Guggenheim fellowship, which was granted me in 1954-1955, enabled me to begin work on this book. Chapter 2 appeared in *Partisan Review* in Summer, 1960; chapter 9 and Appendix B appeared in *Yale French Studies*, Winter, 1957, and Spring, 1960. For permission to reprint in a revised form I wish to thank the respective editors.

To Henri Peyre I am most heavily indebted. He has encouraged and inspired me. To him goes my gratitude, my admiration, my deep affection.

Special thanks are due to Kenneth Douglas for his painstaking and generous help. His incisive comments have been extremely useful to me. The extent of my debt he can easily recognize in these pages. I also wish to thank Edwin Stein, Jr., for reading my manuscript and for making a number of very helpful suggestions.

To Stewart Richardson, of Lippincott, I would like to express my gratitude for his generous interest in this book and for all the cordial encouragement and help he has given me. To him, Corlies M. Smith and Catharine Carver, my grateful thanks for their devoted editorial assistance.

And above all, my thanks to B.A.B. for whom and with whom this book was written.

V.B.

Yale University
March, 1961

NOTE: My analysis of all texts has been based upon a reading of the originals. Translations are my own. I have, however, consulted with profit Stuart Gilbert's translation of *Jean Barois* and Samuel Putnam's translation of *Le Sang noir*

Contents

[10]   The Intellectual Hero

1

Introduction

> *I must confess that ideas interest me more*
> *than men. . . .*
>
> —Edouard in *Les Faux-Monnayeurs*

¶ 1. *Bearings*

"IT IS ALWAYS DANGEROUS to present intellectuals in the novel," warns a character in Gide's *Les Faux-Monnayeurs*. "They bore the reader to death." Few warnings have gone more unheeded. The twentieth-century novel in France has been literally invaded by intellectuals. Never before in fiction has the experience of living been so unremittingly filtered through the *minds* of the protagonists. Never before has it been assessed, rejected, distorted, shouldered or evaded with such professional competence. The proliferation of intellectual heroes is, moreover, symptomatic of a general invasion of all branches of literature by scholars, teachers and professional philosophers. A "literature of *agrégés*" has already become a consecrated expression.[1]

Particularly since the thirties, French literature has been dominated by the figure of the intellectual. The works of Malraux and of the Existentialist writers provide a striking illustration: Gisors, Kyo and Ch'en in *La Condition humaine;* Scali, Alvear and Magnin in *L'Espoir;* Roquentin, the historian, in *La Nausée;* Mathieu Delarue, the professor of philosophy, in *Les Chemins de la liberté;* Perron and Dubreuilh in *Les Mandarins*. Even the minor characters who surround them are "mandarins" of a kind, literati or semi-literati: the Autodidact, Brunet, Boris, Scriassine. Those who are not professional

---

[1] Lovers of statistics will be interested by René-Marill Albérès' assertion ("Romanciers italiens," *La Table Ronde*, September, 1957, pp. 9-24) that 85 per cent of the protagonists in today's French novel have at least their *baccalauréat*.

teachers, philosophers or journalists still conform to a recognizable pattern. Like Blomart, in Simone de Beauvoir's *Le Sang des autres*, they are often typical young *"intellectuels bourgeois,"* ashamed of their social and cultural heredity.

The Existentialist "world," as represented by Sartre and Simone de Beauvoir, seems indeed to be the natural habitat of the intellectual hero. But clearly he did not spring fully grown from their pens. His existence implies a literary tradition, a process of growth and evolution. The figure of the intellectual is, in fact, a characteristically French phenomenon. For side by side with the impetuous artist-heroes and the introspective, highly cerebral young men who tirelessly analyze themselves in the pages of the *roman de l'individu*, there also emerge, in the wake of Balzac's *Etudes philosophiques*, the disturbing figures of the suffering genius, the visionary philosopher, the professional scholar, the dedicated teacher and his "disciple," the dispossessed and uprooted thinker, the revolutionary nihilist and the scholarly dilettante.

Anglo-Saxon readers are at times disconcerted by the importance the intellectual hero and his problems have assumed in current French fiction. "We British don't take our intellectuals so seriously," D. W. Brogan once quipped. More sarcastically, W. H. Auden suggested, in a recent discussion of the work of Sainte-Beuve, that the political opinions and behavior of intellectuals "are seldom to be taken seriously." [2] American attitudes tend to be even more outspoken. The notion of "mandarins" is often met with irritation or downright hostility. "They are the bruised and ineffectual souls who hang around the fringes of the little magazines, the universities, the remnants of Greenwich Village, Big Sur, Rockland County and Cape Cod. They would like to stand aside from American life. . . ." [3] The American novel, on the whole, reflects this deep-rooted suspi-

[2] "Talent, Genius and Unhappiness," *The New Yorker*, November 30, 1957, pp. 221-237.
[3] John Fischer, "Intellectual with a Gun," *Harper's Magazine*, February, 1956, pp. 10-18. The article is an answer to an essay by the French Dominican R. L. Bruckberger, published in the same issue of *Harper's* ("An Assignment for Intellectuals," pp. 68-72), which calls upon the American intelligentsia to live up to a vocation of militant social criticism and universal responsibility. For a more violent attack on the intellectual, see Louis Bromfield ("The Triumph of the Egghead," *The Freeman*, December 1, 1952, pp. 155-158). According to Bromfield, the intellectual is a "self-conscious prig," "an anemic bleeding heart," thoroughly pretentious and un-American.

cion. It would indeed be difficult to find, in the main stream of American letters, many novels which center around the figure of an intellectual. "The intellectual is the only character missing in the American novel," peremptorily affirms Philip Rahv in *Image and Idea* (1949). American writers, according to Rahv, have been so taken with the cult of Experience, so indifferent to the problematical and the speculative, that everything can be found in the American novel except ideas. Irving Howe, in *Politics and the Novel* (1957), also complains of a notion supposedly shared by many American novelists that "abstract ideas invariably contaminate a work of art and should be kept at a safe distance from it." [4]

Criticisms such as these may well betray an unwarranted humility on the part of self-conscious admirers of the European tradition. But they also shed light on the resistance and basic lack of understanding with which writers such as Sartre and Simone de Beauvoir have met in this country. Even a Malraux or a Roger Martin du Gard—at least the Martin du Gard of *Jean Barois*—have rarely *moved* the American reader, who remains recalcitrant to ideological and philosophical themes in fiction, even when the novelist succeeds in transforming them into living and powerful dramatic forces.

It is of course tempting to speculate why the French novel has come to be invaded by intellectuals struggling indefatigably with the Angel (or Demon) of ideas. Perhaps this gradual invasion corresponds to a wider cultural phenomenon which, ever since the middle of the nineteenth century, oriented some of the finest scholars—many of them formed by the Ecole Normale Supéricure—to the field of creative writing and literary criticism. ("Several generations of triumphant *normaliens* have forever shackled our literature," complained Drieu La Rochelle.) [5] But social and economic factors cannot be overlooked. Fewer and fewer writers could, like Flaubert, Gide or Proust, rely on family fortunes and devote themselves to literature with the purist fervor of aesthetes. In ever increasing numbers, writers are forced to seek the security of the stable income that diplomas and a teaching position might provide. Certainly, the number of French writers who have prepared for a teaching career, who

---

[4] Lionel Trilling made a similar diagnosis of the "intellectual weakness of American prose literature." (See "The Meaning of a Literary Idea" in *The Liberal Imagination*, p. 294.)

[5] "Libéraux," *Nouvelle Revue Française*, November 1, 1942, pp. 600-607.

have taught or are still teaching, is impressive and probably equaled in no other country. Romain Rolland, Charles Péguy, Jules Romains, Jean Giraudoux, Jean Prévost, Paul Nizan, Jean Guéhenno, Jean-Paul Sartre, Thierry-Maulnier, Julien Gracq, Brice Parain, Henri Queffélec, Armand Lunel—these are only a few of the better-known writers who were formed by that elite teacher-training institution, the Ecole Normale. If one considers, furthermore, that Roger Martin du Gard was a trained historian, that André Chamson is a trained paleographer, Malraux a full-fledged archeologist, Simone de Beauvoir a former professor of philosophy; that many contemporary novelists (Paul Gadenne, Robert Merle, Jean-Louis Curtis, Michel Butor, Marcel Jouhandeau, Albert Memmi, René Etiemble, José Cabanis, Jean-Louis Bory, Marcel Schneider, Michel Zéraffa) have taught or are presently teaching in lycées or at some university—one is forced to recognize an unprecedented and deeply significant cultural phenomenon.

The emergence of the intellectual hero, and the key position he occupies in the modern French novel, can no doubt also be attributed to the growing prestige of an intellectual elite which, beginning in the late eighteenth century, saw itself further and further estranged in a society whose culture it inherited, but whose moral and aesthetic criteria it felt compelled to reject. Literature reflects the pride of this new aristocracy of the intellect. Rousseau's Saint-Preux, Stendhal's Julien Sorel, the ambitious young men of Balzac, Vigny's Chatterton and Stello, combine passionate temperaments with a fierce nobility that no longer marks a nobility of blood or heroic deeds, but a nobility of the mind. The typical Romantic hero—often non-heroic, self-conscious and hyper-nervous—asserts himself less through physical prowess or striking adventures than through the distinction of his spirit. The irremediable clash between his social condition and his spiritual vocation predestines him to tragedy.

But the primary reason for the key role played by the intellectual hero in the novel must ultimately be sought in the fusion of these social, historical and cultural factors with the fundamental attraction that a *literature of ideas* exercises on French writers. "Literature is, in the noblest sense of the word, a vulgarization of philosophy," asserted the literary historian Gustave Lanson.[6] This pronouncement,

[6] See the "Avant-propos" to the 1894 edition of *L'Histoire de la littérature française*.

hard to imagine outside of France, seems to be particularly relevant
for those works which, in the wake of Romanticism, have been
suffused with a sense of "high seriousness" at times bordering on arrogance. Balzac is not the only one of his period to hold that the
writer is a thinker, and every thinker a "prince," a "sovereign," a
shaper of the world.[7] Vigny, dreaming of the philosopher's reign
of pure spirit, repeatedly toys in his *Journal d'un poète* with the
notion of an "aristocracy of the intelligence" destined to submit
the world to the boundless domination of superior minds. But Vigny,
who at times comes close to deifying intelligence, is also a fine example of a poet-novelist who sees in the act of writing a supremely
serious endeavor. In the preface to *Chatterton*, he calls for the new
era of the *Drame de la Pensée*—the drama of the mind. Elsewhere,
he laments that there are too many writers and too few thinkers.
He claims that his novel *Stello* must not merely be read, but studied.
(Himself he terms an "eternal student.") Insistently, he talks about
his fascination with the "struggle of ideas." Stello's credo is an exaltation of man's capacity for intellectual and moral suffering. ("I
believe in the eternal struggle of our inner life. . . .") Vigny, in
fact, viewed ideas as the main protagonists of his works. "In *Stello*
and in *Servitude et Grandeur militaires*, the idea is the heroine," he
asserted. Toward the end of his life, he even dreamed of writing
an epic poem on *intelligence*: "Intellectual deeds are the only great
deeds." [8]

It is now common belief that every great novel implies a philosophical outlook on the world, perhaps even a unified metaphysical
vision. Yet the deliberate attempt to write "philosophical" novels
was a recent trend in Vigny's time. The eighteenth century did not
take its works of fiction that seriously. Bourdaloue's opinion that
novels sacrifice all higher interests to profane love represented not
only the traditional point of view of the Church, but echoed the
general opinion about the frivolous nature of the genre. The very
"defenders" of the novel rarely dreamed of claiming for it the dignified status of tragedy and epic poetry. As late as the beginning
of the nineteenth century, Madame de Staël, though otherwise convinced of the lofty mission of the writer, protests that "philosophy"
has no place in the novel, that it is a perversion of the genre. The

[7] See "Des Artistes," *Oeuvres complètes*, XXXVIII, pp. 351-360.
[8] *Journal d'un poète*, September 12, 1862.

protest, however, only confirms an ever more powerful trend. The typical young hero in Balzac's novel—a d'Arthez, for instance, in *Illusions perdues*—sets out to prove himself a "profound philosopher" by undertaking a "work of high import in the form of a novel," thereby evidently betraying the deepest ambition of the author.

It was Balzac in fact who, in describing the work of Stendhal, coined the expression *"littérature d'idées"*—an expression which Bourget many years later invoked as he discussed the *"roman d'idées"* in his preface to *La Terre promise* (1892). In the meantime the brothers Goncourt, whose nervous antennae made them perceptive of all new trends, prophesied that the novel of the future was bound to concern itself more with "what happens in the brain of humanity" than in the heart.[9] Certainly, no literary phenomenon of the nineteenth century is more significant than this tendency of the novel to assume the proportions of a *summa*, which ultimately finds its fulfillment in the immense edifice of Marcel Proust. Competition with the other arts and sciences, the desire to annex all the branches of human knowledge and endeavor, at times almost verge on megalomania. Balzac's godlike desire to be the demiurge of an entire world, his claim to be the Napoleon of the pen, have become part of his myth. Zola also, though his brand of megalomania has received less publicity, believed that the novelist must "know everything," that he is bound to have "universal knowledge." [10]

Whatever the definition of the novel of ideas—whether its aim is to intellectualize experience or convert thought into living drama —it is quite clear that the great novelists of the nineteenth century have all been tempted by it. Balzac set the tone. In *Louis Lambert*, in *La Recherche de l'absolu*—in all his works that deal with the tyranny of ideas and the disease of genius—he sings the greatness of man's mind. The very suffering and undoing of his martyr-thinkers testifies to the grandeur of their "tempest of thought." The obsessive thirst to learn, know, think, understand and dominate by dint of intellec-

[9] *Journal*, July 16, 1856.
[10] See the passage in *Le Roman expérimental* (pp. 36-37) where Zola maintains that the novelist is the man who must lean on the greatest number of sciences, since his work represents "a general investigation of nature and of men." See also the article "Les Droits du romancier" in *La Vérité en marche*, where Zola affirms that the novelist deals with history, philosophy and science, that he formulates tomorrow's hypotheses and announces the future!

tual will power is one of his permanent themes. The greatness of intellect is only confirmed, in his work, by its destructive power. Flaubert is perhaps even more obsessed with the tragic potential of man's intelligence. Early in life, he conceived of his double vocation as "thinker" and "demoralizer"—the two were inseparable in his mind. His pessimism (he liked to say that he was born with a complete foretaste of unhappiness) is most oppressive, and most dramatically powerful, in those works which, like *La Tentation de saint Antoine*, or *Bouvard et Pécuchet*, communicate the sadness of all knowledge. His is not only a Faustian disenchantment, as he endlessly catalogues philosophical beliefs and draws the tedious inventory of customs, religions and heresies. These debauches of the imagination are primarily debauches of the mind, as it feels perilously seduced by the dream of self-annihilation. The most powerful temptation of Flaubert's Saint Anthony is not the appetite of the senses, but the appetite of the intellect. And his tragedy is not merely the tragedy of doubt and futility, but the awareness that he cannot cope with this desperate voracity. As the century draws to a close, the disease of thinking becomes an ever more insistent theme of a literature haunted by the notion of decadence.

¶ II. *Intentions*

THE FRENCH NOVEL has remained a great devourer of ideas. Yet there exist profound differences between the philosophical novel of the nineteenth century and the "metaphysical" novel of our times. The works of Balzac, Vigny and Flaubert "dealt with" many important subjects: science, religion, the role of the artist, the suffering of superior minds, the conflict between the individual and society, the tragedy of knowledge. But although these novelists felt the urge to invade other fields, and posed in their own terms the great human issues, their works display none of the metaphysical intensity with which the ethical and political aspects of the "human condition" are dramatized and almost viscerally experienced in the contemporary novel of the intellectual. Jean-Paul Sartre has eloquently stated the passionate nature of this new "metaphysical" literature. "Metaphysics," for these novelists, "is not a sterile discussion on abstract notions which lie beyond experience, but represents a dynamic effort to embrace the human condition from within and in its totality." [11]

The profound significance of the professional intellectual as hero of so many novels since the turn of the century is that his emergence as a literary type, and the stature he gradually acquires, correspond to the development of a novel which no longer merely exploits philosophy, or serves as a conveyance for philosophical thoughts, but in which philosophy itself becomes a dramatic force. This type of novel has little in common with Gide's notion of a "*carrefour d'idées.*" It is far more than a crossroads stage on which ideas meet and perhaps play with each other for the delight of nimble-minded readers. The intellectual novel does not present problems as a spectacle; it is an experience which probes into its own meaning. Few literary phenomena have had deeper significance in relation to our tormented times than this translation into fictional themes of the anguished self-questioning of man and of his tragic obsession with global responsibility.

It is the purpose of this study to examine, within the precise context of representative works, a climate of intellectual tension which, ever since the Dreyfus Affair, and increasingly so under the impact of shattering social, political and economic crises, has oriented the novel toward a permanent questioning of the concepts of Man, the meaning of History and the values of Civilization. The very clichés of our time—words such as "anguish," "predicament," "dilemma," "situation," "engagement," "history" and "despair"—betray a deep malaise and point to a crisis of Humanism. *Bad conscience* is perhaps the outstanding symptom of the modern malady. And the intellectual, vulnerable and articulate, is at the same time the least curable victim and the sternest denouncer of this bad conscience. To give society a sense of guilt, to shock it out of its ethical complacency and make it aware of its bad faith, is indeed for recent generations the primary function of the writer.

The intellectual hero, though aware of his alienation, is thus not committed to a Romantic quarrel with society, to a surface antagonism that pits his pride and his tastes against bourgeois philistinism. He is caught in a deeper, more complex and also more personal drama. For his condemnation of bad faith (the varieties of "*mau-*

[11] "Qu'est-ce que la littérature?" in *Situations II*, p. 251.

vaise foi" Sartre brilliantly analyzes in *L'Etre et le Néant*) is inextricably bound up with the tragic awareness of his own guilt and complicity. Obsessed by the suffering of others, convinced that man's salvation lies in solidarity, he is equally convinced of the walled-in nature of human consciousness and paralyzed by his very lucidity. Dreaming of his high social and spiritual mission, he knows his efforts doomed to defeat, yet blames himself for his own futility. Concerned with the regeneration of mankind, driven on by the urge to speak for and with others, he also flirts with catastrophe and secretly yearns for his own destruction. He is in fact the hero, the victim and the buffoon of a tortured era which has experienced politics as tragedy, freedom as necessity, and where history has assumed the urgent voice of a *fatum*.

It is no doubt because the intellectual has been, by vocation and by temperament, most vulnerable to this political and metaphysical sense of anguish, and most tempted also by the perilous dialectics of our time, that he came to occupy such a privileged position in the contemporary French novel. But this pre-eminence was acquired slowly. At the end of the nineteenth century, the professional scholar was most often a minor literary type—pompous, maniacal, extravagant, at best a whimsical bore. How the intellectual penetrates into literature, how from a minor and often ridiculous character he gradually evolves into a protagonist of stature; through what vicissitudes he becomes the key personage of an entire epoch; how he can be defined in relation to the traditional "hero"; but above all, what themes (psychological, ethical, political and metaphysical) the novelists develop through his presence—these are some of the questions I propose to examine. But first it may be useful to situate historically the concept of *"l'intellectuel"* and attempt to circumscribe the feelings and ideas that cluster around this rather vague term.

2

Toward a Portrait of the French Intellectual

> *Le héros d'intelligence se dit, en ses meilleurs moments, que l'honneur de l'homme serait de vivre selon le vrai, quoi qu'il lui en puisse coûter. . . .*
>
> —ALAIN

L'intellectuel—RARELY HAS A WORD inspired more fervor, arrogance, bitter irony and generous anger. Edouard Berth, ardent royalist and sympathizer with *L'Action Française*, gave vent to some of these violent feelings in a long-forgotten but significant book, *Les Méfaits des intellectuels* (1914), in which he described the intellectuals as an anti-heroic caste of effeminate, knavish and deceitful weaklings, who strive to impose on the modern world nauseating humanitarian ideals and a morality of cowardice. One easily recognizes echoes of Barrès' vituperations against the servile mandarins, imbued with Kantian moral principles and determined to emasculate an already corrupt France.

Without even mentioning the hysterical polemics of a Berth or the strident outbursts of a Barrès, it is easy to draw up a catalogue of unfavorable opinions. Paul Valéry inveighed with much irony against the megalomaniacal, complex-ridden intellectuals; Romain Rolland declaimed against the intolerant "maniacs" in love with ideas; Péguy denounced the *parti intellectuel;* Julien Benda wrote a series of books about the "treason" of the intellectuals. More recently, Raymond Aron diagnosed their addiction to ideological opium and their supposed irresponsibility in the face of history.

It is clear that intellectuals themselves, when they are not openly hostile to the term and the concept "intellectual," are secretly disturbed by it. Much of the fictional work of Sartre and Simone de Beauvoir testifies to this uneasiness. Henri Perron and Robert Dubreuilh, in *Les Mandarins*, proudly affirm that they are intellectuals; but deep in their hearts they are assailed by fears that they may have no function whatsoever, that they are merely sterile windbags, or as Scriassine puts it—guilty of a mental and political "masochism" typical of all intellectuals. Perron is fully aware of the pejorative connotations of the word: "I am an intellectual. It irritates me that this word has been made an insult." And is it not one of the functions of petulant Ivich, in Sartre's *L'Age de raison*, to exacerbate the scruples, hesitations and guilt feelings of Mathieu Delarue—a function which Nadine, Ivich's counterpart in *Les Mandarins*, fulfills with even more gusto by uttering cruel and occasionally even obscene statements about intellectuals?

THE TERM "INTELLECTUAL" (that is, the substantive, *"un intellectuel"*) is a fairly recent word in the French language. One would search in vain for it in the Littré dictionary (1863-1877). To be sure, nineteenth-century writers, groping for the word, made use of certain expressions that vaguely corresponded to this idea. Balzac, for instance, in *Illusions perdues*, calls Michel Chrestien a *"bohémien de l'intelligence."* Yet quite significantly, when the French delegates to the First Congress of the Workers International in Geneva (1866) asked for the exclusion of all delegates who were intellectuals (a Proudhonian attack on the Blanquists), the appropriate term was still wanting: they were forced to use the clumsy expression "workers of the intellect" (*"les ouvriers de la pensée"*). All the socialist literature of the latter part of the nineteenth century bears witness to the absence of the term. There is talk of the *"professionnels de l'intelligence,"* of the *"travailleurs de la pensée."* Zola, in 1897, still employs the circumlocution *"professionnels de l'intelligence,"* [1] and Clemenceau, in his articles for *L'Aurore*, refers to the *"hommes de pur labeur intellectuel."* All tends to prove that by 1895, the term was not yet in common usage. Else, why would Karl Kautsky's pamphlet *Der Sozialismus und die Intelligenz* have appeared, in "Le Devenir Social" (1895), under the title *Le Socialisme et les carrières libérales?* Yet, only a few years later, in the work of Romain Rolland for instance, the term is already very familiar. Why the emergence of the term? What occurred in the intervening years? The answer is spelled out clearly: the Dreyfus case, that "holy

[1] *La Vérité en marche*, p. 103.

hysteria," as Romain Rolland put it. For this ideological war which, eight years after the abortive Boulanger revolution, opposed the two spiritual families of France, was not merely an explosion of all the bitterness accumulated since 1789 by a nation with too good a political memory. It marked above all a great moment in the intellectual history of the country, serving as a catalyst for already prevalent tendencies, but also opening a new era which Albert Thibaudet has aptly called the "*République des Professeurs*," and which, he felt, was brought about by "an insurrection and a victory of intellectuals." [2] The struggle between the two irreconcilable mystiques was probably not followed anywhere with greater intensity than in the little Librairie Bellais, the *Revue Blanche*, the editorial rooms of *L'Aurore*, and in the teaching profession (the *Université*) which, at a time when even Jaurès' Socialist Party was indifferent (or too prudent), constituted the first professional or social group to throw its weight behind the defenders of Dreyfus.

To the intellectual, "the Dreyfus case is the palladium of history," writes Julien Benda, who was himself deeply marked by the crisis.[3] Thibaudet sums it all up: "This Dreyfus case . . . this tumult of intellectuals . . ." It is indeed difficult to think of the French intellectual in historic terms without situating him first in the passionate climate of a crisis which confirmed unequivocally his vocation of moral responsibility. All evidence, moreover, points to the fact that it is during this ideological battle, and more specifically at its moment of highest dramatic intensity (the Esterhazy and Zola trials) that the word "intellectual" is thrown into circulation. Maurice Paléologue, in his recently published *Journal de l'Affaire Dreyfus* (1955), relates an impassioned evening during which a particularly bellicose Brunetière was battling Paul Hervieu, Gustave Larroumet, Victor Brochard and Gabriel Séailles—all of them ardent revisionists. Paléologue records part of Brunetière's tirade (January

[2] After the Dreyfus case, according to Thibaudet, the professor becomes the lawyer's rival in politics. Herriot, Painlevé, Blum, Péguy, Alain, Thomas —all with "academic" training—are cited as examples of this "professors' republic." See *La République des Professeurs,* but also Thibaudet's short article "Pour l'histoire du parti intellectuel," *La Nouvelle Revue Française,* August, 1932, pp. 265-272, in which he suggests that the Dreyfus case crystallized the intellectuals' function as apostles of the "*spirituel républicain.*" Jacques Barzun also notes that the "continual use" of the terms "intellectual" and "anti-intellectual" goes back to the Dreyfus case (*The House of Intellect,* p. 1).

[3] *La Jeunesse d'un clerc,* p. 199.

15, 1898—exactly two days after the publication of Zola's sensational letter to the President of the Republic):

As for M. Zola, why doesn't he mind his own business? The letter *J'accuse* is a monument of stupidity, presumption and incongruity. The interference of this novelist in a matter of military justice seems to me no less impertinent than, let us say, the intervention of a police captain in a problem of syntax or versification. . . .

As for this petition that is being circulated among the *Intellectuals!* the mere fact that one has recently created this word *Intellectuals* to designate, as though they were an aristocracy, individuals who live in laboratories and libraries, proclaims one of the most ridiculous eccentricities of our time—I mean the pretension of raising writers, scientists, professors and philologists to the rank of supermen (pp. 90-91).

The faithfulness of Paléologue's transcription cannot be questioned: one need only glance at Brunetière's articles in the *Revue des Deux Mondes*, or at his militant public lectures attacking what he termed "the enemies of the French soul," to find the same expressions and the very tone of his harangue in Mme Aubernon's salon.

Paléologue's talent as a memorialist is, however, not what matters here. The real interest of these pages is that they testify to the newness of a word which, significantly, appears in italics in this, as well as in most other texts of the period. Brunetière associates the word with the signers of the petitions. That very day indeed —on January 15—a protest in favor of a retrial had appeared in *Le Temps*, signed by Anatole France, Zola, Emile Duclaux (director of the Institut), F. Fénéon (secretary of the *Revue Blanche*), Fernand Gregh, Daniel Halévy, Marcel Proust, Victor Bérard, Lucien Herr, Ferdinand Brunot—and many others. If one follows *Le Temps* throughout these first three months of 1898, one is struck by the frequency with which the word "intellectual" appears. On January 25, an article entitled "Le Prolétariat intellectuel" complains of the plethora of useless mandarins threatening the social equilibrium. Only a few days later, Jean Psichari, dean of studies at the Ecole des Hautes Etudes, sends an open letter in which he demands for "intellectuals" the right to intervene actively in political matters. Rarely has a group become so vehemently aware of itself.

As for the newness of the word, the contemporaries themselves are aware of it. In a pamphlet entitled *Les Etapes d'un intellectuel* (1898), Albert Réville proudly proclaims: "Let us use this word, since it has received high consecrations." Clemenceau, in an article dated January 23, in *L'Aurore*, employs the word in italics. On April 5, Anatole France uses it in an article that appears in *L'Echo de Paris*, and which is destined to serve as a starting point for the third conversation of *L'Anneau d'améthyste*. All the while Maurice Barrès affirms (though with considerable bad faith) that it is Clemenceau who invented the term, and that this "neologism" was very "poor French" indeed.[4] Whatever the exact date of the creation of this word (the Hatzfeld and Darmsteter dictionary, 1895-1900, still fails to include the substantive), it is evident that the word penetrated into the common language during the winter of 1897-1898. Even in Marxist literature, it is only after this date that one commonly encounters the word in France: the pamphlets by Hubert Lagardelle and Paul Lafargue, respectively entitled *Les Intellectuels devant le socialisme* and *Le Socialisme et les intellectuels*, both date from 1900.

¶ STIGMA I: *Voices without a mandate*

BUT PALÉOLOGUE'S TEXT ALSO TELLS US much about the affective value, the color of the new word. Brunetière pretends to be shocked by the presumptuous interference of Zola. Why doesn't he mind his own business? he asks. The reaction is characteristic, and soon becomes a cliché: here are individuals who should be at work peacefully and modestly in their laboratories and libraries, who suddenly get it into their heads to meddle in affairs totally outside their ken. Brunetière is tireless on the subject. In a resounding article in the *Revue des Deux Mondes* (March 15, 1898), he asseverates that a "first comer" has not the right to insult the French army and French justice, that learned compilers do not know everything, that to have written a treatise on microbiology (an obvious dig at Emile Duclaux) does not entitle one to judge one's fellow men, that schol-

---

[4] *Scènes et doctrines du nationalisme*, p. 46. With bad faith, for he himself had used the word some ten years earlier in *Sous l'oeil des barbares* (1888), though in a somewhat different sense. What Barrès disliked by 1898 was obviously not the word but what it had come to stand for. As for Paul Bourget, he had used the substantive as early as 1882 (*La Nouvelle Revue*, XVI, p. 886) in his essay on Flaubert, whom he described as a victim of the corrosive poison of "Thought." It is interesting to note, however, that in his novel *Le Disciple* (1889) the word appears only twice, each time in a derogatory sense.

ars are not equipped to understand such "delicate questions" as individual morality and social ethics, and that (the irony is somewhat
facile) a professor of the Tibetan language may not be the ideal
man to govern France. On April 15, Brunetière is at it again; reviewing Zola's novel *Paris*, he proposes the following definition of
the intellectual: a person who "meddles dogmatically in matters
about which he is ignorant." Brunetière is not alone: other voices
are heard, and in the same key. "The roster of intellectuals is made
up of simpletons," writes Barrès in *Le Journal* (February 1, 1898).
And in his *Scènes et doctrines du nationalisme*, after having defined
the intellectual as a cultivated individual without any mandate, but
who obstinately wants to impose his chimerical ideas on a concrete
reality, he recalls the old proverb: *"A chacun son métier et les
moutons seront bien gardés."* A member of the French Academy,
Emile Gebhart, turns out to be even more violent, showering insults
on what he calls the "battalion of the discontented": virtuosos of
Latin metrics, pale paleographers, embittered metaphysicians, mi-
crobe hunters and other abstracters of quintessences.[5] Echoes of
these reactions will still be felt a few years later in the novels of
Romain Rolland: Jean-Christophe is appalled by the number of
littérateurs who specialize in politics, form leagues, and sign petitions. "I do not trust those who speak of what they don't know,"
he confides to his friend Olivier in *Le Buisson ardent*. As for Daniel
Halévy, he will recall long after, in *Apologie pour notre passé*, how
he and his friends were accused of being nothing but bookwormish
intellectuals in rebellion against an entire people.

¶ STIGMA II: *The death of instinct*

"ONE IS ALWAYS UNFAIR when one attacks professors," Barrès ad-
mits with candor in *Mes Cahiers*, though he does not bother to
analyze his brand of unfairness. There is of course the age-old suspicion of the thinker and teacher against whom the social group
seeks vengeance by means of a caricature based on the conventional
and much-belabored contrast between intelligence and knowledge.
("I'd rather be intelligent than an intellectual," proclaims Barrès.[6])

---

5 See the letter of February 25, 1898, quoted by Barrès in *Mes Cahiers*, II,
pp. 3-5.
  6 *Scènes et doctrines du nationalisme*, p. 45.

But more significant still, as far as Barrès and his contemporaries are concerned, the last two decades of the nineteenth century witness a real offensive against the "pernicious professor": novels such as Barrès' *Les Déracinés*, as well as Bourget's *Le Disciple* and *L'Etape* or Unamuno's *Amor y pedagogía*, all illustrate the thesis that teachers are directly responsible for the actions and even the crimes committed by their disciples. Trends such as these correspond in fact to a general tendency to devaluate pure intellect. Brunetière maintained that intellectual aptitudes had only a relative value, that he, for one, had infinitely more esteem for will power and force of character. Barrès liked to parade his contempt for intelligence as well. Impressed by some remarks made by the physiologist, Jules Soury, he waxed lyrical about the grandeur of "uncultivated life" (he of all people!) and repeated by heart, like a conscientious schoolboy: "Intelligence! . . . what a tiny thing at the very surface of our personality!" [7] Behind this attempt to discredit the intelligence of the "simian mammal" (a pet expression of Jules Soury), it is easy to detect a reaction against the rationalist tradition with its faith in science and progress, and its intellectual cosmopolitanism. Had not Brunetière, in a much discussed article, announced the bankruptcy of science? [8]

To be sure, it was better to be intelligent than intellectual—but even that was not the ideal. Barrès preferred *"l'inconscient national"* and complained that the nineteenth century (Hugo, Michelet, Taine, Renan) had been entirely mistaken about the importance of Reason. "The individual! his intelligence, his ability to grasp the laws of the universe—it's time to quell these pretensions. We are not the masters of our thoughts. They do not spring from our intelligence . . ." (*Scènes et doctrines*, p. 17). This discrediting of intelligence obviously also corresponded to the affirmation of a nationalistic mystique which, in the decades following the defeat of 1870, called the French back to the cult of their ancestors, exploited the primitive allegiance to the "soil," and praised instinctive solidarity with a carnal France. That, unquestionably, is the significance of Barrès' pontifical statement that pseudo-culture "destroys in-

[7] *Mes Cahiers*, I, p. 73. Barrès was very fond of this statement and repeated it on several occasions (see the preface to *L'Appel au soldat*). One of his heroes, Roemerspacher, is also an admirer of Jules Soury.

[8] "Après une visite au Vatican," *Revue des Deux Mondes*, January 1, 1895, pp. 97-118.

stinct" (*Scènes et doctrines*, p. 46). It is, of course, this very kind of "betrayal" that Benda had in mind when he later denounced the clerics for having lent themselves to the intellectual organization of political fanaticism. Ironically enough (though not so ironically for a Benda), a similar devaluation of intelligence and culture can be observed in the socialist literature of the period. Karl Kautsky used to call literary bohemians "vain concocters of projects." Hubert Lagardelle attributed to Greco-Latin education the emergence of a group of dissatisfied, ambitious *déclassés*, out of touch with the masses, and considered the humanities useless and perhaps even harmful to modern man.[9]

¶ STIGMA III: *The hybris of the mandarins*

THE SAME PASSAGE FROM PALÉOLOGUE'S DIARY points to still another sentiment attached to the new word. Brunetière's remark that the "Intellectuals" claim to constitute an aristocracy of supermen clearly echoes a widespread resentment provoked by the supposed arrogance and boundless pride of the "mandarins" (the word is much used at the time). A thoroughly laughable and unjustified arrogance, according to Brunetière and his friends. Paléologue recalls with what suspicion the judges at the Rennes court-martial listened to the testimony of "intellectuals," these "presumptuous pedants who take themselves for the aristocrats of the mind." Similar sounds are heard from all sides: "*caste nobilière*," "*aristocrates de l'esprit*," "*aristocratie intellectuelle*," "*mandarins des lettres*," "*aristocrates de la pensée*," "*élite intellectuelle*"—these are the most common derogatory expressions. Président Méline's most admired speech was probably the one delivered in the Chamber of Deputies (February 28, 1898) in which he thundered against the "intellectual elite" with a sarcastic verve that provoked prolonged laughter and unanimous applause. In an article that appeared two weeks later, Brunetière repeats that nothing seems to him less bearable than the idea of an intellectual aristocracy. In his *Discours de combat*, he grows even more violent, calling Nietzsche "a professor of Greek, delirious with

[9] See *Le Socialisme et les carrières libérales*, p. 265, and *Les Intellectuels devant le socialisme*, p. 51. Extracts from Karl Kautsky, as well as from Paul Lafargue's *Le Socialisme et les intellectuels*, appear in English translation in the very interesting anthology *The Intellectuals; a controversial portrait* (pp. 322-337), edited with taste and imagination by George B. de Huszar.

impotence and pride." As for Barrès, he too, of course, is outraged by these "aristocrats of the mind" who, he feels, are but "a bunch of people crazy with pride" (*Scènes et doctrines*, p. 210). Of this supposed arrogance, Paul Bourget had given earlier a famous fictional example in his Robert Greslou, who believes in an oligarchy of scientists, and who dares to think (and to write) that a man such as he must learn "not to consider as a law for us who think what is and must be a law for those who do not think" (*Le Disciple*).

Many of the anti-rationalistic attitudes of the nineties are in conscious rebellion against the thinking of a Renan who, in *L'Avenir de la Science* and the *Dialogues philosophiques*, had more than toyed with the idea of new spiritual guides for humanity. It is Renan, no doubt, whom Bourget had in mind when, in the preface to *Le Disciple*, he alluded to the all too eloquent master whose paradoxes and intellectualism had charmed, corrupted and spiritually dried up the typical young Frenchman. Brunetière is more blunt in his denunciation of Renan's "odious dream": he shuddered at Renan's future world, controlled by an elite of scientists "placing unlimited terror at the service of truth." [10]

It is true that, in some cases, the statements and attitudes of certain "intellectuals" seemed to justify accusations of arrogance. Zola, during his trial, clumsily answered the judge: "I do not know the law and I do not want to know it." To a somewhat baffled jury he proudly declared that it was he who was the true defender of France, and that his victories would be more meaningful to posterity than those of any general. Even in the calmer atmosphere of his study, he could not refrain from formulating thoughts that exalted the writer over the statesman: "Our lawmakers seem to me inefficient; I would like to see the task entrusted to moralists, writers, poets" (*La Vérité en marche*, p. 118). Opinions such as these seemed to corroborate the worst suspicions of a Brunetière!

Here again it is noteworthy that very similar accusations were fired from the extreme Left as well as from the traditional Right. Proudhon, it is well known, resented all "mandarins." The anarchist ex-nobleman Bakunin tirelessly insisted that it would never be possible to convert to socialism the "aristocrats of the intellect," domineering, caste-conscious and filled with contempt for the working classes. French socialists, at the turn of the century, more than ever

[10] Quoted by E. Duclaux, *Avant le procès*, pp. 23-24.

before express hostile sentiments. In a lecture delivered to a Parisian student group in 1900, Hubert Lagardelle describes the intellectuals as arrogant and thirsty for power.

Paradoxically—as though it were not enough to be caught in the crossfire of the extreme Right and the militant Left—the intellectuals find themselves in the ambiguous position of being classified simultaneously as an aristocracy and as a proletariat. As early as 1860, the brothers Goncourt had noted with a measure of bitterness, in *Charles Demailly*, that the new generation of artists and journalists no longer belonged to the comfortable bourgeoisie as did the generation of 1830, but that instead the new *bohème*, whipped on by economic need, lived, worked and "fought for its soup" with "all the hatreds of a proletariat." At the time of the Dreyfus case, a collective pamphlet appears, *Les Prolétaires intellectuels en France* (among the collaborators are Henry Bérenger, Paul Pottier and Pierre Marcel). Barrès is also delighted by the expression (which he attributed to Bismarck): an important chapter of his novel *Les Déracinés* is entitled "Le Prolétariat des bacheliers." [11]

Aristocrats and proletarians, elite and proletariat—these "accusations" are contradictory only in appearance: according to a Brunetière the intellectuals are precisely a proletariat of *arrivistes* whose totally insane ambition it is to usurp the privileges of an elite. But the importance of such accusations cannot be limited to the intentions of those who formulate them: it is precisely such comments, such judgments which help situate existentially the intellectual and define him to himself.

¶ STIGMA IV: *Enemies of the national "soul"*

PALÉOLOGUE'S DIARY MENTIONS ONE FURTHER SIN attributed to the "Intellectuals." These "aristocrats of the mind" are also accused of having lost their "national mentality"—of having assumed the function of subverters and corroders of patriotic ideals. According to Brunetière, these "enemies of the French soul" (this is the title of one of his many lectures on the subject) are trying desperately to destroy the traditions of France. As for Emile Gebhart's epigrammatic assertion that teachers of German no longer think often

---

[11] In January, 1898, *Le Temps* printed the editorial "Le Prolétariat intellectuel." The expression also appears in Gabriel Monod's *Portraits et souvenirs*.

enough in French—it may seem tasteless and excessive, but it was certainly not an isolated opinion. Countless are the bitter remarks provoked by the so-called Kantian invasion of French education. Here again, Barrès' reactions are perhaps most characteristic. Of this subversive *Kantisme* his Professor Bouteiller, in *Les Déracinés*, is the living symbol: a "modern sorcerer," uprooted and ambitious, who, by means of the intellectual poison he spreads, succeeds in uprooting entire generations of innocent young Frenchmen.

Much of this explosion of chauvinism at the time of the Dreyfus case can be explained by memories of the recent defeat. Dreams of revenge went hand in hand with a hatred for Germany that was further inflamed by unavowed sentiments of inferiority, and by the awareness that France was lagging behind in the Industrial Revolution. Barrès did not have to invent: there were men like Roemerspacher's grandfather, who would not hear of any member of his family studying at a German university. It is against this background that the fictional figure of Professor Bouteiller has to be assessed. Barrès' accusations against intellectuals follow a recognizable and symptomatic pattern: men such as Bouteiller "decerebrate" the nation, they ignore the instinctive faith of the masses, they insist on teaching an "absolute truth" instead of teaching piously the "French truth" (one can see Benda's grimace of pain!). In short, the intellectual is an "enemy of society" (*Scènes et doctrines*, p. 57).

"We must watch the Université," writes Barrès in *Mes Cahiers*. "It contributes to the destruction of French principles." Such a warning, coming from a cultured and sophisticated writer, may surprise. Even more surprising, however, is the impassioned battle cry calculated to arouse a student group: "Will you let us be devoured by these people? Lay your hands on your libraries! To arms, comrades!" That feelings such as these were quite widespread is proven by André Beaunier's satirical novel *Les Dupont-Leterrier* (1900). In order to mock this very brand of militant anti-intellectualism, Beaunier has his Major Joseph say: "The intellectuals! It was already they who betrayed Constantinople to the Greeks—to some dirty little Greeks!" Of course, Beaunier's satire has its limitations: Brunetière, Barrès, Gebhart, Méline and the editorial writers of *Le Temps* have little in common with a Major Joseph. Nevertheless, each in his own way expresses what is at the time a cliché, namely that the "intellectuals" have all "lost the national mentality."

Needless to add that what to some is scandalously anti-patriotic, others interpret as a praiseworthy cosmopolitanism or a generous internationalism. Barrès calls all intellectuals *déracinés* (uprooted). Lucien Herr, in the *Revue Blanche*, rejoins that they are *désintéressés* (selfless). *Déracinés* or *désintéressés*, uprooted or selfless—the argument implies nothing less than a difference of perspective. To the ones, the intellectual is the sworn enemy of the collective discipline, the enemy of the established social order. (Did not an article in *Le Temps*—February 14, 1898—calmly assert that French intellectuals were discontented troublemakers?) To the others, this supposed corrosive and subversive force is but the proof of their moral dynamism, of the integrity of their critical stand and of their competence to serve as liaison agents between one culture and another.

¶ *A few conclusions and a few ambiguities*

CLEARLY, THE WORD "INTELLECTUAL" CARRIES, from the moment of its birth, the stigma of derision, contempt, suspicion, and even hatred. Thrown into circulation during the winter 1897-1898, the term implies the intervention in public affairs of supposedly incompetent scholars without a mandate, and suggests a mentality hostile to the mystique of tradition. Intellectuals are held responsible, retrospectively, for all the ills since the French Revolution—and for the worse ills that lie ahead. Hardly a single expression of disparagement or of sarcasm is spared them: envious bookworms, bitter *ratés*, histrionic anarchists, the dregs of society—these are only a few of the colorful expressions used to designate the "impotent" and "cowardly" mandarins. A few nostalgic souls even went so far as to regret the good old days of Sparta when teachers were slaves and kept in a permanent state of inebriety to serve as a living lesson to the aristocratic youth.

Occasionally, the "intellectuals" of 1898 themselves display a definite distaste for the term. At the *Revue Blanche*—one of their headquarters—there seems to be some doubt as to whether to rejoice over the appellation. Pierre Quillard, in a pungent reply to one of Brunetière's articles, protests against this "ridiculous title." Léon Blum, reviewing a novel by Paul Adam, establishes an implicit equation between "intellectual" and mental unbalance. As for Zola, he does not hesitate to deride the hairsplitting "silly intellectuals." It is true that Zola especially detested the Ecole Normale Supérieure, which he sarcastically termed "the school where one knows everything."

But on the whole—and overwhelmingly so—the intellectuals take up the term with pride. Brunetière's accusations do not go unchallenged during that evening in the salon of Mme Aubernon. Hervieu, Séailles, Larroumet, Brochard—all react with fire, pointing out that it is the intellectuals (they are not ashamed of the word) who today incarnate the true traditions of the French conscience. Elsewhere, Emile Duclaux proudly glories in the very accusation: "Yes indeed, it's the intellectuals who made the French Revolution," adding even more categorically: "I don't know what the choice of my country will be. My choice is made: I remain 'an intellectual' " (*Avant le procès*, p. 35). This militant pride finds many echoes. In a letter to *Le Temps* (February 3, 1898), Jean Psichari proclaims that intellectuals are the glory of a country like France.

A triple ambiguity, however, seems to attach itself to the term from its very inception: (1) The apparently contradictory accusation that intellectuals constitute on the one hand a pitiful proletariat and on the other an arrogant, caste-conscious, self-styled elite. (2) The reactions of the intellectuals themselves, who oscillate between a feeling of uneasiness (and even of shame) and the most undisguised pride. (3) The fact that the battle cries and utterances of contempt from the traditionalist and nationalistic Right are echoed (and even reinforced) by other bellicose cries coming from the Left, revolutionary, internationalist and equally hostile. This early awareness of being caught in a crossfire ushers in one of the most serious predicaments of the twentieth century, and soon becomes a major theme in the modern French novel.

¶ *The crystallization of a concept*

IN SPITE OF NEW HISTORICAL CONTINGENCIES, the word "intellectual" continues, throughout the subsequent fifty years, to bear the traces of its ideological origin. The French concept of the intellectual thus remains bound up with the notion of a social, political and moral crisis. Better still: it implies *the notion of a permanent state of crisis*. Given this state of crisis, the intellectual considers it his obligation to intervene. This sense of moral duty may reach a particularly high pitch during certain periods (1930-1950, for instance)–but it constitutes a permanent trait. Passionately committed to political thinking, haunted by dreams of action, he is, according to Benda, a "traitor" to clerical values (*La Trahison des clercs*). But significantly, even Benda fails to live up to his quasi-monastic ideals: not only does he make specific concessions (such as allowing "political speculation," or granting intellectuals the "social mission of truth," or affirming that the "passion for justice" is not a political passion!), but he will quite regularly denounce the traitors of the Right, while tolerating and even admiring the political passion of Leftist intellectuals on the grounds that they, following the dictates of their conscience as true "*clercs*," protest in the name of justice and out of a pure sense of moral duty. This generous inconsistency in Benda's thinking is symptomatic of a whole climate of ideas.

The intellectual's intervention thus follows a predictable pattern: he considers himself a *voice*. And not merely a voice crying out in protest (Aron calls it the mentality of "permanent opposition"), but a voice that proclaims itself a *conscience*.[12] "To think sincerely, even if it means to think against everybody, still means to think with and for everybody," Romain Rolland was fond of saying. The deep concern here is not with one's private thought or suffering, but with the thought and suffering of others, with the need to respond, to declare oneself, to take one's stand whatever the risk— in short, with the impossibility of remaining silent. In his *Apologie pour notre passé*, Daniel Halévy recalls with undisguised emotion that Emile Duclaux was so haunted by the idea of a possible injustice that he literally could not sleep until he had publicly expressed his qualms and so performed what he considered his clear duty. The anecdote is significant: the intellectual's suffering is not a private affair occasioned by some hidden remorse. If he has to speak up, it is because he feels called upon to become the conscience (which often means the guilty conscience) of an entire group, or even—the ambition is not uncommon—of an entire epoch. Half a century later,

---

[12] This has become a cliché. Anatole France, in his panegyric on Emile Zola, called him "a moment of the French conscience." The term is still fashionable. When Camus was awarded the Nobel Prize, *Le Figaro Littéraire* commented: "The Stockholm Academy undoubtedly wished to honor not merely a writer whom we all admire, but a conscience." Similarly, Mauriac, who thought that Camus was "not only a writer, but a conscience."

in Simone de Beauvoir's *Les Mandarins*, Professor Dubreuilh asks himself: "What does it mean, the fact that man never ceases talking about himself? And why is it that some men decide to speak in the name of others: in other words, what is an intellectual?" But the very question implies the answer: the intellectual is precisely the one who has decided to speak, and speak up, in the name of humanity. This sense of "global responsibility" is one for which intellectuals have been much criticized. But if it is true, as Raymond Aron suggests in *L'Opium des intellectuels*, that this eagerness to think for all humanity does not go without a measure of pride, it must also be added in all honesty that it marks not only moral courage, but a deep and beautiful yearning to reaffirm man's solidarity with man.

Is there a "race" of intellectuals? Vincent Berger, the hero of Malraux's *Les Noyers de l'Altenburg*, observes, during the symposium which brings together philosophers from various countries, that these faces so diversely and profoundly characteristic of the different nations to which they belong, nevertheless resemble one another. "My father discovered to what extent intellectuals constitute a race." But a "race," needless to say, that is to be recognized through moral rather than physical traits.

What are these traits? One hesitates to undertake this moral portrait. Sensibility modeled on thought; faith in the efficiency of ideas as an organizational force in the tangible world; the utilization of culture as an instrument for criticizing tradition; the unselfish, gratuitous pursuit of truth, but simultaneously the pursuit of a humanitarian ideal; the transmission or preaching of moral values; the sensation, now proud, now humiliating, of existing outside the social framework, and yet, on the whole, an obvious sympathy for the laboring groups of the country and a consequent attraction to Leftist political parties; a feeling of "not belonging" and of impotence; jealousy of the men of action; the cult of revolt, sometimes even of anarchy; the nearly obsessive fear of being caught on the side of injustice; nostalgia for the masses coupled with the complexes of a *fils de bourgeois* ashamed of belonging to the privileged classes— these constitute only some of the more permanent traits of the French intellectual.

¶   *Toward a literary "type"*

OUR INTELLECTUALS AND THOSE OF 1898 are of one and the same
family. Yet it is also evident that they existed *avant la lettre*. The
intellectual type could not possibly have penetrated so fast and so
deeply into literature had he not first slowly emerged and become
aware of himself as a social reality. The entire nineteenth century
felt the need for the word.

Is Arthur Koestler right in affirming somewhat peremptorily that
the Encyclopedists, entering the historical stage as iconoclasts and
debunkers, were the first modern intellectuals? [13] To limit the Encyclopedists' role to that of iconoclasts and debunkers may seem
unfair; it fails to account for their sense of mission and their positive
idealism. But Koestler is not alone in pointing to the eighteenth-century *philosophes* as the direct ancestors of modern intellectuals. According to Benda, these *philosophes* with a social conscience, and
socially involved, were the first traitors to the philosophical spirit.
Raymond Aron, for reasons that are also not altogether flattering,
sees in these eighteenth-century philosophers the first clear example
of the intellectual in the modern sense of the word: using their
pens for a living, they assume that they have the right to express
generously their critical opinions on any subject.

The danger of such digging for ancestors is that it leads to the
alluring game of anachronistic generalizations. Yet it is difficult to
deny that there exist parallels and even family ties. The *philosophes*
of the eighteenth century also considered themselves guides of humanity. They too were slandered and sneered at. The word *philosophe* was also discredited.[14] Accused of fabricating doctrines to cover
their narcissistic arrogance, of undermining the highest virtues (such
as love of country), they were said to be a threat to the very existence of society. The *philosophes*—especially at the hour of their
triumph—sometimes replied with rather excessive statements. In his
Essai sur les règnes de Claude et de Néron, Diderot defines the role
of the philosopher as follows: "The magistrate dispenses justice;
the philosopher teaches the magistrate what is just and unjust." Or,
even less modestly: "The philosopher teaches the priest what the
gods are." Generally, however, the *philosophes* are more measured

---

[13] "The Intelligentsia" in *The Yogi and the Commissar*, p. 62.
[14] See Herbert Dieckmann, *Le Philosophe*, pp. 70-72.

in their pronouncements on themselves. In the *Encyclopédie*, for instance: "The philosopher does not consider himself in exile in this world"—a lapidary but moving statement of human solidarity.[15]

Nothing could be more unfair and more unfounded than to view the nineteenth century as the debaser of these ideals. The Encyclopedists did not degenerate into the ludicrous figures of Homais, Bouvard or Pécuchet. Their true heirs are men such as Hugo, Michelet and Renan—and on a humbler level, the underpaid, undernourished, but dedicated country schoolteachers. Prophets and martyrs for the republican mystique, pioneers of the New Regime, these *instituteurs* have shaped generations of French minds, patiently propagating the gospel of progress and civic virtues. Their figures —now already part of a bygone age—have acquired an almost mythological stature. "Saints without hope," Brice Parain calls them in his dense, moving book, *La Mort de Jean Madec*. Charles Péguy was fond of referring to them as "the black hussars of the Republic": one of the *Cahiers de la Quinzaine* he treasured most was that given over to Antonin Lavergne's somber short novel about a pathetic schoolteacher literally throttled by poverty, *Jean Coste*. As for Zola's *Vérité* (a too obvious fictional transcription of the Dreyfus case), it attempted to sum up the virtues of the *instituteur* and raise him to the level of a tragic hero. Dedicated to an apostolate of truth, isolated in his thirst for justice, suffering from all the privations and humiliations of a *déclassé*, Marc Froment is an exalted and frequently naïve portrait of a type that nonetheless did exist in real life.

No less important to literature than the survival of the *esprit encyclopédique* and the emergence of a selflessly devoted body of schoolteachers, is another social phenomenon of far-reaching consequences: the incredible fascination that Paris held for the young

---

[15] The newness of such a concept of allegiance is confirmed by a glance at the many old-fashioned definitions of the word "philosopher" which still appear in the dictionaries of the period. They seem to echo La Bruyère's view of the philosopher ("Des Ouvrages de l'esprit"): a dispassionate observer of humanity. The *Dictionnaire François* by P. Richelet (1680), the French Academy dictionary of 1694 (as well as the 1786 edition), all describe the philosopher as a wise man, leading a tranquil and secluded life, far from the entanglements of business, prudent and detached—though occasionally guilty of "*libertinage*." It is true, however, that with La Bruyère one already senses the emergence of a more impassioned and more engaged concept of the philosopher: he is "accessible," he is deeply moved by the world's "miseries," he wants to "render service," to "become useful" ("Des Biens de fortune").

men of the period, the attraction to the metropolis of countless talented and not so talented provincials—in short, the extraordinary intellectual centralization that took place in the capital. "The French have hoarded all their ideas in one enclosure," complains Paul Valéry's Monsieur Teste, who abhors this paradise of oratory. This centralization is one of the main symptoms of the contagious fever of *arrivisme* racking the young men of the first half of the nineteenth century. This fever spreads through the entire work of Balzac, particularly in *Illusions perdues* which describes the flight to Paris of an unsettled generation, losing itself in the sordid mire of journalism, or forming *cénacles* which express the idealism of the epoch. In this urge to conquer Paris, Balzac saw one of the evil results of the Revolution. To some extent, his bitterness can be explained by his own vexatious experiences with the world of Parisian journalism ("... the journalists in France, the most infamous men I know," he expostulates to Madame Hanska). Balzac moreover remarked wryly that all sorts of mediocrities were now attracted to literature: "When one does not know how to do anything, one becomes a man with a pen," he writes to Zulma Carraud.[16] But though personal bitterness explains the reaction, it does not eliminate the fact that ever increasing numbers of moneyless young men of humble birth launched into literary and artistic careers—a phenomenon which can be attributed to political and social changes, the victory of the Romantic movement, the spread of socialistic ideas, the cult of success, and more generally to the "democratization" of literature.[17]

Many novels since the middle of the nineteenth century—and some of the finest—testify to this ferment and describe the formation of these groups which so often meant the death of individual talent, of these bohemian *cénacles* of artists, journalists and failures with their ambitions and illusions: Frédéric Moreau and his friends in *L'Education sentimentale;* the group centering around the journal *Scandale* in the Goncourts' *Charles Demailly;* the circle of Coriolis, the self-destructive painter in *Manette Salomon;* the youthful and exalted group of young artists dedicated to beauty and suffering in Zola's *L'Œuvre;* the utopian members of the "Union Tolstoi"

---

[16] *Correspondance inédite avec Zulma Carraud*, p. 242.
[17] See Pierre Martino's chapter on the "bohemian" group around 1830 ("Le Groupe de la bohème et les origines de l'école réaliste") in *Le Roman réaliste sous le Second Empire*, pp. 3-25.

in Bourget's *L'Etape;* the young men from Lorraine, Sturel's up-rooted fellow students in Barrès' *Les Déracinés.* Similar groups of artists and intellectuals continue to people the novels of the twenti-eth century: the *"groupe des huit"* in Martin du Gard's early novel *Devenir;* the militant Dreyfusard group of *Le Semeur* in *Jean Barois;* the young *normaliens* of the Rue d'Ulm in Jules Romains' *Les Hommes de bonne volonté;* the anti-bourgeois young bourgeois in search of revolutionary justifications in Paul Nizan's *La Conspira-tion;* the more amenable young bohemians who gather in the Cour de Rohan in André Chamson's *La Neige et la fleur;* the frustrated postwar Existentialist intellectuals in Simone de Beauvoir's *Les Man-darins;* the less engaging young intellectuals style-Saint-Germain-des-Près in Jean-Louis Curtis' ironic novel, *Les Justes Causes.* These "groups" alone—their evolution during the last hundred years, the changing problems they face, the light they cast on the intellectual and moral preoccupations of successive generations—deserve a seri-ous study.

Finally, the growing prestige of the universities, and the emer-gence (especially during the Third Republic) of a *fonctionnarisme universitaire* holding out the promise of a stable though mediocre career, attracting many young men of modest background, created a social phenomenon with far-reaching consequences.[18] The near-obsessive struggle for a diploma became a recognized malady. A growing army of *licenciés,* frequently frustrated in their ambitions, developed side by side with an equally growing white collar prole-tariat, and occasionally merged with it. A bitter Vallès, himself the son of a submissive schoolteacher, has drawn the caricature of these pitiful young men, sons of peasants or petty bureaucrats, who find in the teaching profession a life of humiliations and vexations. Need-less to say, Vallès' picture is very one-sided: some of the freest minds of France—a Taine in philosophy, a Jaurès in politics, a Ro-main Rolland in literature—were the products of this very training. The Ecole Normale Supérieure, in particular, played an immensely important role in determining the intellectual life of the country. But Vallès is not the only one to complain: at the turn of the cen-tury, somber diagnoses begin to come in from all quarters. Serious

---

[18] Paul Bourget's Professor Monneron (*L'Etape,* p. 100) sums up this yearn-ing for bureaucratic security in his advice to his children: "You will all be functionaries (. . .) remember that no one is as happy as a functionary."

newspapers such as *Le Temps*, scientists, writers, professors, politicians show concern over the growing army of young men with diplomas. Not only Barrès, according to whom all Frenchmen dream of becoming bureaucrats, but men such as Gabriel Monod repeatedly call attention to the dangerous plethora of university graduates and to the "bureaucratic plague" which, they feel, sap the energies of the country. "The history of the Third Republic," writes a particularly acid critic, "will be marked by the admittance of all to the liberal professions and by the growth of the army of failures." [19] No wonder Marxist propagandists attempted to exploit this situation, for unquestionably, ever since the middle of the nineteenth century, France had been witnessing a steady proletarization of its intelligentsia—a proletarization which finally led to syndicalist organizations such as the Confédération Générale des Travailleurs Intellectuels and the Compagnons de l'Intelligence.

It is therefore not surprising that, side by side with the intellectuals' idealism and political involvements, the novel should also have mirrored this social phenomenon. From Vallès' pitiful Vingtras *père* to Sartre's Mathieu Delarue, ashamed of (among other things) his "*vie de fonctionnaire*," French fiction is peopled with these shabby-looking "professor types," leading apparently colorless lives: Anatole France's hen-pecked but smiling Bergeret, Bourget's monklike, pernicious Adrien Sixte or his utopian Monneron, Barrès' smug and opportunistic Bouteiller, Malègue's worn-out "*larme-à-l'oeil*" Méridier, Louis Guilloux's clumsy but admirable Cripure, Louis de Villefosse's humble, idealistic and profoundly unhappy Adrien Bruneau —all types which, at first sight, seem to lean heavily in the direction of conscious pathos or caricature.

This curious tendency toward caricature is hardly a coincidence: it is probably the most important single key to the emergence of the intellectual as a literary type. For without even insisting on the significance of an anti-intellectual revolt such as the one led in various countries by intellectuals like Unamuno, Péguy or Papini, it is clear that it is the intellectuals themselves who, with a curious lack of solidarity, have in large measure been responsible for this portrait of the intellectual. Just as it was the anti-bourgeois son of the bourgeois who invented and exploited the hatred of the philistine in

[19] Jean Rabain, "Pourquoi trahissent-ils?", *Revue Bleue*, November, 1929, pp. 657-660.

whom he so often still recognized himself, the intellectual, with self-inflicted cruelty, has created in literature the frequently unflattering portrait of the intellectual. The literary climate of the nineteenth century only encouraged such a paradox: with Romanticism man learns to view himself as a "problem," the novelist casts himself as his principal hero, art gradually becomes a meditation on art, and thought the subject of thought. Even a distorting mirror is still a mirror, and, like irony, can be a useful device where there is fear, shame or duplicity. Thus caricature can be ambiguous: the comic figure projected into fiction by the intellectual-novelist may wear another mask, begin to play a more serious role, cease to be awkward or monstrous, and finally be granted the stature and dignity necessary to emerge as the central character in the modern novel of ideas.

PART I: *From Pathos to Stature*

3

Vallès and the Pathos of Rebellion

Nous étions livrés aux professeurs, c'est-à-dire à la mort sous toutes ses formes.

—LOUIS GUILLOUX

JULES VALLÈS' DISHEVELED EXUBERANCE was not confined to literature. Son of a provincial schoolteacher who sent him to Paris to prepare for the Ecole Normale, he despised diplomas, preferred the more hot-blooded bohemian life, launched into revolutionary activities, gained experience in street fights and in the editorial rooms of militant papers, participated in the 1870 Commune, got a taste of jails and exile, and played until the end the dangerous game of revolt for revolt's sake. His colorful life, however, and even his role as founder of the revolutionary *Cri du Peuple*, might well be forgotten today were it not for the vigorous, succulent pages of his largely autobiographic *Jacques Vingtras* (1879-1886).

This trilogy, written with prankish zest, has not always been taken seriously. The linguistic verve suggests, from the first paragraph on, that the tone will remain truculent throughout. Metaphorical tours de force, onomatopoeic effects, scathing understatements, the abundant use of colloquialisms—all are part of Vallès' comic inventiveness. Indeed, the first volume, *L'Enfant*, appears primarily as a humorous though occasionally bitter series of childhood reminiscences written by a man who is eager and able to recapture the precise reactions of a young boy. *L'Enfant* is appropriately dedicated to all those who died of boredom in school, who were made to cry at home, who were "tyrannized by their teachers and thrashed by their parents."

The bare, raw, freshly whipped buttocks displayed in the opening pages are a concrete image of the petty misfortunes of young Jacques

43

Vingtras. His childhood is not exactly happy. His parents, particularly his mother, seem to delight in punishing him or in forcing him to do what most thwarts him. Yet comic passages abound. The absurd home-made outfit his stingy mother forces him to wear; her grotesque demonstration of a peasant dance at an official party; pathetically amusing scenes at home or in school—in pages such as these, laughter seems to function as a belated vengeance.

For it soon becomes clear that Vallès' comic verve goes hand in hand with the theme of revolt. Vingtras' parents symbolize the petty bureaucratic aspirations of the lower middle class. His father, as well as the greedy director of the pension Legnagna, are part of a moral climate against which the boy and later the adolescent instinctively rebel. The shocking bitterness with which he evokes his mother (a cudgel, he says, could have replaced her!) must be set against the larger implications of his critique. The child feels drawn to every excess. The prison he has visited seems to him less atrocious than his school and he compares unfavorably the sad and smelly classrooms with the corner tavern filled with laughter and good cheer. The brawny adolescent watches with envy the apparently carefree movements of peasants at work. Vingtras' revolt is in fact the revolt of a *déclassé's* son.

It is indeed primarily against the teaching profession that Vallès directs his caustic verve. Vingtras' father thus appears as the pitiful caricature of the exploited, humiliated, regimented intellectual whose sole ambition is to maintain his precarious security, ever threatened by students and superiors. Despised, often hated by his students who persecute him through organized class disorders (the traditional *chahut*), he is in turn forced to scare them in order to have peace and to obtain the much needed private lessons. The slightest scandal could compromise his career. Since he is not even an *agrégé*, he is made to feel hierarchical differences with particular brutality.

There is, however, something besides pity in these pages. Vallès does not really succeed in hiding the bitterness with which he contemplates a cowardly father who, in order to hold on to a job, had his politically compromised son (still a minor) committed to an insane asylum. And yet this caricature is by no means limited to his father. Vallès is one of the many French writers who, in the wake of Balzac's *Louis Lambert*, have evoked their days of suffering at school: the cruelty of fellow students, the obstinate struggle between the boys and their teachers, the sordid hygienic conditions, the arbitrariness of a regime based on physical punishments and privations, the instruction in solitude imparted in this social microcosm, but also the dreams of friendship and emancipation that such a regime fosters. (Vallès himself had suffered and rebelled at the pension Lemeignan, the lycée Bonaparte in Paris and the lycée of Nantes.) Much of the first volume of *Jacques Vingtras* is thus devoted to a bemused, wistful, but also malicious portrayal of pedantic types: the professor who proves the existence of God by displacing beans and matchsticks on a table; the young *agrégé* of philosophy with the obsessive mania for being first everywhere; the Principal who sets greater store by a tidy and obedient servant than by a competent teacher. Very soon, however, the caricature becomes vengeful. It is with undisguised hate that Vallès describes the thick lower lip of one professor, Turpin, who persecutes fellowship students for the simple reason that they are poor. It is with equally undisguised indignation that he tells of the false official report whereby the Principal succeeds in having a defenseless teacher removed.

Examples of pettiness and flagrant injustice stud these pages. But neither the cowardice of the father nor the arbitrariness of despotic schoolmasters can account entirely for the virulence of the caricature. The reactions provoked by reminiscences may be spontaneous, but they are also quite evidently part of a more far-reaching critique of the entire intellectual proletariat. If the young boy seems to prefer rural occupations to those of the classroom, if in his mind he sets the prison and the tavern above the sordid corridors of his school, it is not merely out of an adolescent yearning for a supposedly carefree life. If he repeatedly (and always unfavorably) compares his father to his peasant uncles and cousins, it is because he feels that their healthy allegiance to manual work, far from degrading them, has preserved their dignity. His father, on the other hand, in his very ambition to emancipate himself, in his eagerness to gain elusive "honors" by means of diplomas, has chosen the humiliating path of the *déclassé*.

The personal reproach is, however, less important here than a sense of vicarious shame for a father who has been the victim of a social phenomenon. All around him Jacques Vingtras observes the symptoms of this new social disease. On the very morning he is to take important State examinations, he sees under a bridge a destitute figure busy washing a handkerchief in the river. The figure seems familiar: he recognizes a teacher dismissed some years ago. What had been his crime? Perhaps he had played a prank on the Principal, or written an article that provoked official ire. Who cares! The point is that this former teacher, washing handkerchiefs in the muddy river water, suddenly comes to symbolize his father's whole world: unintelligent headmasters, cruel students, cowardly inspectors, intriguing colleagues—and, most of all, the eternally humiliated and persecuted teacher.

Vingtras' sense of shame thus comprises an entire social class—indeed, the very class that Barrès will soon denounce in *Les Déracinés* and Bourget in *L'Etape*: the unhappy, uprooted and socially unstable *"prolétariat des bacheliers."* At his father's deathbed, Jacques Vingtras once more deplores the willful uprooting that has made him, in his own eyes, less than a complete human being. But it is significant that the sense of shame ceases to be vicarious: Jacques Vingtras himself feels caught up in a professional career, tied to a social reality. Caricature, at first an expression of adolescent revolt, then an instrument of comedy and social critique, finally merges with a sense of personal suffering. The violent accusations he hurls at his father cannot hide the fact that it is a personal drama in which Jacques Vingtras is caught:

> Why did I set foot in this profession! O father! Why did you commit the crime of not letting me become a worker! . . .
> What right did you have to condemn me to this cowardly career!

Not only has vicarious shame been translated into a personal shame, but the comic perspective has made way for a serious, dramatic treatment. The somewhat external critique of a social group becomes a deeply felt experience of loneliness and frustration. But above all—and it is here that Vallès' entire approach is ambiguous —the object of the caricature turns out to be the narrator himself, accuser and accused in one, the half-pathetic, half-heroic, socially determined figure of an intellectual in conflict with society and himself. For Vingtras is the prisoner of his education no less than of a social reality. It is against this double imprisonment that he attempts to rebel, but rebellion is useless: whether he likes it or not, he is condemned to the intellectual's alienation, and this awareness of captivity only increases his shame.

Part of Vingtras' unhappiness is of course nothing more than a healthy discontent which can be traced to immediate material causes. Although he does derive some satisfaction from his activities (the excitement of delivering a shocking lecture, the pride of publishing a book, of founding a review, of writing articles for which he is sent to prison), the nasty truth is that no diploma and no amount of classical knowledge can feed his plebeian appetite. *Le Bachelier,* the second volume of the trilogy, is dedicated to "those who, nourished on Greek and Latin, died of hunger." It cannot be said that Vingtras does not try. His attempts, however, only amount to a long series of mortifications and minor catastrophes. As tutor in a boarding school, he spends his time wiping children's noses, cannot obtain his pay, and is falsely accused of assaulting the virtue of the headmaster's wife. He then gives private lessons, but that too leaves his stomach grumbling. As his stomach continues to protest, he becomes less and less proud. "I offered myself dirt cheap." But no school wants him, and he has to turn to other occupations: private secretary to a rich Austrian who treats him like a manservant; drama critic with instructions to interlard his column with advertisements for a coat factory; contributor to a charlatanic dictionary for which he concocts alleged quotations from Bossuet and Charron—these are only a few samples of what Vingtras considers an inescapable prostitution. When at long last he seems settled for a while in a semi-honorable position—at the *Mairie,* he verifies the sex of children brought in for birth certificates—he loses even that job when the scandal of his revolutionary lecture on Balzac becomes known.

Far more disturbing, however, than this sequence of minor calamities and the material hardships they entail, is the feeling that he is ensnared in a rootless social class which has all the claims and none of the rights of an authentic proletariat. Jacques Vingtras knows he is the victim of his background: a plebeian, who has betrayed his origins; heir to a bourgeois "humanist" culture, but at the same time irrevocably cut off from all bourgeois comforts and hostile to bourgeois ethics. He is in fact the typical representative of a social group which rapidly was expanding during the last decades of the nineteenth century—a group with which even an increasingly bureaucratized and bureaucracy-conscious France could not quite cope. No wonder Vingtras attempts to escape his depressing social fatum. But everything seems to conspire to maintain him in his social confinement. He wants to be an ordinary worker. But what has he learned to do with his hands? When he tries, his fellow workers make fun of him, convinced that he is a common criminal hiding from the police. He enters a commercial firm, but considered "too educated" he is dismissed after one month. He visits a printing shop, dreams of becoming a printer or a typographer, proposes himself as apprentice, but is told by the owner that it is too late, that he should have come at the age of twelve, that no one cares for *déclassés* who abandon school for the workshop!

Déclassé—that is indeed the key word here. Even the extreme Left suspects the "workers of the intellect." Though masking his self-pity behind the biting, exuberant style, Vallès does not succeed in disguising his sadness. Any contact with the proletariat—his brothers in suffering—is denied Vingtras. Nothing perhaps reveals more movingly his yearning for brotherhood than his joyful surprise when invited by the old rag-picker Gros: "He does me the honor of inviting me from time to time to a family dinner; and I am so happy to feel that I, the *déclassé*, am esteemed and loved by this professional rag-picker." There is little doubt: much of Vingtras' revolutionary zest, many of his insurgent activities, can be explained by this need to find and to affirm his solidarity.

One could, of course, point to a great deal of exaggeration in Vallès' trilogy. There is too unremitting an effort to attain hearty comic effects, too much metaphoric verve. The adolescent mood is somewhat artificially maintained. And after all, the lot of the "*bachelier*" was really not quite so hopeless as Vallès would have us believe. Yet in spite of aesthetic flaws and overstatements, it cannot be denied that at the root of this work there is a tragic sentiment, if not a tragic vision, which most often takes the form of rebellion.

To be sure, the myth of revolt at first appears as a manifestation of childish exuberance. The books on the French Revolution which the schoolboy discovers on his arrival in Paris impress him because they make Roman history seem pale by comparison. The discovery is an early revenge against his stuffy, despotic teachers. And there is still a great dose of puerility in the organization of the *Comité des Jeunes* which binds together a group of eighteen-year-old boys who, in a fake revolutionary atmosphere, exalt each other with fiery speeches that sound like imitative exercises. But in the last volume, significantly entitled *L'Insurgé*, the myth of the Revolution becomes more serious, the game is over: rebellion against family and school, and revolt against his own social condition, now take the form, for Vingtras, of direct participation in revolutionary activities. These pages, written much less as fiction than as a lyrical document of events witnessed, sing the heroic hours of La Villette, the street fighting, the glorious days of the Commune. In *L'Insurgé*, the theme of Revolt converges on political action, the myth of the Revolution bursts forth triumphantly. It is still with a sense of adolescent joy that Vingtras heralds the Commune, as though its only purpose were to offer ebullient young men an opportunity for excitement:

> Arise! It's the Revolution. So there it is, the moment longed for ever since the father's first cruel gesture, the first slap in the face by the teacher, ever since the first breadless day, the first homeless night—there it is, the revenge against school, misery, against the December *coup d'état*.

It is significant that the political reason should come last, that the real justification of his militant enthusiasm is exclusively emotional. Here, however, there is a grave danger of misinterpreting the Vallèsian attitude by confining it to childlike effervescence. Paul Bourget's article, written on the occasion of Vallès' death, is a fair example of this sort of interpretation.[1] Perceptively, Bourget attempts to explain Vallès by means of a shrewd stylistic analysis which brings out the childlike imagination of the author (his fondness for direct, concrete suggestions, for onomatopoeic effects) and his inability to formulate an abstract idea. Vallès thus appears as the opposite of the philosophic or scientific mind that sees all things in terms of formulas. "The gift of intellectual metamorphosis was denied him because of the very energy of his immediate animal sensations," writes Bourget, in an obvious effort to convince the reader that Vallès' taste for revolution was merely the unreasoned, destructive revolt of a child.

Clearly Vallès' yearning for a revolution was not an intellectual one. He found Marx's ideas cloudy. Ideologies interested him little indeed. Marcel Cachin, who wrote a preface to *L'Insurgé*,[2] voiced

---

[1] "Jules Vallès," in *Portraits d'écrivains et notes d'esthétique*, Etudes et Portraits, I, pp. 139-155.
[2] Les Editeurs Français Réunis, 1950.

a typical Marxist point of view when reproaching Vallès with having been an isolated rebel, lacking the guidance of a specific political doctrine and unaware of the value of political discipline. But what neither a Bourget nor a Cachin were willing to recognize is that Vallès, in spite of his apparent dynamics of pure rebellion, is really not at all out to destroy, but to preserve, or rather to recapture something infinitely precious for him. ("All that which, in his case, looks like hatred, is only another form of love," writes Louis Guilloux.[3]) His quest may be above all emotional—yet it cannot be reduced to mere petulance: it is the deep yearning to be with others, to suffer for and with others. It is this yearning for some form of solidarity which explains in part his fascination with the destitute:

> *Je suis l'ami du pauvre hère*
> *Qui, dans l'ombre, a faim, froid, sommeil.*[4]

It also explains the particular excitement with which his hero receives letters from admirers after the publication of his book, and his deep joy as he becomes aware that his journalistic battles have endeared him to the workers. Finally, it is this very yearning to belong or join with the underprivileged that explains his militant attitudes.

The irony of the situation is that even in the midst of the virile fraternity of a revolution, Jacques Vingtras remains a stranger, a fleetingly accepted pariah. Alone in his pacifism, alone in his anti-militarism, he remains alone even under shell fire and in the midst of brave deeds. Attached, in spite of himself, to bourgeois values and to a bourgeois culture he would be happy to repudiate, Vingtras remains conscious throughout of his status as *"bachelier."* The ministers of the Commune, his comrades, cannot understand what he means when he speaks of freedom of the press. Is he not forced to admit that revolutions are best organized and fought by those who, like Deputy Mayor Grêlier, display an utter contempt for the laws of grammar? He admires these leaders, these self-appointed ministers, who dictate revolutionary manifestoes studded with barbarisms,

---

[3] "A propos de Jules Vallès," *Nouvelle Revue Française*, October 1, 1930, p. 441.
[4] "I am the friend of the poor wretch/who, in the dark, is hungry, cold and sleepy." Quoted by Henri Avenel, *Histoire de la presse française depuis 1789 jusqu'à nos jours*, pp. 546-547.

and who, while fighting tyranny, also organize a thorough insurrection against French syntax.[5]

But there is more than facile humor in this situation. Vallès is indeed broaching here one of the significant tragic themes of our day: the unhappy marriage between the Leftist intellectual and the revolutionary parties. Others, coming after him, have undoubtedly explored this subject with more self-consciousness, or greater depth and artistry. In Vallès' work the theme frequently remains only half formulated or marred by a touching naïveté. But although Vallès' treatment may at times be out of focus (historically, also, the subject was a little premature), it is undeniable that there is pathos in this tension between the *déclassé* intellectual's yearning for dignity through common action and the proletarian's suspicion of such a free choice. Caricature has given way to the old conflict between thought and action. If the already graying "schoolboy" shakes his fist at his lycée, it is because he feels that it did not teach him what he most needed to know, that the culture which he now carries like a burden has betrayed him. There is bitter irony in the fact that Vingtras is ordered by the Commune to organize the military defense of the university quarter. For this university, he feels, has failed to teach him what he most needed to learn: how to be a man among men.

[5] How wrong Maupassant was in suggesting that Vallès felt discouraged and *disgusted* by the stupidity of his comrades-in-arms! ("Va t'asseoir," *Le Gaulois*, September 8, 1881.)

4

Bourget and the Guilt of the Teacher

Let us never accuse pure thought of impiety.

—ANATOLE FRANCE

¶ 1. *The reaction against positivism*

ADRIEN SIXTE, THE WITHDRAWN PHILOSOPHER in Bourget's *Le Disciple* (1889), may at first remind the reader of certain pedants described by Jules Vallès:

> A high and receding forehead, a protruding, willful, thin-lipped mouth, a bilious complexion, eyes sick from too much reading and hidden behind dark glasses, a slender body with heavy bones . . .

There is nothing flattering in this portrait. The receding forehead suggests evasiveness, perhaps even falseness. Thin lips are usually associated with frigidity, indifference or downright cruelty. The bilious complexion points to a disordered functioning of the organism—an idea which is further reinforced by the allusion to the sickly eyes. Finally, the description of the lank body in contrast to the heavy bones underlines the notion of a basic lack of balance.

Compared with Vallès' caricatures, Adrien Sixte however reveals a more systematic hostility on the part of the author, a hostility that is both more closely reasoned and more strictly limited to intellectual issues. Adrien Sixte is indirectly guilty of a crime. Bourget's novel indeed propounds the thesis that a teacher is morally responsible for the far-reaching consequences of the philosophy he teaches, that a philosopher is responsible for the thoughts and deeds of his disciple, whose crime, especially if committed in the name of a philosophy, must be attributed to his pernicious influence. More precisely, *Le Disciple* describes the dangerous moral effects of positivist thinking on an ambitious young plebeian who, inflamed by an arrogant desire for intellectual domination, seduces the daughter of a nobleman in order to experiment with emotions and test the limits of will power.

One easily detects Stendhalian echoes: Robert Greslou, the scheming, cerebral seducer is, like Julien Sorel, a tutor in a noble household; he too poses as a cold strategist and is in reality a timid, hypersensitive adolescent. But although Bourget wrote some delicate pages suggesting Greslou's complexity of character, he was more interested by far in the abstract tragedy of Sixte's philosophic and moral influence on a "disciple" he did not even know—a tragedy which leads the philosopher to doubt the validity of his system. For Bourget's attacks are aimed not merely at a fictional character, but at the entire positivist, scientific outlook that dominates the period.

The publication of Le Disciple was immediately recognized as an important event. Theodor de Wyzewa recalls the surprise that greeted this fictional proclamation of the writer's moral and social responsibility.[1] The novel does indeed mark a turning point in the career of Bourget who, until then, had been primarily concerned with sophisticated psychological analyses in novels such as Cruelle énigme, Un Crime d'amour or Mensonges. The event has greater significance, however, as a conscious and coherent repudiation of naturalist aesthetics, as well as a frontal attack on positivism, scientism and, more generally, the prestige of science.

Viewed in this light, Le Disciple is not at all an isolated phenomenon. All through the eighties, and particularly in literature (Villiers de l'Isle-Adam, Huysmans), it is easy to sense a growing dissatisfaction with the religion of science. The curiously well-timed publication of L'Avenir de la Science (written when Renan was a young man, but published only in 1890) increased the alarm already widely felt, and was soon answered by Brunetière's resounding article on the bankruptcy of science.[2] But long before Brunetière challenged Renan and Taine (who were by then most obligingly in their graves), at a time when the prestige of science seemed to be at its zenith, disturbed voices had made themselves heard. Villiers de l'Isle-

[1] Introduction to Le Disciple, Edition Nelson, p. 8. Victor Giraud, in his Paul Bourget (pp. 76-77), also recalls the importance of the event: ". . . this simple novel has had on the inner lives of many of us a unique and decisive influence."

[2] "Après une visite au Vatican," Revue des Deux Mondes, January 1, 1895, pp. 97-118.

Adam—this "fellow of infinite jest," as Anatole France calls him—while secretly enthralled by the poetic possibilities of science, protested, on the aesthetic plane, against a tendency to view man and the universe totally apart from the metaphysical problems of God and human freedom. Earlier still, Flaubert had been obsessed throughout his life by the siren song of knowledge and the barrenness to which intellectual voracity seemed to lead. If his *Tentation de saint Antoine* as well as his grotesque philosophic epic *Bouvard et Pécuchet* are deeply moving works, it is largely because both of them are haunting accounts of the nausea that overcomes the mind when it surveys the multiplicity of phenomena—for such an inventory of knowledge leads only to the hallucinating denial of the intellect by the intellect.[3] It is significant that Bourget, in an essay on Flaubert written some eight years before *Le Disciple*, should have laid particular stress on this very theme, and that he should have attributed the defeat of Flaubert's characters to the abuse of the intellect, the frenetic exaggeration of thinking, the "ravages" of science, the steady erosion of their personalities by excessive cerebration. All Flaubert's characters, according to Bourget, are victims of the "fateful goddess" *Thought*.[4]

After the defeat of 1870 Flaubert's bitterness against science increased, as he found a concrete object of aversion in the vandalizing German soldiers whose victory was due, allegedly, to their scientific superiority. "What good is science, since this people of scientists commits horrors worthy of the Huns?" Flaubert asks in a letter to George Sand. He fulminates against these "white-gloved" officers, who know Sanskrit, smash windows, steal clocks and guzzle champagne.[5] Flaubert's anger concerns literary history since it found expression in the writing of *Bouvard et Pécuchet*—but his reactions to the German victory and his disillusionment with science also herald attitudes that will emerge much more clearly in the eighties and the nineties. The outcome of the war had indeed not only been a severe blow for the contemporaries of Taine and Renan, it affected much of the intellectual history of France for the next forty-five

---

[3] J.-P. Richard in his remarkable essay on Flaubert (*Littérature et sensation*, p. 150) suggests that Flaubert is a direct ancestor of Sartre's great practitioner of intellectual nausea, Antoine Roquentin.

[4] *La Nouvelle Revue*, June, 1882, pp. 865-895. The essay was later reprinted in *Essais de psychologie contemporaine*.

[5] Letter to George Sand, March 11, 1871 (*Correspondance*, IV, pp. 50-51).

years. But whereas men such as Taine and Renan counted on science to regenerate France, the succeeding generation (Bourget, Barrès) questioned this faith in a new idol and came to associate nationalism and traditionalism with an avowed anti-positivist attitude. That in 1889 the events of 1870 were still meaningful and very much on Bourget's mind is demonstrated by the preface to *Le Disciple*, which attributes to the 1870-1871 crisis the emergence of a new sense of responsibility, and inveighs against sterile "intellectualism" à la Renan.

Bourget's hostility to this "intellectualism" is in fact a double hostility. On the abstract, philosophical level, it is a reaction to the arrogant claims of the positivist and deterministic methods. On the social level (and increasingly so as the century draws to a close), it is the concern over the growing social group of *"bacheliers"* or *"intellectuels"* who represent, as far as the class-conscious, traditionalist Bourget is concerned, one of the deplorable consequences of the university bureaucracy set up by the Revolution and the Napoleonic regime. These *universitaires républicains*, with their maladjustment, uprootedness, ferocious anti-clericalism and utopian naïveté, constitute for him a direct threat to the health of France. In *L'Etape* (the very title is a program of social conservatism), Bourget sets out to demonstrate the dangers to the individual and to society inherent in a competitive system that makes it possible for the son of a peasant to become a Parisian lycée professor. Joseph Monneron, the former fellowship student who has risen to the post of professor at the lycée Louis le Grand, becomes the symbol of all the free-thinking, academic functionaries (the "Monnerons" of France, as Bourget puts it) who, like Adrien Sixte (also the son of a modest clockmaker), are symptomatic of a moral and intellectual disease that is sapping the best traditions of the country. Bourget had obviously read Vallès with great care; there are clear echoes of *Jacques Vingtras*. Monneron's son also blames his father for having left his farmhouse ("We should have remained in Quintenas, my father a peasant like his father, and I too, a plowman, a farmer . . ."). But Bourget had also read very attentively Barrès' novel *Les Déracinés* (1897), in which his younger *confrère* (in turn influenced no doubt by Bourget's *Le Disciple*) tried to expose the dangers of the French educational system, centralized, abstract, unconcerned with regionalistic differences, politically committed to a Republican mystique.

Bouteiller is the very embodiment of this mystique. In fact, in *L'Etape* there are allusions to Barrès' Bouteiller as well as to other university professors who combine an admiration for Kant with doctrinaire ideas and corrupt political deals. Joseph Monneron of course is no Bouteiller; he is deeply honest and idealistic. But the education he gives his children is not only inept, it is criminal. The moral disorders to which they fall prey symbolize the danger this new class of "intellectuals" represents for France.

¶ II. *The techniques of dehumanization*

HOSTILITY TAKES AT FIRST the form of caricature. Bourget follows here some traditional patterns, though at times he weights the scales too heavily. Comedy is not his strong point. His tone is never more forced and off key than in his attempts at verbal realism—in those passages, for instance, which are given over to the vulgar colloquialisms of a Parisian concierge. The portrait of the "egghead" Sixte is more successful, no doubt, but in great part because little inventiveness is needed to depict an already familiar *type* in literature. What could be more conventional than his physical description? (Monneron also, with his black carefully buttoned frock coat and his narrow, sunk-in chest, looks exactly the way one expects him to look!) As for the moral traits, they are equally conventional and innocent at first. Bourget emphasizes the maniacal habits of his intellectuals. Every minute of Sixte's day is regulated according to a strict schedule of work. Every letter he receives is automatically classified in a folder labeled "Contemporary Documents." He is obsessed by the fear of losing time. His ineptness in daily living and ordinary human contacts is much stressed. He is a "dreamer," an "abstracter of quintessences" (Bourget makes sure the reader does not miss the reference to Rabelais!); he is, like Monneron, an eccentric adherent of all that is nebulous. Monneron himself is treated in an even more grotesque fashion: his unvirile thinness is contrasted with the physical opulence of his southern wife, who domineers over him in the best comic tradition. Monneron is not only a pathetic schoolteacher, he is an incapable father, blind to the goings-on in his house, fooled by his ruffianly son—mistreated above all by Bourget himself, who seems to take a malicious pleasure in having him make truly stupid pronouncements. The same sort of author's malice breaks through at the beginning of *Le Disciple*, when a simple-minded woman, terrified by Sixte's enigmatic, motionless face, takes him for a police spy: *"Dieu! qu'il a l'air faux . . ."*

This "false" look of Sixte's is no meaningless detail. It not only stresses the distance that separates a man like Sixte from ordinary humanity, it also suggests an inner lack of balance which Bourget points up ironically elsewhere. Sixte's emotional life is singularly sterile (has he even loved his mother? asks the author). And yet he does not hesitate to analyze the sexual instincts of man in two hundred bold pages which are, to say the least, incongruous, since they are written by a "very chaste, if not virginal man." This lack of balance between the intellectual and the emotional is further brought out by Sixte's refusal of family life and of friendship; by the refusal of his duties and prerogatives as a citizen (he never reads a paper, he does not vote) and even of normal social activities. Bourget goes quite far, no doubt, in the demands he makes on the reader's willingness to suspend his disbelief. Sixte, we are told, never once accepted a dinner invitation, never once went to the theater. But the author's aim is clear. He overdraws the supposedly ludicrous traits of Sixte in order to bring out the *inhuman* element in him. This inhumanity is part of a system. Did not Sixte write in his *Anatomie de la volonté* that "social ties must be reduced to a minimum by those who wish to know and speak the truth in the field of psychology"? This systematic dehumanization goes still further. Not satisfied with dismissing Christianity as a disease of mankind, he invokes Spinoza to abolish the very concept of charity. His favorite pastime is to spend hours watching monkeys in the zoo, and to laugh deeply and silently at the cynically ferocious traits of the macaques while all around him children and nurses are totally unaware of his "misanthropic thoughts."

The ascetic, absent-minded scholar, with his physical and emotional atrophy, his fear of the world, his indifference to human suffering, are hackneyed themes in Western literature. Their significance in *Le Disciple* is that they serve to cast discredit on the contemporary philosophy embodied in Sixte. Just as Monneron is far more than yet another inadequate father of another French family, being the representative of a new class and a new attitude (in fact Bourget goes so far as to ally his beliefs with those of the "worst enemies of France"), so Adrien Sixte, author of *La Psycho-*

logie de Dieu, La Théorie des passions, and *L'Anatomie de la volonté,* incarnates the deterministic, positivistic thought of his period. The very titles of his works bring to mind the names of Renan, Ribot and above all Taine, to whom he is compared on more than one occasion.

Bourget's approach obviously leaves little room for a fair assessment of a philosophy on its intrinsic merits. The argument, from the very start, is *ad hominem* (the dehumanization of the intellectual), and doubly perfidious in view of the fact that Bourget attacks a bogeyman he himself had dehumanized. Even the intellectually more respectable argument concerning the philosopher's moral responsibility is singularly devious, since it rests exclusively on the flimsy connection between an abstract philosophic position and the distant, exceptional effects of his theories on an isolated, exceptional individual. Bourget's technique is worth noting. Once again it proceeds from caricature (the concierge's suspicions that Sixte has somewhere an illegitimate son) to the serious theme of the philosopher's awareness and acceptance of guilt. This guilt, or spiritual paternity in relation to the criminal, is at first merely affirmed from the outside. The concierge's slanderous gossip *(". . . il y a quéque fils illégitime là-dessous")* is corroborated on another level by the *juge d'instruction* who informs Sixte that he is the *"directeur intellectuel"* of the accused, hence morally involved in the crime.[6] Is there not an uncanny analogy between the handwriting of the disciple and of the master? Would not graphology reveal the same "propensity to rapid discouragements"? Finally, there is even the appeal to pathos: Greslou's mother blames Sixte to his face. "If he has lost his faith, whose fault is it? Yours, sir, and your books'."

The author's devaluation of Sixte's humanity and the "external" accusations give way, in the central portion of the book, to what might be termed a subjective affirmation of responsibility: the letter of confession Greslou writes to his chosen master, in which this tormented character who has inherited many Romantic traits (sense of isolation, paralysis of the will, ineffectual longing) affirms that

---

[6] The grotesque elements are again stressed in this scene, for instance in the magistrate's remarks after Sixte's departure: "There's a madman who'd better be put away." "It's ideas like those of this intellectual anarchist that corrupt young men." The old anti-Socratic argument is reinforced by the pejorative use of the word "intellectual." Robert Greslou is, at one point, called a *"scélérat intellectuel."*

there exists between him and Sixte an unbreakable bond which
ordinary human beings could not understand. There is more than
a little irony in Greslou's desire to show himself worthy of his
master by writing a perfectly sincere confession. Even in this analysis
of the effects exerted by a "dangerous" philosophy on an impressionable young mind—and here Bourget's evaluation and technique
are infinitely more subtle—one senses a malicious tendency to discredit by means of distortion and exaggeration. "I paralyzed my
heart by dint of ideas," writes Greslou. This losing of the heart's
resources, which in turn leads to loss of faith, in no way upsets the
disciple. On the contrary, in his yearning to idolize the intellect
(the *"funeste déesse,"* as Bourget calls it elsewhere), he bends all
his efforts on transmuting the visceral forces, including sexual desire,
into pure cerebration. It is obvious that Bourget, in spite of a latent
fondness for Greslou, attempts at nearly every point to make him
as unpalatable as possible. Greslou's pride, exacerbated by this idol-
atry of the intelligence, leads him not only to view himself as different from ordinary mortals, but to dream out a system in which the
so-called "barbarians" (he gives this name to all those he judges
"irretrievably alien to intellectual life") are subject to the rule of
a new intellectual elite: "I dreamt, with the author of the *Dialogues
philosophiques,* of an oligarchy of scientists, a despotism of psy-
chologists, economists, physiologists and historians." [7] This explicit
reference to Renan shows how thoroughly, in Bourget's mind, the
Renanian dream seemed tainted with arrogance. To leave no doubt
concerning the nature of such arrogance, Bourget has Greslou state
quite bluntly the "basic principle" which underlies his view of life,
namely "not to consider as a law for us who think what is and
must be a law for those who do not think." [8] Bourget uses every
weapon to blacken the philosophy that seduced Greslou. The very
notion of remorse or guilt, the very foundations of moral awareness
and responsibility, are corroded by the theories that have poisoned

[7] The use of the word "barbarian" in this context brings to mind Barrès'
Sous l'oeil des barbares, which had appeared one year earlier, in 1888. Together
with a certain passage of the Preface, it probably is a dig at the young confrère's *"culte du Moi."*

[8] I have already referred to this statement in Chapter 2, in relation to the
"hybris of the mandarins" as seen through the eyes of hostile critics at the
time of the Dreyfus case. But clearly the hatred of a new *"caste nobiliaire,"*
delirious with pride, existed before that crisis.

Greslou: ". . . the doctrines in which I believe, the truths which I accept, the convictions that constitute the essence of my intelligence, make me consider remorse as the silliest of human illusions."

Even Sixte's ultimate awareness of responsibility in this "sinister seduction story" seems unfairly contrived by the author. It is too obvious that Bourget is interested in this acceptance of guilt primarily in order to bring Sixte to the point of questioning the validity of his entire philosophic system. The bias, here again, distorts what might have been a moving account of an intellectual's discovery of spiritual paternity. It is one thing to have Sixte admit that a mysterious bond ties a master and his disciple, even when the master does not desire this responsibility. It is another to affirm the existence of such a tie even when the disciple misunderstands or distorts the teaching. But the otherwise rational Sixte seems convinced by precisely this kind of logic. He has the "awful vision" of the corrupting force of his ideas, he understands that he has "committed wrong," he has the "lightning revelation," the "indisputable proof" that his work has poisoned a soul, that his philosophy carries the very principle of death in it. At the end of the novel, Bourget imagines the total defeat of the intellect in the face of the unknowable. Sitting at his disciple's deathbed, watching Greslou's mother pray, the "great negator" Sixte finally loses himself in a meditation which augurs well for his eventual return to religious faith: ". . . for the first time, aware that his mind was powerless to sustain him, this analyst so logical that he was nearly inhuman, humbled himself, bowed, lost himself in front of destiny's inexplicable mystery."

¶ III. *From caricature to nobility*

HIPPOLYTE TAINE WAS SO PAINED BY THE NOVEL that he delayed for several months thanking Bourget for the complimentary copy he had sent him. Not only did Bourget's unexpected attack against positivism sadden him, but he felt personally implicated. When he finally did answer (September 29, 1889), he did not hide his strong objections. On the one hand, he felt, the character of Greslou had been treated with far too much sympathy, which placed the entire burden of guilt on the teacher and paradoxically reaffirmed an intellectual determinism in complete contradiction to the basic anti-deterministic thesis of the book. Taine pointed out what he considered the weakness of the novel: the reader is forced to choose between a discrediting of morality and a discrediting of science. Not surprisingly, however, it is the portrait of Adrien Sixte that most disturbed Taine. He accused Bourget of having created the absurd caricature of a monumentally ignorant pseudo-philosopher rather than an honest portrayal of a scientific mind. "You have given him an insufficient intellect and an insufficient scientific education," Taine complained. "He knows only surfaces." How can a man who reads no newspapers, who has traveled nowhere, whose knowledge of society, politics, literature, economics is more limited than that of the "most narrow-minded grocer" or most obtuse peasant —how can a man with such "colossal ignorance" pronounce judgments on social and moral problems?

Taine was evidently too close to the novel and too upset by its implications to assess it in the proper perspective. Some very curious aspects seem to have escaped his attention. It is true that Robert Greslou has an endearing side to him: his extreme sensitivity, the fervor with which he discovers Shakespeare and Musset, his intellectual honesty, his courage and dignity at the end of the book. But it is equally true that Bourget—probably with very little premeditation—has endowed Adrien Sixte with likable and even admirable character traits which, at nearly every point in the novel, contradict or undo the effects created by hostile caricature. Sixte, in spite of his ultimate acceptance of responsibility, early in the book very bluntly denies the possibility of such guilt in terms that certainly should have pleased Taine.[9]

Contradiction or ambiguity? To some extent Bourget was no doubt aware of the dual nature of his character. As the omniscient author he intrudes, at one point in his novel, to explain that the *juge d'instruction* Vallette could not possibly understand this unusual combination of an "all-powerful brain" in the realm of ideas with a "naïve," "timid," and even "comical" nature in the realm of facts. This duality of conception, it would seem, is not limited to the character of Sixte. It occurs nearly every time an "intellectual" appears in Bourget's as well as Barrès' work. The very word "intellectual," stirring up mixed feelings, seems to point to an am-

[9] "To impute to a doctrine the responsibility for the absurd interpretation of that doctrine by an unbalanced mind is like imputing to the chemist who discovered dynamite the crimes for which this substance is used."

bivalent concept. At the beginning of *L'Etape*, the reader learns that Jean Monneron has "the slender, beautiful fingers of an intellectual"—an observation that leads to a brief digression on the term "intellectual" which, we are told, is the only adequate term to designate human beings who are sometimes hatefully arrogant, but whose inherent "nobility" also makes of them the "admirable" victims of their own intellect.

Some of this ambivalence can no doubt be attributed to Bourget's sincere desire to be honest and fair—scruples that may appear somewhat naïve in the light of his so obviously slanted *romans à thèse*. It is noteworthy, however, that as late as 1927, in *Nos Actes nous suivent*, the "enemies" of the traditional French values (the anarchist-philosopher Edouard Péreuse, and even the political terrorist and assassin Sitnikoff) are given what appears on the surface to be a "fair" treatment. A more significant, more personal reason is probably the fact that Bourget's own father, an ex-*normalien*, was a university professor (his idealized image briefly appears in *Le Disciple* as the father of Greslou, who takes long walks with his son and initiates him in sound scientific methods), and that Bourget himself, though he stubbornly refused to enter the academic profession, had nevertheless obtained his *licence*, prepared for the entrance examinations of the Ecole Normale and been a student and great admirer of Taine, whose ideas he most successfully applied in his *Essais de psychologie contemporaine*.[10] It is easy to detect in Bourget's work a permanent tendency to create noble intellectual figures such as the "admirable" Professor Victor Ferrand or the much "admired," morally pure philosopher William James so frequently evoked in *Nos Actes nous suivent*.

Anatole France called Sixte the hero of *Le Disciple*.[11] Of all the contemporary critics, France was unquestionably the most perceptive. For Sixte is not only the principal character (even this was not so obvious to many readers: much more space in the book is devoted to Greslou's tragic adventure), he is at nearly every point, consciously or unconsciously, and frequently in seeming contradiction

---

[10] During the winter of 1871-1872, Bourget audited, at the Ecole des Beaux-Arts, Taine's lectures on the Venetian painters. Albert Feuillerat (*Paul Bourget*, pp. 28-29) believes that these lectures confirmed him in his literary vocation.

[11] "La Morale et la Science. M. Paul Bourget," in *La Vie littéraire*, 3ème série, pp. 54-78.

to the basic thesis, glorified by the author. He is a "great manipulator of ideas," a "powerful worker." Even as a puny child, he astonished his schoolmates with his strength of character. Robert Greslou places Sixte among "the princes of modern thought." Bourget himself informs the reader that in his very first work Sixte already displayed an extraordinary intellectual "power" coupled with a "breadth of erudition" and a multiplicity of viewpoints the like of which had not been seen in many years. He belongs, we are told, to the family of great thinkers. His modes of being and of thinking can give us an insight into the existence of a Descartes. The image of Spinoza, whose life by Colerus Bourget knew by heart, constantly hovers over Sixte like an admired master or interceding saint. Sixte is particularly fond of an old acacia bearing the inscription "1632"—the year of Spinoza's birth. Greslou writes: "You appeared to me as a sort of modern Spinoza, so completely true to your own books in the nobility of a life entirely devoted to thought." Elsewhere, the author praises his "magnificent sincerity," his "noble" (though naïve) heart and the "holy virginities of his conscience." For Sixte, the positivist teacher, is also a "poet of ideas," living with a daily ideal of purity, losing himself in contemplation with a sort of dizziness, "feeling" thoughts with all his being and participating quasi-mystically in the permanent labor pains of the cosmos. "He lived life in all its forms. He assumed all of its shapes."

This paradoxical exaltation of the very personage whose life, thoughts and influence Bourget on one level explicitly disapproves of, even takes the form of a mild hagiolatry which expresses itself in recurring images and comparisons. In his Preface, Bourget calls the positivist philosopher and philologist Emile Littré "nearly a saint." From the very beginning of the novel, heavy stress is laid on Sixte's "ascetic" life. Robert Greslou explains to his mother: "If you knew him, mother, you would venerate him. He is a saint." The intruding author voices similar feelings when he describes Sixte as a "lay saint" and his pure "monastic" life as that of an "intellectual hermit." That these images and comparisons must be taken at face value is made clear. Bourget explains that this man, so utterly afraid of petty disturbances, has the makings of a hero and a martyr: "This thinker, so heroically independent . . . would, at another period, have walked to martyrdom for his convictions, with the resolution of a Bruno or a Vanini. . . ." The key words of the passage leave no doubt as to the deeper feelings Bourget experiences for a human type who has "sacrificed" everything (here too the choice of words is significant) to "serve" the cause of "truth." His honesty, his "magnificent" sincerity may lead Sixte to the acceptance of responsibility and guilt—but in this very acceptance Bourget admires the philosopher's dignity and the generosity of his mind.

Even Monneron, in spite of his incurably utopian temperament, his chimerical outlook; in spite of his intransigence, drunkenness with ideas and political allegiance to ideologies that ally him with the "enemies of France" (he was, of course, a Dreyfusard!)—even Monneron displays a nobility of soul and intellect which Bourget generously bestows upon him at the very moment he does his best to discredit him and his ideas. In spite of his "worst intellectual aberrations," he is an "excellent man," capable of "true tenderness." This "senseless" father is also a "magnanimous" one, a "noble" heart, "simple," "true" and "sensitive." Bourget does not stop at such a sentimental rehabilitation: his Monneron has not only authentic enthusiasm for the best literature (he is a *"délicat lettré"*), but, like Sixte, he also has an "ascetic nature," is completely devoted to school and students, punctual and conscientious like a good soldier, irreproachably honest, incorruptible, stoical in his suffering and proud of his "admirable" profession. Above all, he is a citizen of the world of ideas, to which he feels committed with true poetic fervor. "You and I, we are two beings passionately in love with ideas," he proudly explains to his son at the end of the novel. The author himself seems to applaud the "delicate scruples" and the "energetic integrity of his conscience," the ardor and sincerity of this "selfless believer."

Monneron remains, however, a pathetic figure despite his moments of greatness. The same is not true of Adrien Sixte, whose intellectual defeat in the face of the deeper mystery of life has tragic grandeur. His is the humiliation that accompanies the acceptance of a revealed reality (Bourget significantly uses the words "vision" and "revelation"). When Anatole France called Sixte the true *hero* of the book, he may well have come closer to the truth than he intended. Behind Bourget's didactic purpose, another voice can indeed be heard which describes with sympathy the cruel shock experienced by a man of good will and proclaims his disappointment, his suffering and his sadness.

That Bourget seems to have been haunted until the end of his life by this theme of the intellectual's tragic responsibility is evidenced by the very title of his last novel, *Nos Actes nous suivent* (1927), in which the culprit for whose sins the following generation still has to pay is once more a scientist (an ex-*normalien*, in fact) who lives in an "atmosphere of lofty ideas" and is the victim of "intellectual anxieties." Albert Feuillerat suggests that the main theme of *Le Disciple* was derived in part from a very personal, though indirect sense of moral implication Bourget may have experienced in the *affaire* Chambige. This was an illicit love affair which resulted in an attempted *Liebestod*-suicide (only the woman died), involving a hypersensitive young writer whose literary talent Bourget had encouraged, and who seems to have been led astray by too much reading of fiction (including the novels of Bourget!).[12] It is not unlikely that Bourget was shaken by this *crime de passion*, and that, with a measure of self-dramatization, he conceived his novel in part as an act of atonement.

Obviously, however, Bourget's vision is not limited to such a personal, half-imagined and half-exaggerated sense of guilt. His concern in *Le Disciple* and elsewhere is clearly with a more permanent theme that provokes his meditation, with the *tragique de la pensée*, the tragedy of intellect—and more specifically with the dialectics of thought and action, which, in a totally different form and context, had haunted Balzac. Thought and action, *Denken und Tun*, Goethe wrote in *Wilhelm Meisters Wanderjahre*, is the sum of all wisdom, like the rhythm of question and answer. Yet the corruption of thought by action, and of action by thought—all thinkers, all religious or revolutionary leaders have had to face it. Greslou, the disciple, in a way symbolizes the intellectual's double yearning for both poles of human experience: he feels "tormented by longing for this despised action." It is Bourget himself who seems to add (and the remark is, I believe, deeply significant) that "Goethe has created all of his *Faust* out of this nostalgia." Is there not an implicit glorification of the power of ideas in the very condemnation of their effects? For what greater tribute can there be to their efficacy than this insistence on their potential danger?

The tragic undertones behind Sixte's character and experience are thus successful to the extent that he effectively embodies Bourget's personal and also his abstract concern with the problem of the

12 *Paul Bourget*, pp. 139-140.

intellect. The opening onto mystery at the end of the novel only ennobles the human attitude in the face of this mystery. It is no defeat, but a victory. The ultimate impotence of thought implies also the grandeur of this impotence. Bourget might have agreed with Anatole France: living (like thinking) cannot be innocent.

It is no coincidence that intellectuals—writers, historians, scientists, philosophers—so frequently people Bourget's fiction. Already in *Mensonges* (1888), the writer Claude Larcher views the artistic sensibility as a self-inoculated experimental field. In *Nos Actes nous suivent* Bourget's concern is still with an emotional and spiritual crisis, but his primary interest has lain for some time now in what he himself terms a *"drame intellectuel"*—a crisis of the intellect. Like Louis Savignan, the central character of *Le Démon de midi*, the intellectuals offer a double advantage to the novelist: they are lucid and competent judges within the novel (Savignan is an "intellectual athlete" who evaluates, condemns and jousts with modernistic trends in religion), but their conscience is also a convenient and even necessary locus for the unfolding of the *"drame intellectuel."* Ideas, Bourget seems to imply, have a life of their own. Crémieu-Dax explains in *L'Etape*: "One cannot prevent ideas from leading us where they themselves move." One must wrestle with them, of course, but this struggle with the angel is also an admission of faith in the power of ideas (Bourget even uses the expression *"corps à corps"* in relation to such a purely ideological struggle [13]). One expression perhaps sums up all that Bourget wanted his principal characters to be: *héros de la conscience.* This unquestionably was Bourget's intention in *Le Disciple* and it explains why the portrait of Adrien Sixte is far indeed from being as simple, as grotesque or as hostile as it may at first appear. Bourget's aim was the novel of ideas, the tragedy of the mind and of the conscience. In a speech delivered to the Académie Française in 1907, he himself explicitly condemned the *roman à thèse*: "Let us condemn thesis literature, an essentially false genre; we must clearly set apart the literature of ideas, a legitimate, a necessary genre. If our novels and our plays do not lead to it, then we are nothing but entertainers." [14] Did Bourget succeed

[13] *Le Démon de midi*, II, p. 59.
[14] Speech delivered on the occasion of the reception of Maurice Donnay at the Académie Française. Quoted by Charles-Brun, *Le Roman social en France au XIXème siècle*, p. 63. Bourget expressed his views on the *"roman d'idées"* in the preface to *La Terre promise.*

within his own work in maintaining this distinction? That is another question. But it is certain that this ambition, as well as his permanent attraction to the intellectual as hero, make him a direct ancestor of our modern metaphysical novel.

5

Emile Zola and Anatole France:
The Lay Apostle and the Lay Saint

¶ 1. *The apostolate of Marc Froment*

Vérité (1902) IS AN UNSOPHISTICATED PANEGYRIC to the glory of a schoolteacher who, urged onward by his republican mystique, fights obscurantism and lays the foundations of the new City of Truth and Justice. Characteristic simplifications and amplifications leave little doubt as to the author's own fervor. Zola's intellectual hero, Marc Froment, has a quasi-primitive heroic stature.

> There was a measure of heroism in his deed and he accomplished it with simplicity, out of enthusiasm for the good work he was undertaking. The highest role, the noblest, in a young democracy is that of the primary schoolteacher, so poor, so despised, who is entrusted with the education of the humble and who is to make of them the future happy citizens, the builders of the City of Justice and Peace. His mission suddenly became clear to him: his apostolate of truth, his passion to penetrate the positive truth, to proclaim it loudly, to teach it to everyone.

The tone of the passage, words such as "mission" and "apostolate," the idea of a "truth" to be discovered and disseminated, clearly point to an ideological passion as absolute as a religious faith. The millenaristic social dream is repeatedly suggested by direct references to the *cité future*. Not only are the schoolteachers of the Third Republic called "modern apostles," "apostles of reason," "missionaries of the new humanity," but the novel is part of a tetralogy entitled *Les Quatre Evangiles* (*The Four Gospels*), the individual titles of which are *Fécondité, Travail, Vérité* and *Justice*.[1] Mathieu, Luc and Marc are the respective heroes of the completed *Evangiles*. As for the name Froment (from the Latin *frumentum*, the richest

[1] *Vérité* appeared posthumously. The final volume, *Justice*, was never written.

type of wheat), it serves to remind us of Zola's obsession with the theme of fertility. In *Vérité* the fertilizing is exclusively intellectual: the hero sows the seed of enlightenment, the "good word" which will free peoples' minds from error and lies.

The specific error, the specific lie around which the novel crystallizes and against which Marc Froment sets out like a true crusader is the scandal of the Dreyfus case—which Zola transposes by making of a Jewish schoolmaster, a colleague of Marc Froment, the innocent victim of local superstitions, mental indolence and chauvinistic bias. A schoolteacher and a Jew: a predestined target of all the forces of darkness! It is no doubt with a certain measure of contentment that Zola made his "apostle" the defender of a Jew. But although the fictional version of the Dreyfus case is at the heart of the novel (in 1902 all the incidents were still fresh in readers' minds), Zola seems much more concerned with his own humanitarian dreams than with the legal issues raised by the famous *Affaire*. The attitude of Zola is not unique. Péguy and his friends also experienced this national crisis above all as a spiritual adventure. "*L'affaire Dreyfus, c'est la mystique républicaine,*" Albert Thibaudet explained many years later.[2] Indeed, once the battle had been won and the true culprits denounced, there remained the abstract quest for justice and for the myth of Republican Purity. The priest-ridden town of *Vérité* gives way at the end of the novel to the harmonious city, a new version of Eldorado made secure for future generations by the schoolteacher (now the most honored citizen), by science and by the "irresistible power of ideas."

An unmitigated seriousness inspires the book. One finds here none of the ambiguities that characterize Vallès', Bourget's or Barrès' treatment of the intellectual. Yet there is incongruity in Zola's enthusiasm for Marc Froment and for the "irresistible power of ideas." No one, in a sense, was less prepared than Zola to exalt the heroic virtues of the intellect, or less suited temperamentally to be a leader of the *parti intellectuel*. But literary history is full of such ironies. Just as Bourget, the son of a professor and himself endowed with a potential for scholarship, became sharply critical of much that intellectualism and science stood for; just as Barrès, the dilettantish aesthete, posed as an enemy of culture and was consequently ac-

2 "Réflexions—Péguy et Bergson," *Nouvelle Revue Française*, April, 1931, pp. 580-592.

claimed by those whom he himself had termed "barbarians"—so Emile Zola, by a twist of fate, found himself at the head of a group with which he had little in common.[3] For Zola felt scant tenderness for professors and for the academic life. He left school after having twice failed the *baccalauréat*. His writings display a consistent suspicion of the academic scholar and are often outspokenly hostile. Particularly unpalatable to him was the spirit that prevailed at the Sorbonne and at the Ecole Normale Supérieure. Professors and professional critics do not fare well in his novels. In *Le Docteur Pascal*, the retired teacher living in symbolic isolation in the house next door embodies egoism, cowardice and sterility.

Zola became even more bitter after the unfavorable reception of his novel *Rome*. Pierre, the hero of *Paris*, launches into a lengthy disquisition against the *normaliens*: they are not satisfied with teaching, but want to rule over the world of art, of journalism and of society; they pose as dilettantes, are haunted by the desire to charm, become masters of paradox, and strive mightily to appear skeptical, frivolous and very "Parisian." Even in *Vérité* there are echoes of this same prejudice. Marcilly, the ever-smiling young Député, a former *normalien*, is nothing but a pleasure-seeking *arriviste*. As for Le Barazer, the Inspecteur d'Académie, he is an ardent republican and consequently defends Marc Froment. But his very adroitness is a moral blemish: the prudent "diplomat" is also an "opportunist."

More strictly literary reasons—his concept, for instance, of the modern epic novel—also explain why Zola denied the thinker and the drama of thought any important role in the Rougon-Macquart cycle. When the critic Jules Lemaître, after the publication of *Germinal*, spoke of Zola's "pessimistic epic of human animality," Zola replied: "You place man in his mind, I put him in all of his organs. You isolate man from nature, I can't conceive of him away from the earth, whence he comes and where he will return. . . . I firmly believe that I have taken into account all of the organs, the brain as well as the rest. My characters think as much as they should think, as much as one does think in ordinary life." [4] This dialogue with Lemaître he carried into *L'Œuvre*, where Sandoz, who is in part

---

[3] Characteristically the young intellectuals in Roger Martin du Gard's *Jean Barois*, while filled with admiration for Bernard Lazare and Emile Duclaux, are somewhat irked by the well-meaning "lyricism" of Zola.

[4] *Correspondance (1872-1902)*, pp. 633-634.

an idealized self-portrait, explains why he does not want to write metaphysical novels or novels of ideas: "What a joke, this continuous and exclusive study of the activity of the brain, on the pretext that the brain is the noble organ! . . . Thought, thought, damn it all! thought is the product of the entire body. Let's see a brain think all by itself, let's see what happens to the nobility of the brain when the belly is sick! . . ." Observations such as these are significant. The "thinker" simply did not fit Zola's requirements for heroic stature. Commenting on Théodore de Banville's play, *Deïdamie* (1876), he very seriously asserted that contemporary writers wishing to emulate works of antiquity should use as characters peasants and workers. "Only our workers and our peasants have the simple and sturdy build of Homer's heroes." [5]

The trilogy *Les Trois Villes (Rome, Lourdes, Paris)* thus marks a turning point in Zola's career as a novelist, a bridge between the completed Rougon-Macquart cycle and *Les Quatre Evangiles*. The "intellectual" Froment family, in sharp contrast with the Rougon-Macquarts,[6] imports into Zola's fictional world a new series of themes: crises of conscience, social indignation, intelligence as a dynamic force, moral dedication, spiritual conversions and reconversions. This renewal and, to some extent, broadening of Zola's themes can be diversely interpreted. Malevolent voices immediately suggested that Zola's powers had declined, that he had lost his creative vision and in its stead was purveying artificially contrived "problems." It is still customary today to point to the waning of Zola's imagination and artistic powers after 1892 or 1893. Certainly nothing he wrote after that date can even be compared with the movement and color of *L'Assommoir*, *Germinal* or *La Débâcle*.

To equate intellectual themes with artistic decrepitude constitutes, however, a dubious critical judgment. In reality, there are other reasons why Zola turned his energies to the novel of ideas. First among them perhaps was the intellectual mood prevalent in French letters at the turn of the century. Convinced that in spite of her prosperity France was really undergoing a grave moral crisis, many of the serious writers (Barrès, Claudel, Maurras, Anatole France, the young Romain Rolland) set out to diagnose her ills and prescribe appro-

[5] *Nos Auteurs dramatiques*, 1881, pp. 297-303.
[6] Docteur Pascal is an exception. But he acts more as an epilogue to the entire series. He is a fictional "observer" within the fiction, a living "index."

priate remedies.[7] Bourget's *Le Disciple* had set the tone. More specifically, Zola's ire had been aroused by Brunetière's polemics with Berthelot and by his crusade against science. *Paris* is studded with direct and indirect allusions to Brunetière's article on the "bankruptcy of science."[8] Zola felt compelled to counter-attack, and his fiction became ideologically militant. But it is also true that as early as 1890 Zola starts to toy with the idea of a totally different type of novel. "I begin to be tired of my series"—he confides to Jules Lemaître in a letter thanking him for his review of *La Bête humaine*.[9] And, after explaining that he must finish it, he adds this curious remark: "Then I will see, if I am not too old, and if I am not too much afraid of being called a turncoat." This "turncoat" aspect of his work is manifested in *Les Trois Villes* and *Les Quatre Evangiles;* Zola himself has best defined it in a letter to Octave Mirbeau: "All this is very utopian, but what do you want? I've been dissecting for forty years; I must be allowed in my old days to dream a little."[10] To embody his dreams in fiction, Zola needed a new type of character: the thinking (or dreaming) protagonist capable of free choice, or critical distance, and driven onward by an urge for syntheses and global visions.

Perhaps Zola himself exaggerates the newness of what he wrote after 1893. His renunciation of the aims and methods of pure naturalism is less far-reaching than he thinks. "Dream" and "dissection" are, in his case, not really irreconcilable. The utopian characteristics of *Les Trois Villes* and *Les Quatre Evangiles* only bring to the surface a natural and, at one time, predominant tendency of Zola's character. For Zola's early admirations went to idealistic and visionary artists: Dante, Ronsard, Chénier. He even enjoyed the delicate dreams of a Musset. The Romantics, against whom he openly rebelled, had not only been his spiritual masters, but could claim him as their direct and secretly most faithful heir. He had been brutally unfair to Hugo—but owed him far more than he would ever dare acknowledge: a taste for grandiose visions, sympathy for the "peo-

---

[7] For a comprehensive study of these "clinical" approaches to contemporary social problems, see Micheline Tison-Braun, *La Crise de l'Humanisme*, I (1890-1914) (1958).

[8] Zola takes a malicious pleasure in referring constantly to the "bankruptcy of charity."

[9] *Correspondance (1872-1902)*, p. 720.

[10] Letter of November 29, 1899, *ibid.*, p. 855.

ple," a tendency to self-dramatization and self-glorification, and, above all, that inner conviction that the poet is prophet, *vates*, seer, a fierce magus, a voice that announces the truth. Like Hugo, he might have proclaimed:

> Peuples! écoutez le poète!
> Ecoutez le rêveur sacré!

His earliest projects, for instance the long poem in three cantos to be entitled *La Chaîne des êtres*, betray epic ambitions and call for a significant mixture of the scientific and the poetical. In a letter to his friend Baille (June, 1860), Zola explains that the scientific account of creation and the historical account of the progress of civilization are to lead up to a "*magnifique divagation*" in the final canto. The very choice of terms is revealing: "Thus, in the first canto, the scientist; in the second, the philosopher; in the third, the lyric bard; in all three, the poet.—A magnificent idea. . ." [11]

The distance separating the "scientist" from the "lyric bard," the cold observer from the utopian dreamer, never gaped very wide. The naturalistic novels of Zola are saturated with moral and moralizing undertones which point forward to the revolutionary lyricism of his later period. This explains perhaps his determination to equate science with revolution. Docteur Pascal's credo is still a typical eighteenth-century belief in progress, toughened somewhat by Darwinism. In *Paris*, however, the scientist Bertheroy goes much further, proclaiming the religion of science: "Science alone is revolutionary." Hostile to the anarchist intellectual who reasons out murder cold-bloodedly in order to alleviate his boredom (one recognizes Zola's own anti-"intellectual" bias), Bertheroy explains: "Isn't science enough? . . . she alone sweeps away dogmas, carries away the gods, brings light and happiness. . . . It is I, a pensioned and decorated member of the Institute who am the only true revolutionary." These poetics of science, this sentimental, vague, optimistic fatalism were not exactly to the liking of Zola's new socialist friends. It has been suggested that it is in part their admonitions which oriented him toward the "fideistic" characters of *Les Quatre Evangiles*. [12]

[11] *Correspondance (1872-1902)*, pp. 98-99.
[12] Cécile Delhorbe, *L'Affaire Dreyfus et les écrivains français* (1932), p. 56. For a more specific discussion of the fictional transpositions of the Dreyfus case, see Renée Riese Hubert, *The Dreyfus Affair and the French Novel* (1951).

The hero of *Vérité*—an intellectual with a non-intellectual temperament—is thus the fictional product of many contradictory strains in Zola's make-up: a long-standing suspicion of the scholar and yet a faith in the revelations of science; a need for epic simplifications and yet the ambition to be a subtle moral diagnostician of France's ills; utopian leanings and militant tendencies colored by an obsession with the physical aspects of human life; a propensity for obvious symbols aggravated by scant gifts for analysis; the temperament of a visionary allured by sweeping syntheses in which science, poetry and revolution all merge—these are some of the reasons that account for Zola's apostolic free-thinker Marc Froment. They also cast light on the idyllic simplicity of his character.

Even the manner in which Zola magnifies and glorifies his character reveals a curious lack of focus. On the one hand, there is a systematic attempt to cluster around the figure of this defender of Truth and Justice some of the conventional tragic themes and attitudes. Marc Froment, an "alien" in the town he adopts, is the solver of a riddle (the novel, at times, takes the form of a detective story) and the healer of a moral disease. His drama is personal (a moral crisis that involves a seeming choice between honor and happiness); but it is also communal: the drama of social responsibility in which the individual assumes and ultimately purifies a common guilt. His is moreover a tragedy of progressive loss and loneliness, as his wife temporarily abandons him and he is deprived of his daughter and of his friends.

Marc Froment's courageous acceptance of personal loss in the pursuit of a higher aim, his ability to dominate his grief for the sake of a passionate commitment to an ideal, soon cease, however, to be presented in the light of an individual experience. The hero, struggling against ignorance, founder of the new City that embodies Zola's dream of a revitalized France, dedicated to the happiness of the community, loses his identity and dissolves into an epic abstraction. Even Zola's style—his mania for recapitulations and repetition of epithets—contributes to the epic climate.

This tendency to proceed from the individual to the group is of course a permanent feature of Zola's novels. In *Vérité*, there is however a more precise reason for this shift in emphasis. Zola's fictionalized account of the Dreyfus case was to be above all a dithyramb in honor of the primary schoolteacher, the *instituteur*. And not only in honor of the *instituteur* Marc Froment (whose humility and sense of vocation are merely representative), but in honor of the entire *"bataillon sacré"* who, in the remotest villages of France, struggle valiantly to conquer ignorance.

Zola's paean of praise to the *instituteur* is of course not an isolated phenomenon. Ever since Condorcet coined the word in 1792 the name has been synonymous with republican virtues. Hugo and Michelet repeatedly proclaimed that this shaper of minds and torchbearer lighting the road to a better future embodied the highest values of France. During the Third Republic (1870-1940), the *instituteur* truly came to symbolize the myth of Revolution, love of democracy, the religion of progress and the cult of civic virtues. Ferdinand Buisson, himself one of France's idealistic educators, called the *instituteur* the "pioneer of the new regime," and asserted that in a Republic the schoolteacher should be *"chose sacrée."* [13] Clemenceau, in *Le Grand Pan*, spoke of the prophets of the New Logos! Caught between the grandeur of his mission and the misery of his condition, the *instituteur* was eventually surrounded by a special mythological aura. Albert Thibaudet recalls a version of *Prometheus Bound* (performed at a Université Populaire in 1903) in which the heroic Prometheus was a persecuted socialist *instituteur*.[14] The *instituteur* also found his way into the novel: Eugène Sue's "lay Parsifal" in *Martin, l'enfant trouvé* (1846); the poor young teacher in Erckmann-Chatrian's *Histoire d'un sous-maître* (1871); the hungry, disheveled hero, driven to madness, in Antonin Lavergne's *Jean Coste* (1901); the idealistic Clauricard, in Jules Romains' *Les Hommes de bonne volonté;* the austere, demanding schoolmasters in *La Mort de Jean Madec* (1945), whose purity of heart and unshakable faith in the eminent dignity of the common people Brice Parain so powerfully evokes—all moving portraits, no doubt; but none as ambitious as Zola's.[15]

[13] "L'Instituteur et la République," *Le Radical*, December 31, 1907. Reprinted in *La Foi laïque*.
[14] *La République des Professeurs*, p. 226.
[15] For a colorful though sketchy historico-social portrait, see Georges Duveau, *Les Instituteurs* (1957). Jean L'Hote's *La Communale* (1957) is a series of humorous scenes involving a family of *instituteurs* in Lunéville. More recently, Jean Boorsch, in an excellent article on French primary education, has written some very suggestive pages about the *instituteur* (*Yale French Studies*, No. 22, Winter-Spring, 1958-59, pp. 17-46).

For Zola's treatment is not limited to the lonely struggle and ultimate victory of a representative type. *Vérité*, like *Jean Coste* (and perhaps more convincingly), also insists on the pathos of the *instituteur*, which is brought out by means of a minor character, the embittered Férou who, persecuted by the local priest as well as by the brutal peasants, lives in heroic misery. Son of a shepherd, he is a typical *déclassé*, permanently humiliated and literally spat upon. Through this somewhat excessive image of misery Zola attempts to give his social victim a tragic dignity. Expressions such as "heroic courage," "tragic gravity" are only a prelude to the sordid dénouement. Exasperated to the point of rebellion, Férou is dismissed from his teaching post, then deserts from the army, and is finally shot down like a mad dog by a sergeant in a disciplinary battalion, leaving his wife and two daughters in utter destitution. But if Zola presents this destiny with somewhat clumsy insistence, it is not at all to back the view that rebellion is the only answer to this moneyless and honorless career, but to bring out the martyrdom of his "apostles." For martyrdom is the proof as well as the price of their ideal. If things turn out well in the long run for Marc Froment it is not because his hero must suffer less, but because the truth of the new Gospel has to be victorious. "Glory be to the *instituteur* stricken down in the exercise of his function, a victim of his effort toward more light! . . ." The very tone of such sentences—and they are not rare—suggests once again the evangelic style, and serves to remind the reader that the worn-out Gospel is to be replaced by a newer and better one: the Gospel of Intelligence, which supposedly proclaims the inanity and danger of the Christian "Blessed are the poor in spirit. . . ." No wonder certain contemporary critics, like Lucien-Victor Meunier, considered *Vérité* a "superb book of republican and lay education."[16] Gustave Téry, in *La Raison* (May 10, 1903), called the novel "our gospel, our lay breviary"! To more sober readers, however, the end of the novel may well seem a little exuberant, even faintly comical in its very note of triumph. Not only does Marc's own daughter become an *institutrice*, but the fecundity of the new gospel is such that nearly everybody, one gathers, becomes a schoolmaster, marries a schoolmistress and gives birth to a swarm of future sowers of the Truth.

But Zola was not content with this abstract triumph of the *institu-*

16 *Le Rappel*, February 26, 1903.

teur. Beyond the tragic dilemma of Marc the individual, beyond the glorification of the "sacred battalion" which ultimately dissolves into mere propaganda, Zola was also quite evidently out to glorify himself. His outline for the novel contains this revealing note: "And at the end he [Marc] is right. *It is my triumph.*" [17] The reference is clearly to Zola's role in the Dreyfus case. Curiously enough, Dreyfus himself, in all the literature inspired by his plight, never appears as a hero or even as an important character. Partly this may be due to his pale, unheroic figure which so much disappointed his most ardent defenders. Nearly all the writers who dealt with the case squarely or episodically (Zola, Anatole France, Romain Rolland, Proust, Martin du Gard) were in fact primarily concerned with the broader political or social issues, or with their own ideological commitment. Zola is one of the few who has at least attempted to present Dreyfus as a suffering creature and not merely as a symbol. But he it is, too, who pushed the furthest his efforts at self-glorification.

Malicious pens and tongues have suggested that all Zola really saw in the famous *Affaire* was the providential occasion to remain in the public eye at a time his muse was deserting him—and that he exploited this occasion to the hilt. Nothing, however, could be further from the truth. What in reality first seduced Zola was neither the abstract problem of Truth and Justice, nor even the role he might play, but the human drama. It is with a novelist's eye that he first surveyed the scene: "What a poignant drama, and what superb characters! In front of these tragically beautiful documents which life brings us, my novelist's heart pounds with passionate admiration." [18] Only later—and gradually—did Zola conceive of the heroic role he might be called upon to play as a writer, as an "intellectual."

There was great *literary* potential in this personal and intellectual involvement. The dramatization of the artist, of the intellectual *self*, was, moreover, not alien to Zola. *Le Docteur Pascal* describes the struggle of a scientific mind against the prejudices of family and society, and on another level, the autumnal love affair of a sexagenarian which is not without some echo of Zola's own *arrière-*

[17] See the "Ebauche" of *Vérité, Fonds Français*, Bibliothèque Nationale, Nouvelles Acquisitions, 10343, p. 566. Reproduced by Maurice Leblond in his edition of *Vérité*, Bernouard, 1928, p. 673. Italics mine.

[18] "M. Scheurer-Kestner," *Le Figaro*, November 25, 1897. Reprinted in *La Vérité en marche.*

saison adultery. Docteur Pascal is perhaps the only character Zola extols as an alienated individual (*"je suis à part"*) whose solidarity with the human family is colored by the pride of being "different," "without any communion." Pascal's death is a Socratic death (he continues discussing and dissecting), and this death scene was probably the one Zola had dreamt for himself: sustained by the "heroic idea of work," Pascal dies at his desk.[19] Sandoz, the generous, fertile writer in *L'Œuvre*, is another, though less dramatic, self-portrait, whose primary function is to provide Zola's "healthy" views on art as contrasted with Claude Lantier's fatal obsession with beauty unattainable. Centering on the artist's demonic struggle with the angel, filled with theoretical digressions on art, *L'Œuvre* takes its place in the tradition of the artist's novel that runs from Balzac to Romain Rolland and Proust. It is to a large extent an echo to Balzac's *Chef-d'œuvre inconnu* and an answer to the Goncourts' *Manette Salomon*. But although Zola succeeds in contrasting Lantier's diseased passion for art with Sandoz' redeeming passion for life, the treatment of the intellectual themes is here also strangely blurred. Sandoz and Lantier represent two different *physiologies*, never the two conflicting poles of a single consciousness. Even Lantier's own grandeur and decadence remain strangely out of focus, for it is never clear whether his anguish and defeat are the result of a Promethean quest for absolutes which drives him to madness and suicide in the best Romantic tradition, or merely—as Zola repeatedly suggests—the price he must pay for his heredity. Thus Zola (perhaps because his theories were at odds with his deeper nature) never truly exploited the drama of the mind. For it is one thing to glorify, and another to dramatize. In spite of the latent themes in *L'Œuvre* and in *Le Docteur Pascal*, Zola has not succeeded, it would seem, in paying more than lip service to the tragedy of thinking, doubting, or creating.

The case of Marc Froment, in *Vérité*, is conclusive. Surely, Zola has not been sparing in his use of epithets and in his attempts to magnify the figure of his hero. He has in fact rarely been so prodigal with the terms *hero, heroism, heroic* and other laudatory expressions. Though Marc's family life is in danger, he silences this

---

[19] The scene is really quite powerful. Docteur Pascal, before dying, describes his own death like a professor dissecting in an amphitheater. Did Vercors remember this scene when he created, in *Colères*, the courageous figure of the professor of chemistry who dies on his feet from a lung cancer while continuing obstinately to write formulas on the blackboard?

personal anguish with a "heroic effort." He accepts the struggle
with a "brave gesture." At the height of the crisis, he shows an
"admirable and valiant serenity" and continues teaching with "marvelous" spirit and integrity. He is an "unknown hero" who feels a
deep "need for heroism." When victory is at long last achieved, he
becomes a "patriarchal" grandfather and indulges in nostalgic reminiscences of the "heroic days." And yet, in spite of these ponderous
efforts, in spite of a dramatic situation rich in possibilities and of his
own personal involvement—Zola did not succeed in creating, as
Bourget had done, a convincing drama of ideas. The moral crisis
is merely stated. One finds here no inner conflict.

The sources of this failure must be traced ultimately to Zola's
artistic temperament and to the peculiar limitations of his talent. But
part of this failure is also self-willed. Zola was so afraid to describe
a human being merely as an ambulatory thinking machine, he was
so easily antagonized by what he considered the inhuman, arrogant
depravity of the thinker, the very concept of the intellectual was in
short so alien to him, that he devoted far more effort to "human-
izing" Marc Froment than to bringing into sharp relief his supposed
anguish. A modest pedagogue in a small provincial town, Marc had
originally planned to become a printer. He is a husband, father,
grandfather, and finally a venerable patriarch. Zola tirelessly underlines his simplicity, his modesty, his generosity of heart. But, paradoxically, this effort at humanization only waters down the portrait
to the point where no psychological tension is possible. The very
humanity of the character is obliterated by his exemplary qualities.

Yet Zola's flair for great subjects, which even a Barrès admired,
brought him very close to a new theme: *the suffering of others.* It is
easy enough to catalogue some of the glaring defects of the novel:
clumsy transposition from fact to fancy, unnecessary repetitions, a
coarse, unenlightened anti-clericalism, the naïveté of the beliefs.
All this is obvious. The real pity, however, is that Zola did not
exploit the drama of human solidarity he repeatedly broaches
throughout the work. For Marc Froment is a characteristically
"modern" hero in his refusal to pursue an exclusively private happiness, his conviction that he is responsible for all the pain and injustice that exist in the world, and his "religion of human solidarity"
which is a more apostolic version of that *"fraternité douloureuse"*
already experienced by Docteur Pascal.

¶ II. *The* bon maître *or the exercise of "indulgent virtues"*

IT IS DIFFICULT TO IMAGINE a writer more alien to this apostolic mood than Anatole France. Irony, sophistication and urbanity are not exactly Zola's strong points, nor are they criteria which display his work to best advantage. Nothing is more of a contrast to Zola's genius for amplification than Anatole France's nuanced art of understatement. One of France's most representative characters, Jérôme Coignard, is a hedonistic priest, a Christian Socrates, for whom wisdom lies in the blending of the unique qualities of Epicure and Saint Francis of Assisi, and who himself combines in artful doses enough epicureanism to protect him from sorrow and a sufficient "sainthood" to provide him with innocent joys. The theme of the lay saint is a recurring one in France's work. This *bon maître*, a flexible, dialectically gifted teacher who knows how to be at the same time a traditionalist and a moral subversive, obviously does not speak the language of Zola's apostles. Nor does Professor Bergeret, who teaches that indulgence is preferable to justice, nor Bretteaux des Ilettes, the philosopher of *Les Dieux ont soif*, who cynically observes that innocence is a matter of luck, not of virtue.

Though the Dreyfus case found both writers fighting side by side, a true dialogue between them was impossible. *Vérité* and much of *L'Ile des pingouins* treat the same subject. But neither the tone, nor the technique, nor the intentions, nor the over-all effect can even be compared. France's remark in his Preface concerning the "levity of the mind common to all serious men" gives the reader a foretaste of the apparent frivolity with which important matters are here treated. This surface resilience, characteristic of all his works, can be irritating. France knew and exploited this. Madame Bergeret impatiently reproves her husband: "You laugh about things that are not laughable and one never knows whether you are joking or whether you are serious. Conversation is impossible with you."

This difference in temperament between the two writers explains Anatole France's severe and even unusually brutal reactions to some of Zola's novels. *La Terre*, Zola's novel on peasant life, angered France to such a point that he called it a monument of filth and hailed it as the Georgics of vice.[20] In an article on *L'Argent*, published in *Le Temps* (March 22, 1891), he compares Zola to Shake-

[20] *La Vie littéraire*, I, p. 235.

speare's Caliban who walks with lowered head, seeing nothing. What offended France was not only the naturalistic dogma of Zola, but what he considered his "bad taste" (the one unredeemable sin, according to France) and his non-intellectual, "instinctive" nature. Even much later, when a common action brought them together and France had learned to prize the other's courage, he could not, when he decided to evoke Zola's intervention on behalf of Dreyfus, refrain from presenting him in a slightly malicious manner: Colomban, the hairy, myopic little man with a single-track mind is, we are told, the author of one hundred and sixty volumes of penguin psychology!

Anatole France's background certainly prepared him far better than Zola to portray the intellectual and deal with the excitement or drama of ideas. Son of a Parisian book dealer, he was from childhood a voracious reader, acquired a genuine erudition, and remained throughout his entire life irrepressibly fond of books. Intellectual activity was to him synonymous with pleasure, but it had also been a lesson in sadness. It is in the study that he felt most at home. Like his hero Bergeret, he was timid with other men, but "never feared ideas." Addicted to the peaceful *voluptés* of the mind, he cultivated, much like his genial Satan in *La Révolte des anges*, a private garden in which intelligence and sensuality heightened each other. But his father's bookstore also seems to have helped intensify his inborn pessimism.[21] The browsing habitués who gathered there to discuss politics or literature taught him that opinions are subjective, fragmentary and ultimately irreconcilable. The books he saw, reposing dusty and forgotten on their shelves, reminded him how evanescent, how perishable life and customs are. Repeatedly he set the action of his stories and novels in bookish atmospheres. Bookstores and libraries are the *luoghi ameni* of his private poetic world: Astarac's library in *La Rôtisserie de la reine Pédauque;* Blaizot's bookstore in *Les Opinions de Jérôme Coignard;* the bookshop of Paillot, in *L'Histoire contemporaine*, where Bergeret finds respite from his shrewish wife; the private library of Baron Esparvieu, whose pedantic librarian is tormented by prankish angels in *La Révolte des anges.*

[21] Concerning the importance of his father's bookshop (and in general the fascination with libraries), see George Brandes, *Anatole France*, p. 13, and Haakon M. Chevalier, *The Ironic Temper, Anatole France and His Time*, pp. 92-93.

This love for books is more than a form of intellectual hedonism. As time went by, Anatole France acquired real faith in the dynamic power of ideas—a faith occasionally echoed by his favorite characters. To his daughter who wishes to know how the world can be changed, Bergeret enthusiastically explains: "Through the Word, my child. Nothing is more powerful than the Word. The link of strong reasons and of lofty thoughts is a bond that cannot be broken. The Word, like David's sling, lays low the violent and the mighty. It is the indivisible weapon." But earlier than this, long before the Dreyfus case enlisted his enthusiasm and directed him toward socialism, Anatole France proclaimed the glory and the "inalienable rights" of Thought. In his lucid discussion of Bourget's *Le Disciple* —primarily a stirring answer to Brunetière's attempt to subordinate metaphysics to the accepted social code—France affirms with great eloquence man's duty to speculate, no matter what the danger.[22] Invoking Pascal ("all our dignity is in thinking"), he asserts that intellectual courage is man's greatest pride. For Anatole France knows that thinking is an *act*, that nothing in life can be innocent and no thought totally harmless.

"Where do you lead me, thought"? sighs the fallen (or falling?) angel in *La Révolte des anges*. In fact, thinking is to France synonymous with doubting—and doubting is the beginning and end of subversion. This propensity to question and doubt, France explains in *L'Ile des pingouins*, is "singular, exquisite, philosophical, immoral, transcendent, monstrous, full of malice, harmful to citizens and to property, contrary to the good order of the country and the prosperity of empires. . . ." The appanage of the happy few, this talent for doubting is a dubious blessing: painfully cultivated, it most often rewards the doubter by making him a victim of his own lucidity. Critical intelligence is thus doubly subversive. On the one hand, it is the principle of all rebellion: liberty, curiosity and doubt are the cardinal virtues in the eyes of Lucifer and his followers. It is science, France reminds his readers, that inspired the angels with the desire to free themselves from bondage by rebelling against the impostor-oppressor Iahveh. "I knew, I thought, I lost faith," is the angel's lapidary account of this liberation. But on the other hand, this same talent for doubting predestines the thinker, angel or man,

22 See "La Morale et la Science—M. Paul Bourget" in *La Vie littéraire*, III, pp. 54-78.

to be a victim. Like Prometheus whose symbolic figure looms over the entire nineteenth century, the intellectual chooses to stand and fall with the vanquished. France's Satan has nightmares about displacing God; he fears that by acquiring power he will lose his intelligence and his compassion. For it is a privilege to find oneself among the defeated—a privilege as well as a title of tragic nobility. Not only are scholars, from Pythagoras to Poincaré, "the greatest of men, heroes, demigods," [23] but Nectaire, another fallen angel, explains: "The independence of the mind is the proudest aristocracy." It is only natural that Anatole France's authentic sympathy for the scholar and his high regard for the subversive and noble mission of the intellect should have induced him repeatedly to portray the intellectual in his fiction.

His very first novel, *Le Crime de Sylvestre Bonnard* (1881), centers on a maniacal philologist, a passionate hunter of rare manuscripts, whose gentle nature and generous heart make him an endearing figure. Anatole France has justly been credited with the creation of a new genre: the "bookish" novel, in which the scholar's temperament, tastes, thoughts, preoccupations and anguish—whimsically bound up with the exigencies of daily life—have become the very subject matter. Quite early also, France's imagination began to toy with the figure of the *bon maître*, the private tutor, the gentle, original, life-loving philosopher-teacher, full of paradoxes and sparkling digressions. Such a one is the extravagant political exile, the Marquis Tudesco di Venezia, lover of poetry and good wine, who undertakes the education of the poor bookbinder's son, Jean Servien. But it is *La Rôtisserie de la reine Pédauque* that marks the full blossoming of this particular type so dear to France.

This novel, which taps the picaresque tradition and exploits the eighteenth-century taste for philosophical dialogues, remains one of France's most brilliant achievements. Its real hero, however, is not at all Jacques Ménétrier, the *rôtisseur's* son who becomes a book dealer: it is the Abbé Jérôme Coignard, humanist and theologian, who leads a disheveled life, whose stoical, skeptical, indulgent nature and dialectical gifts enable the author to display the pyrotechnics of his own bold and malicious thinking. Ernest Seillère, in his biased

<hr />

[23] See *La Vie en fleur*, p. 81. Quoted by Micheline Tison-Braun, who analyzes France's rational and epicurean "messianism," in *La Crise de l'Humanisme*, I, p. 318.

study, was no doubt right in insisting on the importance of Coignard whose "satanic perversion" and inveterate iconoclasm he interpreted as ultimate manifestations of the Romantic disease.[24] France was indeed so delighted with his own creation that, in spite of Coignard's violent death, he immediately revived him in Les Opinions de Jérôme Coignard (1893).

As though aware of the significance this type was to have in the larger context of his work, France set out to describe Jérôme Coignard in an ample preface. The pattern which emerges will indeed become a recurring pattern. Jérôme Coignard, professor of eloquence at the Collège de Beauvais and curator of the Astarcian library, is "simple," "candid" and "lovable." His charm is due not only to the enticing mixture of epicureanism and "franciscanism," but to an "indulgent wisdom" and a "generous skepticism." He is a dreamer, but likes to remain awake during his dreams. He is an enemy of all nocturnal phantoms, but even in his opposition to all forms of superstition he prefers to show himself benevolent. For his wisdom is incompatible with "systematic" thinking. "All principles seemed to him equally controvertible." He is too critical to have a "sense of veneration." Anti-dogmatic and anti-superstitious, the good abbé remains nonetheless staunchly faithful to Christian tradition and doctrine. Is this a sly inconsistency on the part of France? It is more likely that the author wished to underline the basic philosophical equilibrium of Coignard, in contrast to Rousseau's unrealistic belief in man's innate goodness. For Coignard's benevolent, indulgent irony is rooted in his acceptance of "human infirmity." It is the key to his particular brand of sainthood: his non-orthodox charity depends on a belief in original depravity.

Of the saintly attributes, Coignard inherited above all gentleness. His "benevolent irony," his "indulgent" philosophy, his preaching of the "indulgent virtues" go hand in hand with a predilection for disreputable characters, in imitation—we are told—of "the One who lived among publicans and prostitutes." This blasphemous parallel is not the only equivocal aspect of Coignard's virtues. His "purity of heart" as well as his "treasures of mercy" are not devoid of ambiguities. In the first place, part of this gentleness is but a form of softness and self-indulgence. Even his boldest excursions into the realm of thought turn out to be not much more than the pastimes of a

24 See *Anatole France, critique de son temps*, pp. 23-55.

peace-loving *promeneur*. Sentimentally (or is it prudently?) attached to time-tested attitudes, he finds old errors less vexatious than new ones, and considers that, since err we must, the safest is to stick to decayed illusions. This curious defeatism is further aggravated by a contempt for humanity which, in a putative saint, may seem a little less than holy. For we are told that Jérôme Coignard "despises men with tenderness" and that, conversely, it is his "benevolence" that leads him to denigrate his fellow men. In short, it is his charity, France explains, which prevents him from holding too high an opinion of humanity. Coignard is not only a virtuoso at paradoxes, he is a living paradox: rebellious but faithful to tradition; pleasure-loving but alive to the demands of the spirit; a specialist of systematic doubt and yet a staunch believer in the Christian dogma; a humanist who lacks true solidarity with the rest of humanity; a cynical priest whose favorite occupation is to discuss serious ideas in a tavern; a gentle soul who smiles approvingly when the police are roughly handled. "Never was there a mind at once more intrepid and more peaceful."

Much of this indulging in paradoxes stems no doubt from France's inveterate and slightly perverse need to debunk. As Seillère points out, there is duplicity in France's method: his subversion depends in part on his ability to reassure the bourgeois in himself. Obviously, a character such as Coignard, a sophist through and through, constitutes an invaluable tool for juggling with important issues. The book is really given over to a series of discursive digressions or essays in dialogue form on selected themes: Revolution and Tradition, Democracy and Autocracy, public morality, sociology, science, the Army, civil and military justice—all of which, in spite of the eighteenth-century setting, very maliciously allude to contemporary problems. But the deepest root of Coignard's paradoxes is neither his teasing, subversive make-up, nor the author's desire to raise controversial issues, nor even a brand of cynicism which is not devoid of charm—but a form of pessimism which no amount of irony can cure. This may explain his severe judgment on Rousseau, whose dream that man was originally good nettles him. We must not forget, the good abbé explains, that men are "evil monkeys"! Optimism, according to him, is furthermore a dangerous aberration since it usually leads to utopian fanaticism.

It is easy to draw a catalogue of "pessimistic" pronouncements in *Les Opinions de Jérôme Coignard*: all governments govern badly (only some govern worse); life is a "pitiful comedy"; knowledge is a bitter cup; man is naturally obedient and sanguinary, and can be adequately defined as an "animal with a musket" who is obviously "not made to think." Bitterest of all paradoxes: man's very intelligence appears as an incongruity—a punishment inflicted on some by a cruel divinity. For in spite of Coignard's "joyful and proud liberty," he is *condemned* to suffer from this intellectual freedom. The sadness of all knowledge, the awareness of thought's incompatibility with action (and hence with life) thus constitute a *basso continuo*, a steady drone which graceful arpeggios cannot muffle. Occasionally the pessimistic note is made explicit. Coignard evokes his amorous hatred of learning: the suffering of having yearned to know too much. In the commerce of books and scholars he has lost his spiritual peace and his "holy simplicity." What remains after knowledge is "proud bitterness" and majestic sadness. "My mind is altogether spoiled by thinking." There is a militant irony in this quip. But there is also a self-diagnosis: thought is a corruption which not only makes him unfit to decide and act, but which gnaws away at the very core of his being. Like most spiritual diseases, it takes the shape of a temptation. Coignard knows that the serpent of Genesis is the oldest of philosophers.

But the intellectual incarnated by Coignard is not altogether devoid of coquettishness. His attitudes and pronouncements, often excessive like his vitality, come at times dangerously close to being mere poses. Much more nuanced, realistic and socially rooted is the portrait of Professor Bergeret in *L'Histoire contemporaine*.[25] Son of a lycée teacher who had courageously refused to swear allegiance to the Second Empire, he was brought up in the cult of the Republic. He is a typical *fin de siècle* intellectual. Character and subject matter are indeed so bound up with a historical and social context that *L'Histoire contemporaine*, as the title suggests, often reads like a series of chronicles or essays about the life and political intrigues of a provincial town—a true microcosm in which we witness the clash of interests between a vulgarian Préfet, the Church

25 The four volumes of this work are: *L'Orme du mail* (1896), *Le Mannequin d'osier* (1897), *L'Anneau d'améthyste* (1899), *Monsieur Bergeret à Paris* (1901). Most of the chapters were published separately, first in *L'Echo de Paris*, then in *Le Figaro*, over a period extending from January, 1895, to August, 1900.

authorities and the forces of reaction. France was of course aware of the discursive nature of his novel as well as of its *unfictional* quality: in apparent self-justification he immodestly invoked Rabelais, Cervantes and more frivolous *conteurs* of the sixteenth century.

Bergeret may well at first appear as a comic type—one of the numerous incarnations of the eternal professor. Clumsy, anemic, bilious, incapable of interesting his students, he is tyrannized by his wife and persecuted by his dean who forces him to lecture in a humid basement. Cuckolded by his own disciple, he metamorphoses his anger into an ironic meditation on the vanity of things and on his own mediocrity. Professor Bergeret belongs to a recognizable type in the Western tradition: the scholar whose physical and intellectual non-conformism provokes an instinctive aversion translated into laughter. Such scorn is the price he has to pay for that inner freedom, more precious by far than respectability, which makes him relish rather than deplore his solitude. "He had a free soul," writes France, in whose eyes this is a virtue greater than all his other qualities: his finesse, his erudition, his civilized control over his emotions, his respect for the individual, his curiosity in the face of new ideas. This inner freedom is perhaps not of the purest mettle: it is dependent on certain private pleasures which it in turn selfishly protects. More mildly epicurean than the Abbé Coignard, but equally addicted to the *voluptés paisibles* of the intellect, Bergeret escapes into the private dream world of the humanist, surrenders to the enchantment of the Homeric and Virgilian landscapes, and meditates on the customs of Rome.

Yet the "profound peacefulness" which Bergeret discovers in solitude is to some extent a compensation derived from necessity. His solitude is not so much chosen as inflicted. The elm tree on the mall which provides the title of the first volume is a poetic symbol: under its shade Bergeret surrenders to his erudite daydreams. But it is also a bitter reminder of Bergeret's loneliness. In *L'Histoire contemporaine* Anatole France broaches a theme that Louis Guilloux and Jean-Paul Sartre will later exploit: the tragic solitude of the thinker in a hostile community. France came very close to a rich subject. Bergeret's socratic qualities—his questioning of basic assumptions, his ironic and provoking observations— make him a sort of moral gadfly whose function, it seems, is to irritate and alienate his fellow citizens. "By the mere fact that he thought, he was a strange being, disturbing and suspect to all." This sentence, which appears in *L'Anneau d'améthyste*, was first published in *L'Echo de Paris* in August, 1898, when, at the height of the Dreyfus case, the word "intellectual" was charged with emotional significance. Bergeret thus not only suffers from the perennial misunderstanding between the philosopher and Caliban, but he is a victim of an intellectual integrity that forces him to play an unwanted role.

Unfortunately, as though determined never to make use of his own momentum, France does not explore the dramatic possibilities of this theme. He prefers instead (lack of tragic vision? shyness that translates itself into irony?) to utilize Bergeret—as he has already utilized Coignard—to vent a misanthropic mood that only thinly disguises an inherent but timid idealism. Bergeret's "literary and moral pessimism" depresses his students. His conclusions are indeed bitter. We are ruled by our instincts. Man is an "evil beast" for whom killing is natural, for whom even love is as ruthless as the will to survive. Civilized societies are no gentler in their relations to each other than well-trained "hunting dogs." Not only is war infamous, but there are no armies of heroes. Bergeret's opinions of military prowess are reminiscent of the pungent tone of *Candide*: it is fear that makes soldiers fight; the art of the general consists in making it impossible for his troops to flee. Humanity is crawling on a tiny little mud ball which turns clumsily around an already half extinct sun. In sum, life is a "catastrophe." Bergeret's most permanent need seems to be to deflate and then to smile a wry smile. "The sufferings of our fellow human beings make us laugh, provided they are presented to us gaily." But the smile is at the hero's own expense: it is his very intelligence that eats at him. His is a flawless art of hurting himself. France comments: "M. Bergeret is to be pitied, for he thinks." [26]

Individually successful as *L'Ile des pingouins* (1908), *Les Dieux ont soif* (1912) and *La Révolte des anges* (1914) may be, they add no new dimension to this portrait of the intellectual. The most curious figure is unquestionably, in *Les Dieux ont soif*, the generous and mildly philosophical Bretteaux des Ilettes, ex-financier of the Old Regime, who traverses the turmoil of the Revolution reading Lucretius while waiting to be arrested and guillotined. But his opinions —his cult of pleasure, his urbane anarchism, his somewhat aristocratic

[26] *L'Echo de Paris*, December 29, 1896.

belief in the corruption of man—give the impression that France is imitating himself.

The modern reader is perhaps more acutely aware of the repetitiveness and the triteness in France's fiction. But, ironically, this loss of novelty may well be a tribute to France's success in creating a type whose familiarity proves his significance to the French imagination. Bergeret is to some extent a *new* character: he has sired a whole progeny of non-heroic commentator-heroes who, within the novel of which they are the moral center, comment on an action in which they can never wholly participate.[27] Proud, yet at the same time obscurely ashamed of their detachment, they symbolize the peculiar *dédoublement* of European thinking in the wake of Romanticism: the mirror-disease of thought, the narcissistic auto-hypnosis of the intellect, that self-inflicted and paralyzing wound of modern man. Gisors in *La Condition humaine* and Alvear in *L'Espoir* are Bergeret's distant brothers-in-exile: they too are doomed to be tired repositories of a sterile wisdom.

The real originality of Bergeret is thus not his idealistic disbelief and indulgent pessimism (some of which is directly inherited from Renan, himself a great master of the philosophic dialogue); nor is it that urbane and somewhat irritating misanthropy which makes him despise "Pecus" and prefer the company of his dog Riquet, in whom he recognizes human prejudices and the obscure goodness of Caliban. Bergeret's real significance is that he embodies a turn-of-the-century intellectual *tedium*, a form of philosophic sadness which accompanies the quasi-pathological fascination with decadence so typical of the period. Flaubert had already found much of his inspiration in the deep sadness of all knowledge—a sadness that reaches a point of exasperation in *Bouvard et Pécuchet*. Much of Anatole France's work is a refined but edulcorated "Bouvard et Pécuchet" written by a disenchanted Encyclopedist who cannot quite believe in his own disenchantment. France, at times, is no less bitter than Flaubert. Speaking of his puppets, Bretteaux des Ilettes says: "I am a kind God: I did not give them Thought." But France's most characteristic note is not bitterness: it is a mellow fatigue, a poetic nos-

---

[27] Haakon M. Chevalier, in *The Ironic Temper*, p. 99, points to the "serene, worldly-wise, witty, disillusioned, detached and unimpassioned" characters that appeared in European literature after 1900 (the ironic "commentators" of Schnitzler, Proust, Pirandello, Gide, Mann, Huxley) who are, he feels, to some extent derivative from France's prototype.

talgia for lost hopes. Flaubert may have been the prophet of a moral crisis. Anatole France is its diagnostician, its poet and its disconsolate victim.

The struggle between the humanist and his hostile environment (symbolized by the city) is thus at the core of France's work. The Dreyfus case only confirmed the author's intuition concerning the intellectual's destiny to fight a losing battle. Long before writing *Crainquebille*, Anatole France knew that men of learning were in discredit. The awareness of moral estrangement creates within his fictional world a sense of fraternity between minds which—like Bergeret and the Abbé Lantaigne, for instance—are otherwise hardly made to understand each other. Their very loneliness, the very quality of their intellects create between them the same current of sympathy that Stendhal establishes between a Julien Sorel and an Abbé Pirard. Neither belongs with the common herd: that is why they seek and find each other. Like Stendhal, on whom he wrote a perceptive essay, France admired republican virtues, but disliked the smell of crowds. His eventual conversion to socialism further complicated existing tensions: his love for social justice did not always live happily with his distaste for the plebeian mentality. But in Stendhal and Anatole France, similar dichotomies tended to represent private tensions which both writers valued and cultivated. The broader tragic possibilities are left unexplored. It remained for our own period to witness the collective widening of the gulf which, on the part of the politically conscious intellectual, has led to shame, guilt and self-maceration.

The most original trait of Anatole France's intellectual is, however, a yearning for authenticity that carries with it the dignified repudiation of pride. Bergeret's diagnosis of his own *mauvaise foi*, his self-contempt whenever he betrays human solidarity for the sake of a private satisfaction (be it generosity), is not unworthy of a Sartre. Having given money to a street beggar, he immediately blames himself: in his charity he detects a joy in degrading another human being. "I have tasted of the shameful joy of humiliating a fellow human being; I have agreed to the odious pact which assures power to the powerful and weakness to the weak. . . . I have contributed to this man's having only half a soul. . . . I have humiliated myself by humiliating him." Such an indictment of counterfeit brotherhood seems to prefigure the animosity of Sartre's Roquentin for the world of *salauds*, as well as the permanent guilt feelings with which Mathieu Delarue moves through *Les Chemins de la liberté*. In *L'Ile des pingouins* this tendency to debunk the intellectual's satisfaction with his own courageous commitment is particularly noteworthy. Bidault-Coquille, the astronomer who has left his meteors and celestial spaces to rush to the defense of Pyrot, assesses his action with lucid modesty: "You believed you were doing a fine moral deed. You said to yourself: 'Here I am, just and courageous once and for all. I will be able to rest afterwards, secure in the public esteem and in the praises of future historians.'" This summons to modesty, this advance repudiation of smugness, serves as an antidote to the hidden self-seeking that corrupts the noblest deeds. Intellectual courage—France suggests—is the most readily liable to such corruption. Justice is never a matter of a single moment: the next hour can undo all. This demanding integrity and self-denunciation are to become one of the outstanding characteristics of the twentieth-century intellectual. When Bidault-Coquille goes so far as to qualify his courage as *imprudence*, and then proceeds to minimize even this ("Your imprudence was small; it exposed you to moderate dangers; you did not risk your head"), France seems to be motivated by the very same humility which, some fifty years later, after an even greater national crisis, will compel Sartre to confess: "When we were writing in the underground, our risks were minimal . . . I was often ashamed of it. . . ." [28]

Certainly, this is not the language of a Zola. Marc Froment could not possibly have such doubts, nor would he dream of denigrating himself. Any such disavowal he would deem a form of treason. And yet, in spite of its greater richness, France's treatment of the intellectual hero is lacking in power and scope. Partly this may be due to certain chronic weaknesses of his art: surface grace, absence of a unifying vision, overdoses of erudite allusions, coquettish stylistic effects. France flirts with the *cultured* reader: he seeks to conquer him through charm. "He has nothing at stake. He has no wager with destiny." Haakon M. Chevalier's diagnosis of the ironist's vagabond mentality may well explain the fragmentary nature of the novelist's outlook, his inability to conceive his characters on a grand

[28] "Qu'est-ce que la littérature?" in *Situations II*, p. 260.

scale.[29] Perhaps because nothing appeared to him as quite authentic, he was also unprepared to believe fully in his own fictional creatures and could not surround them with that wall which, according to Ortega y Gasset, immures the characters as well as the reader in a dense fictional world. France preferred instead to establish a direct dialogue with his reader.

This constant presence of the author, this shifting attitude toward his personages, is not merely an aesthetic flaw. Fielding, Stendhal and Gide intervene perhaps more frequently in their works. Their ironic intrusions are, however, more than a technical device: the ambiguous commentary is part of the very texture of their novels. France's interventions are digressions: they suggest that his characters are for him a *pretext*. Abstract discussions—on God, democracy, justice, miracles, the writing of history or the power of lies—interest him far more than individual destinies. "You produce lovely sophisms and your reasonings seem to be modulated on the flute of Pan," says one of the characters to Bergeret. Anatole France also likes nothing better than to play musical improvisations on ideas.

Finally, the character of the intellectual himself, as he appears in the work of Anatole France, is disappointingly weak. The smiling acceptance of turpitude and of his own frailties removes the possibility of conflict and precludes a tragic experience. One finds here, for instance, none of the demonic, Faustian tensions which make of Valéry's Monsieur Teste a disembodied High Priest of the Intelligence. Even the mental suffering of a Bergeret hardly ever amounts to anguish; it rather takes the form of a persistent migraine. The "saint" in him overcomes the temptation of pride; but such a victory is hardly glorious for one who never loses sight of the vanity of all things. An Ecclesiastes without faith, Bergeret is led by his very intelligence to an apparent abdication. It would seem that Anatole France was aware of the defeatist nature of his humanism. "The truths discovered by intelligence remain sterile," explains Jérôme Coignard on the very last page of Les Opinions. Only the heart, he reminds his disciple, can fertilize our dreams. The warning, however, is profitable only if we can generate our own dreams. Anatole

---

[29] Chevalier goes so far as to accuse France's work of *senility:* "His is an old man's philosophy. His tolerance, his smiling skepticism, his urbanity, his delicate licentiousness, his 'silent orgies of meditation' are an old man's virtues and vices" (*op. cit.,* p. 216).

France and his characters suffer from a perfidious disease: the fear of being duped by their own emotions. Perhaps they have read too many books and come to understand too much! Some vital source seems to have dried up. Of them, as of Eliot's Gerontion, it could be asked: "After such knowledge, what forgiveness?"

6

Martin du Gard's *Jean Barois*
and the Challenge of History

> *Where is the poet who will reflect this*
> *sacred anguish?*
>
> —ROMAIN ROLLAND

FEW NOVELISTS HAVE BEEN AS SUCCESSFUL in dramatizing ideas as Roger Martin du Gard. The epigraph to *Jean Barois* (1913) announces the main theme of the novel: the struggle between man and ideology. "The sick conscience—there is the battleground of modern fate." The hero of this struggle with ideas may be looked on as a prototype of the modern French intellectual. Son of a professor of medicine, Jean Barois is attracted to the broader field of the philosophy of science, obtains his *licence* and *agrégation*, teaches for a while, but soon prefers the more dynamic role of lecturer and propagandist. He becomes the director of a militant publication and sets out to "emancipate" his contemporaries. *S'Affranchir* was the title Roger Martin du Gard had originally planned for the book.

The plot of the novel is deceptively uncomplicated. Reduced to its simplest terms, it is the story of faith lost and faith regained. Equally simple, on first sight, are the style and the technique employed. The form is that of dramatic dialogues supported by terse objective notations that read like stage directions, and which the author uses with great effect to set the scene and to allow the reader brief glimpses into the inner drama of the protagonists. Martin du Gard's lasting achievement is not, however, this technique, which has its limitations, but his ability to orchestrate the moral crisis of an individual with the crisis of an entire generation.

¶ 1. *The battle of the individual*

THE STORY OF JEAN BAROIS follows a classical pattern. As a young boy, his sensibilities heightened by a latent malady, he experiences religious fervor. Soon, however, his active mind begins to raise questions which eventually turn into theological doubts. He is distressed by the problem of Evil and suffering. Studies at the Sorbonne further corrode his faith. His initiation into the world of science exalts and dizzies him. In these Parisian lecture halls where universal laws are discussed without any reference to God, he succumbs to what his confessor calls "the poison of scientific pride." His contact with modern exegesis creates further anguish; all of modern scholarship seems to be in absolute contradiction with the basic articles of faith. For a while, Barois tries desperately to hold on. He finds a temporary compromise and some respite in symbolic interpretations of the Bible. But this sapping of fundamental beliefs cannot be arrested. Very soon, the total collapse of his faith leaves him with an exhilarating feeling of liberation, but also with a bitterness and belligerence à *rebours* characteristic of all those who have lost their faith, yet still need to believe.

This need is now directed against religion and against his former self. The second phase of Barois' life is a permanent act of rebellion. Unable to tolerate any longer his wife's superstitious religiosity, he separates from her after bitter quarrels, and gives up the security of an irksome teaching position. He now dedicates himself exclusively to research, to working out and propagating a gospel of "free thought." When the time comes, he throws himself and his group into the maelstrom of the Dreyfus case. This period of his life is one of struggle and ideological commitment. Barois becomes a renowned scholar and polemicist, the acknowledged leader of an intellectual movement of which his paper, *Le Semeur,* is both the instrument and the symbol.

After battles have been won and lost, after the excitement of success and failure, comes frustration and loneliness. The third phase of Barois' existence is marked by disenchantment. A nearly fatal accident brings to his lips, at the peak of terror, a long-forgotten prayer to the Virgin. From that point on, despite the stubborn resistance of a still rebellious intellect, his fear of suffering and of death gradually lead him back to the fold. Aware that the religious experience remains untouched by the onslaught of reason, Barois gradually repudiates his life work and becomes an apostate for the second time. Age and sickness make him yearn for appeasement, for the secure world of his childhood. He withdraws to the old family house in Buis, accepts his wife's care, renounces his pride and is finally converted by a priest who, ironically, regains his own lost faith when he witnesses the pathetic happiness of a mind consoled by the Cross.

IT IS CHARACTERISTIC of Martin du Gard's art that Jean Barois should rediscover his faith at the very moment that the priest who consoles him is on the point of losing his. Such irony is far from gratuitous. It mirrors one of the author's favorite subjects of meditation: the cyclical recurrence of events, the interplay of action and reaction, the ebb and flow of human relationships. The very structure of *Jean Barois* suggests a cyclical movement. Martin du Gard's skillful use of atavism (the hero's father, when weakened by disease and the fear of death, also returns to religion) is only one of many structural devices. Barois' death is the re-enactment of a scene which operates retrospectively as a prefiguration. Martin du Gard makes use of ironic contrasts: the boy believer who should rejoice over his father's deathbed conversion feels the same unvoiced regret as the priest from whom he himself will receive extreme unction, in very similar circumstances. The entire novel is thus carefully built up on a series of parallels and contrasts, of departures and returns. The novel begins in an atmosphere of disease. The opening pages describe the boy's struggle against tuberculosis. From disease to health and back to illness; from death to life and back to death; from faith to atheism and back to faith—the ineluctable nature of the cycle is reinforced by the structural patterns of the book. Martin du Gard seems to play a number of symmetrical variations on the same fundamental theme. From Buis to Paris and back to Buis: Jean Barois not only returns to his wife after a long separation, but he insists on settling in his father's house, and dies in the very room and in the very bed in which his father died. The somewhat formal architecture of the book serves to strengthen the theme of the return. The Abbé Lévys, who confesses Barois at the end of the novel, takes the place of the Abbé Joziers who confesses him at the beginning.

    This formal structure may suggest that the central part of the novel stands for health, intelligence and emancipation. But this is only an illusion. Barois actually betrays his rationalism at the moment his rationalistic fervor attains its highest pitch. The structure of the book is thus more involuted than may appear at first glance. Barois falls into hybris at the midpoint of his existence. On the very page that follows the account of his public lecture on "The Future of Irreligion," an accident which nearly kills him forces him to cry out in anguish: *"Je vous salue, Marie, pleine de grâces. . . ."* The man who proclaimed the revolutionary role of intelligence and hailed the era of irreligion once more becomes, without warning, the timid and fervently religious boy who constitutes the core of his personality. Ironically, he was closest to prayer at the moment he prided himself on his remoteness from it. The exultation of the intellect is suddenly metamorphosed into defeat. But even this defeat remains ambivalent: it may turn out to be a victory.

Ideologically, of course, the adventure of Barois ends in failure. The figure of Michelangelo's *Slave*, which appears as a frontispiece to the novel, is clearly symbolic: the gesture of liberation, as though petrified by the sculptor's material, remains forever uncompleted, doomed to frustration. The plaster cast standing on Barois' mantelpiece foreshadows his destiny; it functions as an ironic commentary of which Barois himself, in moments of crisis, is unavoidably aware. The struggling figure, exerting all his strength, expends himself in sterile effort. Lonely and naked, he remains eternally frozen in his desperate tenseness. "Look at him!" Barois cries out. "He cannot even raise one free arm! . . . Perhaps, like him, I have in all these years acted out a sham emancipation. . . ." Martin du Gard obviously looked on the statue as a key symbol. During his own illness, he asked to have a reproduction placed in front of his bed so that the image of Barois' destiny—the pathetic story of a rebellious individual who remains prisoner of his myths—might serve as a warning.[1] Barois' defeat is indeed a nearly total abdication. During the last months of his life, haunted by fear of death and longing for reassurance, he abandons all intellectual effort. On his large desk, now symbolically empty, only two objects remain, a small crucifix and a handkerchief, as though to suggest that faith regained is dependent on disease.

The author's severity toward his character reveals itself in a num-

[1] See Jean Delay, "Dernières rencontres," *Le Figaro Littéraire*, August 30, 1958.

ber of ways. But it is not an unmitigated severity. Martin du Gard never casts discredit on the quest for emancipation and social justice. Moreover, Barois exhibits some truly admirable traits. He is among those happy few who have known the "intoxication of reason and of pure thought." He displays an impressive capacity for work; in fact, his unremitting, selfless dedication to causes is in part responsible for his untimely physical collapse. He is a victim of intellectual labor. As a fighter, he is at his toughest and most inspiring when others begin to lose hope. Despising easy victories, he relishes the struggle against public opinion and overwhelming odds. His comrades—before his final conversion—certainly do not consider his life a fiasco: "You have helped uproot some errors and maintain a few tottering truths."

What his companions have overlooked—even Barois is unaware of it—is the extent to which this ideological life-struggle is based on self-delusion. Temperamentally, he is unfit for the role he assigned himself. Very subtly (Martin du Gard's art here is rich in nuances), the reader is made to suspect that Barois' Jacobinic attitude, his dogmatic anti-dogmatism, his intolerant assertion of the metaphysics of Tolerance, all stem from a deep need to *believe*. In fact, his aggressiveness can be attributed to the intransigence of youth; life will mellow him and teach him that truths and errors may be provisional. Yet even in this youthful ardor there is something excessive. His lyrical hymns to intellectual liberty are no less disquieting than his "proud insolence." Far from freeing his mind, his so-called "*affranchissement*" only leads to an uncompromising attitude. All becomes for him a matter of principle; his relations with his wife, the education of his daughter—everything involves his "dignity," his "self-respect," his "fidelity" to himself and to his ideas. Free thought, paradoxically, turns into a doctrine. The apostate transmutes himself into a proselytizer. Such fanaticism casts doubt on Barois' ability to free himself. And, deep within him, he knows well what a strong hold these spurned beliefs still have on him. His very militancy bears witness to the resilience and elasticity of the Catholic faith.

But Barois' failure as a free-thinker has broader implications. It carries with it the corollary suggestion that religious faith thrives on the humiliation of the mind. This is perhaps the point at which the myth of Martin du Gard's "objectivity" seems least founded. For it is hard to detect here that "nearly inhuman impartiality" of which Claude-Edmonde Magny complains.[2] An artist's severity toward his own fictional creatures (and Martin du Gard is severe not only with Barois, but with Antoine and Jacques in *Les Thibault*) may appear as a form of impartiality; most often, however, it is a form of intervention involving the author's own emotional response during the process of creation. Undeniably, Martin du Gard views Barois' conversion in a pathological perspective. When Breil-Zoeger coolly surveys the effects of Barois' illness, he is less distressed by the fallen hair, the hollow eyes, and the sluggish body than by what he senses to be a pitiful moral breakdown. Contrary to Bourget's thesis that conversion is the prerequisite for individual and collective regeneration, Martin du Gard seems to imply that religion is at best an individual consolation. Far from being morally rehabilitating, religion appears doubly discredited. It marks the frightened submissiveness of those who prefer blind faith to the lucid inventory of their human condition. Or else—but this is hardly less damning—it is chosen deliberately as a device for maintaining the social and political status quo. Without ever imposing his view on the reader, Martin du Gard subtly orients him toward a feeling of pity and contempt. The very structure of the book lays stress on the combined themes of debility and religion. Adults return to infancy; age and disease reduce them in stature. The father-son relationship further increases the pathos by making the son first a witness and then a victim of this untimely decrepitude. As Barois hears his father's decision to commune, he feels, in spite of his attempted smile, "a poignant, unreasoned, confused disappointment." [3]

Yet Barois' intellectual abdication remains ambivalent. Disappointing in terms of fortitude, the circumstances of the conversion are nonetheless theologically sound and correspond to a religious truth which Martin du Gard was scrupulous enough not to betray. Not only is Barois objectively *right* when he explains that the religious experience by its very nature transcends the limits of the critical intellect, but he is properly at his most *Christian* when obsessed by death and lost in anguished meditation on the transitoriness of physical existence. His weakness thus also marks his worth: metaphysical

[2] *Histoire du roman français depuis 1918*, I, p. 63.
[3] For a radically different treatment of an intellectual's return to faith, see Appendix A: Joseph Malègue's *Augustin ou le maître est là* appears in part like an answer to *Jean Barois*.

anxiety is a noble disease. Unable to face any longer the concept of nothingness, Barois sets out on the tortured quest for meaning. He knows that by humiliating his mind and repressing his *libido sciendi* he stands to gain more precious possessions. Martin du Gard is fully aware that the *credo quia absurdum*, attributed to Tertullian, as well as the *Dieu sensible au coeur* of Pascal, are simultaneously the weakness and the strength of Christianity. According to Christian dialectics, Barois' apparent defeat is truly a victory. All this the author has honestly tried to convey. Nor did he hide the aridity of scientism which, blindly equating intelligence with disbelief, allows no room for spirituality or even poetry, for man's need to love and be loved, to console and be consoled. Barois discovers that *being with others*, even if it means fighting for a common ideal, can become an obstacle to spiritual growth, that human solidarity has its limitations. To Camus' question "Can communion with men, which sometimes helps us to live, also help us to die?" Barois seems to provide a negative answer.[4] But even this answer is in perfect accord with the Christian doctrine of the individuality of souls. Every spiritual crisis is a lonely experience.

It is precisely this individual anguish, this human crisis which, more than any ideological consideration, imbues the living substance of *Jean Barois*. Though fully aware of the metaphysical implications, Martin du Gard sensed that abstract discussions in a novel soon grow pale and wither. His aesthetic instinct warned him against his own scholarly bent: he knew that over-conceptualization can utterly destroy the dramatic qualities of fiction. How much he was preoccupied by these questions is revealed in a recently published posthumous document of major importance—a "Consultation littéraire," in which Martin du Gard, on the eve of undertaking *Les Thibault*, examines some of his own tendencies.[5] "*One cannot be too suspicious of one's own Bovarysm*," he warns himself. Bovarysm, the willing to see oneself other than one really is, meant in his case the tendency

[4] "Roger Martin du Gard," *Nouvelle Nouvelle Revue Française*, October, 1955, pp. 641-671.
   [5] This "Consultation littéraire" (or "Lettres à Pierre Margaritis") was published in the special issue of the *Nouvelle Revue Française* (December, 1958) devoted to Roger Martin du Gard. These letters to Pierre Margaritis (to whom *Les Thibault* are dedicated) were written in 1918, shortly before Margaritis' untimely death, and are further proof of the intense seriousness and integrity with which Martin du Gard meditated on questions of literary technique.

to negate his natural talent (his creative sensibility) and to force himself instead into the role of thinker. It is no doubt ironical to imagine a Martin du Gard suspicious of ideas. When one considers, however, that historical research on the Dreyfus case alone occupied him for ten hours a day during a period of six months, that it took him three years to write *Jean Barois*, and that ten years of note-taking and of classifying newspaper clippings went into its preparation—one can see why Martin du Gard felt concerned lest his inspiration dry up. In order to combat the encyclopedic tendencies of a "half-thinker," as he calls himself, Martin du Gard seeks to bear in mind that his real function as a novelist is to follow with "brotherly attentiveness" the destinies of individuals. The passages he preferred were clearly those least stuffed with ideas: the scenes between Barois and his wife, the death of the Doctor, the promenade and conversation on marriage with the Abbé Joziers, Barois' emotional response to his grown-up daughter, the death of Luce . . . But what satisfied him most were the "moving" pages describing Barois' growing old—and not so much his intellectual fatigue, as the pathetic lassitude of heart and body.

A question comes to mind: how honest is Martin du Gard with himself? Is there not a surreptitious philosophical intention in the very insistence on Barois' physiological weakness? Does the case history not allow for an implicit link between weakness and faith? Martin du Gard is undeniably fascinated by the subject of debility, which he dramatizes by means of a number of interwoven themes. Barois' fear of failure is related to his heredity, which in turn manifests itself through terror of disease and death and, ultimately, makes it possible for the author to exploit thoroughly the pathos of aging, the drama of decline and decrepitude. Repeatedly throughout the novel, Barois expresses misgivings concerning either his efficiency or the worth of his achievement. He feels that he has wasted his life. He complains to Luce that he has reached a dead end, that even his past now seems futile to him. "When I look back, what do I see there? What have I really done?" But much earlier, his self-pity, his need to shift the blame on his wife (*"par ta faute, je suis foutu"*), his self-justification—all point to a defeatist attitude more corrosive even than the dormant bacilli which undermine his body. Barois knows himself doomed to failure, *"Je ne serai jamais qu'un raté."* There is great sadness in the apparently casual remark made during his first conversation with the Abbé Lévys: "I think the world is somewhat unfair to failures. . . ." [6]

Just as the tubercular lesions are hereditary, so is this fear of failure. Atavistic forces are used by the author not merely to cement the formal structure of the novel, but to strengthen the thematic development. Martin du Gard explores this moral-biological determinism with the curiosity and perseverance of a historian. "You have inherited from your mother a tendency to the same illness," Dr. Barois explains to his son. The deeper fears, however, he has inherited from his father: ". . . an instinctive anguish which has its roots in my childhood and in my atavism, no doubt—the terror of losing my faith." This notion of atavism constitutes a permanent theme in Martin du Gard's work. In *Devenir*, the author describes the "private atavism" of the neophytes dedicated to the cult of Art. Mazerelles struggles in vain against the bourgeois heredity of his family—their *"notariat congénital."* Similarly, in *Les Thibault*, the sensualist Daniel Fontanin takes after his father Jérôme; Jacques, in spite of his rebellion, discovers in himself and in his brother hidden affinities with Oscar Thibault ("Later he will have exactly his father's voice"); and Antoine, as he is about to die, places all his hopes in young Jean-Paul who, he feels, will unite Fontanin and Thibault in a common heredity. Fathers and sons: Martin du Gard repeatedly inserts individual tragedies into the broader context of a family fate. The Mazerelles, the Barois, the Thibaults, the Fontanins—each novel is really a family drama and betrays the author's own literary heredity, namely the influence of Zola and of the naturalistic novel.

In *Jean Barois*, the theme of atavism takes on a particular importance, not only because scientism is one of the key issues and biological life the true battlefield, but because it enables the author to present religious faith as a subconscious necessity. Jean Barois, the intellectual, can scarcely be said to exercise a free intellectual choice.

[6] Few thoughts haunted Martin du Gard more than this notion of failure. His first published novel, *Devenir* (1909), is the story of a talentless young writer—a *"raté intelligent"*—who slowly discovers his delusion. Curiously, this novel was written in part as a therapy to exorcise Martin du Gard's private anguish concerning his artistic impotence. The very fear saved him: his ability to describe the "sterile velleities" of Mazerelles proved to him that he was not condemned to share the destiny of his hero. ("Souvenirs," in *Oeuvres complètes*, I, li-lii.)

"I believe that one is born predisposed to doubt or to believe," he says. "All the reasoning in the world cannot alter this." As though to insist on the predetermined nature of metaphysical convictions, Martin du Gard introduces, in the person of Dalier, the innate disbeliever: "My atheism is innate. Both my father and my grandfather were atheists."

This implicit intellectual defeatism is related, in the case of Barois, to his pathological obsession with death. It is no coincidence that both father and son have studied medicine: forces beyond their control drive them to a tête-à-tête with disease and mortality. Martin du Gard's own fascination with medicine is certainly one of the keys to his personality. Hospitals, sickrooms, patients, the progress of a malady always held for him a quasi-seductive appeal. Though his formal training, at the Ecole des Chartes, had been in history and archeology, he attended with far greater excitement, it would seem, clinical lectures given by foremost specialists at the Pitié, Salpétrière, Hôtel Dieu and Sainte-Anne hospitals. Antoine, who emerges as the hero of Les Thibault, is a practicing physician. An entire volume of the series, La Consultation, is devoted to his professional routine. Few novelists have written more powerful scenes describing illness and death: in Devenir, the physical suffering of Mazerelles' wife and her death in childbirth; in Les Thibault, Jenny's meningitis, the death of the father (occupying an entire volume), the scene of the ligature during which Antoine meets Rachel, the atrocious death of Jacques at the front, Antoine's slower, serener death, which he himself observes with a detached clinical curiosity.

Pain and lucidity are excellent tragic associates. The intellectual hero faces the widest range of suffering with the maximum degree of awareness. Jean Barois is indeed spared few bitter experiences: the tragedy of doubt that lays waste the soul, the nocturnal terrors, the desperate gestures of revolt, the search for one's true self that leads to self-destruction, the poison of ideas which makes him a victim of "negative intelligence," the drama of loneliness. But all these are only a prelude to the bitterest experience of all: the intellectual's abdication of his own intelligence, the progressive indolence and numbness that set in as the mind, still lucid, takes stock of its own decline. Martin du Gard himself was convinced that the depiction of Barois growing old was the true achievement of the novel. "This theme of 'growing old' has always obsessed me," he writes in his "Souvenirs." It is possible that this fascination with age and time is partly responsible for his subsequent interest in the *roman-fleuve*. Certainly, the drama of change and erosion occupied his mind at an unusually early age. He himself retrospectively marvels at the fact that when he described Barois' mental and physical degradation, he was at the point of fullest vitality, "a robust young man, confident in the future, carried daily by the pleasure of living, and who had barely reached his thirties."

But *Jean Barois* is uncannily prophetic: the author harbored, deeply hidden, the very disease from which Barois had suffered so much. In later years, Martin du Gard was wont to remark that he was a "contemporary of the past." For this became his own private obsession: the fear of being *out of touch*, of no longer belonging, of watching his own mind go stale. His vain struggle, after the defeat of 1940, to write another great novel, will probably remain one of the saddest chapters in literary history. Significantly, the *Journal du Colonel Maumort* was to be "*le livre du vieillissement*," the novel of the "final discouragement." [7] The history of this failure can be followed, or guessed, in the pages of the "Souvenirs." Tragically, his very inspiration became a cause of paralysis. Nearly every page of the "Souvenirs" bears witness to the author's depression. His project appears to him presumptuous: "It suits neither my age, nor my present working capacities." On his sixtieth birthday, he writes: "This year, I have, very sharply, the feeling of a marked aging." Again, a few pages later: "A year of marked aging, physical and intellectual." But more disheartening even than this persistent awareness of age and fear of senility, is Martin du Gard's feeling of isolation, of intellectual exile. He is haunted by the conviction that he no longer has anything to say that could possibly interest the new generation. To André Gide —who probably did not relish hearing such truths—he wrote: "We are survivors, living 'anachronisms.'" He added, with sadness: "I looked forward to another kind of old age, less inexorably lonely." [8] At one point, in 1946, he attempted to transcend his intellectual loneliness by writing about contemporary youth—a pathetically

7 Letter to André Gide, in *Oeuvres complètes*, I, xcix.
8 *Oeuvres complètes*, I, cxxiii-cxxiv.

aborted enterprise. "These young people are . . . *fundamentally* alien
to me." [9]

Jean Barois, anticipating by thirty years the personal tragedy of
the author, thus seems to stand in a reverse causal relationship to
his life. But if the tragic theme thus precedes the private experience,
if life seemingly patterns itself on art, it is because the literary work
was secretly fecundated by a seed which, though perceptible to
the young artist's intuition, required a whole lifetime to ripen into
living tragedy. An inner necessity drives men to *their* death. In his
"Consultation littéraire" (1918), Martin du Gard came even closer
to his own truth than he could possibly know. The mainspring of
his talent is indeed not ideology, but a sober compassion for physical
suffering and for moral anguish. This is why the novel's most successful passages, the most moving also, are those which describe
the hero's weakening and progressive sense of isolation. He too feels
out of touch. He undertakes a study of the growing generation, but
is soon discouraged: "The young are a puzzle to me." Talking with
two young intellectuals: "I could be your father; we no longer
understand each other." He no longer even feels qualified to be
the director of *Le Semeur*: "Daily I am losing my grip; it's the
young who now impose their views." There is resignation and a
measure of bitterness in the tone. But there is also something else,
more difficult to describe, which the author touches on early in
the novel. At the tensest moment of the father's agony, the dying
man's eyes fix abruptly on his son "with a clear expression of animosity, a sudden flash of rancor . . . then a heart-rending entreaty
which immediately fades away." Jean understood the flash. It meant:
"You are alive. . . ." The tragedy of the individual flows into the
broader drama of the conflicting generations.

¶ II. *The battle of the generation*

BAROIS' DESTINY IS NOT THE SUPREME MESSAGE conveyed by the novel.
Martin du Gard denies himself and the reader the right to draw
conclusions from this private failure. The fate of the individual
merges with the fate of his generation, and cannot be evaluated
apart. The epigraph thus carries a double meaning: the "sick conscience," the battleground of modern fate, is in large part a collective

[9] *Ibid.*, I, cxxviii.

conscience. In his Trocadéro lecture, Barois asserts with passion that he and his public belong to a privileged generation confronted by the arduous task of bringing about a scientific evolution. "We are one of the tragic moments of the painful agony of the past." Similarly Luce, at the end of the novel, assessing the hero's moral situation: "Barois, like so many others, is a victim of our times. His life has been that of many of my contemporaries:—tragic." Every character in the novel seems to be aware of his immersion in a particularly critical moment of history. They are not merely historical witnesses, but active participants in the political gest. Martin du Gard's studies at the École des Chartes are no doubt largely responsible for the historical perspective. "It became impossible for me," he confides in his "Souvenirs," "to conceive a modern character detached from his time." [10] Claude-Edmonde Magny's contention that the Dreyfus case and the issue of modernism constitute "unhappy screens" between the reader and the inner life of Barois takes into account neither the originality of the author nor his success in binding together a private and a collective fatum.[11]

Martin du Gard's non-religious, deterministic cast of mind goes a long way toward explaining his unwillingness ever to look on tragedy as an absolute. Each drama, for him, is tributary to a broader drama. He is, moreover, permanently fascinated by *groups;* they are, in his fictional world, as much a symbol of solidarity as a dissolvent of individual energies. Mazerelles, the young hero of *Devenir*, is enthused by the discovery of Barrès' *Les Déracinés*, and aspires to become the historian of his own generation. This interest in the life of a group, in its struggle and ultimate failure, owes much, it would seem, to the nineteenth-century novel: *Illusions perdues*, *L'Education sentimentale*, *Manette Salomon*, *L'Œuvre*—all portray successive generations, their dreams and their defeats. But no French novelist before Martin du Gard—not even Flaubert—has situated the human drama as unequivocally in its political and social context. "I will have had three somber dates in my life," Dr. Philip confides to Antoine in *L'Eté 1914.* "The first revolutionized my adolescence, the second unsettled my mature years, the third will probably poison my old age." Characteristically, all three crises, though profoundly personal, evoke the experience of an entire generation. The first is

10 *Ibid.*, I, xlviii-xlix.
11 See *Histoire du roman français depuis 1918*, I, 286.

the discovery of the rift between science and faith; the second is the Dreyfus Affair; the third is the mass tragedy of the First World War.

Man—and more particularly the intellectual—is thus for Martin du Gard what Sartre was later to call an *être-en-situation*: a human being condemned to responsibility. First of all, responsibility in the face of inescapable issues. In *Jean Barois* these issues are so clear and so numerous that the editor Bernard Grasset hesitated to publish it, saying that it was less a novel than a "dossier." They are the problems which tormented serious-minded men at the turn of the century: Justice versus national interests; the clash between the temporal powers and the rights of the individual conscience; the prestige of Science (can an ethical system be derived from the scientific method?); the struggle between religion and free thought; the issue of Modernism (traditional Christian apologetics versus symbolist interpretations); popular universities and the duties of the intellectual toward the working class. . . . The clash of ideas, in *Jean Barois*, takes on heroic proportions; thought wrestles with thought. "A nation still capable of such effervescence over ideas," says Jean Barois as the fever of intellectual excitement reaches its highest pitch, "is far from declining."

"Barois découvre les hommes," writes Camus—meaning that in the process of personal evolution he is led from his individuality to the awareness of a common history, the experience of human solidarity.[12] This may only be partially true of Barois himself: his discovery of the community of men is soon followed by a withdrawal. But it is certainly true that the general movement of the book, even when it is most deeply rooted in an individual conscience, projects us toward the world of men and ideas. The lesson of Dr. Benassis in Balzac's *Le Médecin de campagne* applies directly: "Our conscience is the point of departure. We always proceed from ourselves to other men, never from other men to ourselves." The moral implications are clear. The intellectual, especially, has a debt to society. The privilege to devote himself to peaceful research and meditation— one of the protagonists explains—implies "inescapable obligations." He does not have the right to remain silent. Twenty-five years ahead of time, Martin du Gard uses the very vocabulary the Existentialists

12 "Roger Martin du Gard," *op. cit.*

will wear threadbare in their praise of authenticity: *"Il faut que chacun de nous consente à sa vie."*

The structure of the novel points to the constant interpenetration of self and others, to the subsumption of the individual in a collective destiny. *Jean Barois* is divided into three parts: Part I ("The Will to Live," "The Symbolist Compromise," "The Ring," "The Chain," "The Rupture") deals with Barois' private problems, his religious doubts, his unhappy marriage, his separation from his wife; Part II (*"Le Semeur,"* "The Wind is Rising," "Storm," "Calm") centers primarily on the ideological war which is rending France; Part III ("The Flaw," "The Child," "The Critical Age," "Twilight") again stresses Barois' personal tragedy, his relation with his daughter, his illness, his religious conversion and his death. The novel seems, structurally, to move from Barois to the world of men and ideologies, and then back to Barois. Yet this is not altogether the case: the inner architecture of each section, and the very titles used, reveal that the author set out deliberately to alternate and intertwine the individual and the collective themes. Part I contains the obviously philosophical chapter "The Symbolist Compromise." Part III deals with such collective issues as the betrayal of the Dreyfus mystique and the rift between successive generations. As for the central portion of the novel, though primarily concerned with the storm into which Barois leads his group, it also suggests personal reasons for Barois' militant behavior and relates his encounter with death and fear in a chapter ironically entitled "Calm."

The collective theme finds its fullest orchestration in the lyrical passages that sing the enthusiasm, ideals and combativeness of the young intelligentsia. Subject and treatment alike are completely original. Only a few years earlier, Romain Rolland's Jean-Christophe remarked to his friend Olivier that the real poet of the Dreyfus case had as yet not appeared on the literary horizon. "The Dreyfus case has lifted your nation to the stars and plunged it into abysses. Where is the poet who has been inspired by the storm? The most beautiful struggle is taking place in religious minds between the authority of the Church and the rights of the individual conscience. Where is the poet who will reflect this sacred anguish?" [13]

Jean Barois seems to answer this call. Certainly, no other work of fiction so movingly recaptures the epic climate of this battle of

[13] *Dans la maison,* p. 40.

ideas. Léon Blum, who witnessed this "holy hysteria," considered *Jean Barois* an astonishing artistic re-creation of the *âme dreyfus-arde*.[14] Martin du Gard was no doubt well served by his objective-historical technique which not only permitted factual authenticity, but lent the occasional lyric outbursts the added intensity of re-straint. The organizational meeting for *Le Semeur* is one of the most stirring episodes of the novel. The symbolic title echoes the spirit and aims of such actual publications as Péguy's famous *Ca-hiers*. The youthful group discusses its projects with a timid, clumsy idealism. They all wish to give their intellectual life a social and political direction. With a common vibration, they respond to some lines quoted from Lamennais' *Paroles d'un croyant* which appear to sum up their own sense of prophetic mission. "Son of man! Ascend to the mountain top and proclaim what you behold!" Animated by a joyous and virile defiance, their first meeting culminates in a hymn to Progress. But the most solemn moments are to come. The decision to throw their energies into the Dreyfus battle is an apoc-alypse of commitment which makes all hearts beat in proud unison. "It is the beginning of superhuman exaltations. . . ." In passages such as these, the novel far transcends the problems or exploits of the individual protagonist. A whole generation is involved. "Many of us were heroes." [15]

But this collective heroism also ends in collective frustration. The common *élan* is destined to lose its momentum and degenerate. This process, which parallels Barois' private decadence, is presented in three phases. The first is Luce's speech at the 1900 Exposition, his funeral oration of the Dreyfus case. Surveying the achievement of their group, Luce points to a number of disheartening facts. Agita-tors have exploited their victory; the flag of justice has been torn out of their hands and is now used by political opportunists to betray their idealism. A handful of pure *dreyfusistes* has been sub-

14 *Souvenirs sur L'Affaire*, p. 131.
15 It is significant that Martin du Gard never intended to name his novel after the protagonist. It was Gallimard, Fernet and Gide, according to the author, who insisted that he use the name of the protagonist as title. Eager to have his novel published by the NRF, Martin du Gard agreed against his better judgment. This decision, because it betrayed his deeper convictions, he calls "one of the shameful acts of my life." *S'Affranchir*, the title he had in mind originally, clearly pointed to a universal problem going far beyond the destiny of a single individual. (See the "Consultation littéraire," *Nouvelle Revue Française*, December, 1958, pp. 1117-1135.)

merged by an army of *dreyfusards*. So many illusions have been lost along the way that it has become difficult, Luce concludes, not to surrender to pessimism. The second phase is the transfer of Zola's remains to the Panthéon—a vulgar, theatrical parade that marks the official exploitation of their victory. A great sadness weighs on the group: the very sadness experienced by a Péguy when he realized that the *mystique* of the crusade had degenerated into a *politique*. *Le Semeur* is losing its most faithful subscribers and mourns a "general bankruptcy." The third phase coincides with Barois' decision to resign as director of *Le Semeur*. With bitterness, he recapitulates the group's disillusions and concludes with the futility of their efforts. "Everywhere I see lies, self-interest, social injustice as before." Nothing has changed; nothing can change. A profound historical pessimism seems to be the answer to the loftiest ideals. "All the injustices, all the errors are reborn with each new generation; it will always be the same struggle, the same victory of the strong over the weak, of the young over the old—eternally." Cresteil's suicide is like an open proclamation of the group's tragic failure.

The futile antagonism between successive generations is given masterful treatment in the long scene that opposes an aging though still resilient Barois and two aggressive university students whose Catholic nationalism and virulent anti-liberalism have a strong Maurassian flavor. Martin du Gard never dramatized more brilliantly a conflict of ideas. The altercation is presented with such stark economy, with such a concentration on essentials, that ideas no longer seem to require human beings to express them, and the antagonists appear to be there only to incarnate them much as an actor may assume a role which transcends the performance. Martin du Gard's private obsession—his intuition of the loneliness that comes with old age—is unquestionably at the center of this scene. Grenneville and Tillet, the two students, are insolent and unfair. Their deference is only another form of hostility. Their "impertinent smile" wounds Barois. But the personal suffering is less important here than the historico-philosophical implications of this *agon* of ideas.

Irresistibly impelled to view individuals and entire generations in the broader perspective of history and the necessary conjunction of Time and Circumstance, Martin du Gard seems to regard the outcome of collective effort no less pessimistically than he does that of the individual. Michelangelo's struggling *Slave* is also the adequate symbol for the group of *Le Semeur*. No generation can liberate itself. This is so partly because generations also are subject to the laws of atavism, and partly because even the most dynamic movement is only a reaction, and consequently part of the eternal ebb and flow. This is precisely Barois' most telling answer to the juvenile arrogance of his two young visitors: "Don't delude yourselves, gentlemen, as to your role. . . . You are nothing but a *reaction*. And this reaction is so inevitable that you can't even pride yourselves on having caused it: it's the oscillation of the pendulum. . . ." No conclusion is ever possible because of the very necessity of movement. The pessimism is both philosophical and historical: the deterministic forces of the Universe make even rebellion synonymous with heredity.

¶ III. *The drama of history*

A DOUBLE DEFEAT—the score so far seems hardly encouraging. The struggle of the individual and the struggle of the generation meet a like fate. But if they both are subject to the rigorous laws of History, does it follow that History itself is devoid of meaning? The key to the problem is provided, it would seem, by a figure who does not appear very often, but whose presence in the novel is all-pervasive, and experienced as a living lesson by the other characters. The central importance and exemplary value of Luce (the very name seems to imply lucidity and hope) has been confirmed by Martin du Gard in his "Souvenirs" where, some thirty years later, he calls his "exemplary" hero Maumort ("who will be like my testament") a "great figure" conceived "in the tradition of Luce in *Jean Barois*." [16]

Luce is first mentioned when the editorial board of *Le Semeur* decides with unanimous enthusiasm to dedicate the first issue to him. This "Tribute to Marc-Elie Luce" is to honor a man who stands unqualifiedly for probity and uprightness, who has been for all of them a moral guide and an inspiration. Thus he immediately appears as one who transcends a given generation. Their elder by about fifteen years (he is forty-seven, they are barely over thirty), he fulfills the double function of mentor and senior comrade. In and out of the group, he is also above it. At first he has the distance

[16] *Oeuvres complètes*, I, cii-ciii.

of an ideal: no one knows him personally; those who have heard him speak at public gatherings cannot shake off the spell of his ardor and seriousness; the others know him only through his works. Gradually, however, the ideal ceases to be an abstraction and he emerges as a warm human being. Son of a clergyman, Luce at first studied theology, then became interested in history and philosophy. His remarkable books earned him, at an unusually early age, a professorship in the History of Religions at the Collège de France. Active as a social worker, dedicated to the mission of the *universités populaires*, he soon enters into the political arena and becomes a senator respected by all parties because he has sold himself to none. It is not unlikely that Scheurer-Kestner, the vice-president of the Senate at the time of the Dreyfus case, was one of the models for Luce. Luce, like Scheurer-Kestner, once he is convinced of Dreyfus' innocence, regards it as his bounden duty not to remain silent. This requires more than ordinary courage. He has a family of nine children, and his intervention endangers not merely his reputation, but his career and security as well. In fact he is soon ostracized in the Senate and politely asked to give up his course at the Collège de France. It is significant, however, that if Luce hesitates at all, it is not out of personal fear, but because he is fully aware of the enormous responsibility that falls on anyone who, though it be in the cause of Justice, disturbs the peace of the nation.

It is precisely such scruples that distinguish Luce from a Barois. No private vindictiveness ever mars his judgment. Even in the heat of ideological combat, when prejudice has attained epidemic proportions, Luce warns his friends against intolerance. His belief in freedom is so far-reaching that he would grant error the right to function freely. In all things he asks for measure, balance, objectivity. "I always believed that life was like one of these maps of countries I do not know: to find one's way, one only has to try reading it. . . ." There is perhaps in all of French literature no more exalted incarnation of the liberal virtues.

Though intrinsically beautiful, the virtues of Luce—his sense of proportion, his moral equilibrium—permit Martin du Gard to measure the interdependence of private and collective values, and shade subtly the relationship between the individual and his group. Thus Luce warns young Barois of the dangers of collective associations: "Don't let yourself be influenced too much by others. . . . A community of thought is necessary, to be sure, and that you have. A common *élan* brought you together and threw you into action. But do not throw your personality into the melting pot. Remain true to yourself, no matter what. Cultivate in yourself only that which is truly yours." (The advice is reminiscent of Grosdidier's own fear of groups in *Devenir;* he warns the *raté* Mazerelles against these "common treasures" in which individual talents go waste.) But, on the other hand, Luce is equally suspicious of the prerogatives of the individual sensibility. He detects in Barois an unhappy tendency to let systems crystallize around emotions. In this partisan ardor he senses too much subjectivity. "You feel, as it were, a private satisfaction, something like a personal revenge. . . ." Similarly, at the point of death, as he catches an old friend in the act of crying, he consoles him chidingly: *"We should not let ourselves be blinded by the individual."*

It is precisely his death which—in direct contrast with the death of Barois—establishes Luce as the true hero of the novel. The very method chosen for presenting this scene betrays the author's desire to lend it a majestic beauty. Not described directly, but reported by an admiring witness, the death of Luce is endowed with a quasi-mythical grandeur. It is a serene, smiling death which, in its sense of autumnal fulfillment, brings to mind Shakespeare's words: "Ripeness is all." For Luce knows that death can sum up a life and constitute its ultimate message. "I always attempted to pattern my life on my ideas in order to give them vigor; all that remains for me to do is to die without wavering." Was not the noblest lesson of Socrates his death? Luce experiences fear, but he dominates it with all the magnitude of his intellect. "The repercussions of a serene death are very great on our pitiful brotherhood of men condemned to death." An ennobling sense of peace pervades the scene. His is not a resignation made easy by hope of future bliss, but a lucid appraisal of life, of man's limitations and possibilities. To philosophize, the Stoics felt, was to learn how to die. Luce's end clearly demonstrates that death need not be degrading, that it can carry with it the most princely image of the human condition.[17]

[17] There is little doubt that this death scene was inspired largely by Martin du Gard's beloved master, the Abbé Marcel Hébert, to whom *Jean Barois* was dedicated, and whose beautiful pronouncements on death Martin du Gard recorded in the moving pages of "In Memoriam" (*Oeuvres complètes*, I, pp. 561-576), which is as much a testimony to Hébert's unusual personality as to the author's shy and tender idealism.

Some critics feel that Luce, though admirable in a Cornelian manner, is somewhat removed from ordinary humanity, that there is a nearly inhuman element in his dauntlessness and intellectual resilience.[18] When Luce affirms that it is easy to find one's happiness in Reason, Martin du Gard obviously opposes the senator's rational approach to Barois' sentimental reactions. The antithesis is perhaps at times a little too schematic; it is the price the author pays for wanting to demonstrate that Rationalism also has its martyrs and its saints. But Luce is not a cold, statuesque ideal to be admired from a distance. He dynamically embodies the few important, positive affirmations by means of which Martin du Gard seems to answer his own philosophical pessimism. There is not pride but humility in Luce's cult of Reason. He refuses to pass final judgment on life. Unlike Barois, who needs reassuring absolutes, Luce is willing to live with "insoluble problems." Paradoxically, it is he who clearly is the more religious of the two; to Barois' *fear*, he opposes his *faith*—a faith in the life process itself and in man's role in it. "We are a fragment of universal life." That is why Luce can envisage death as naturally as birth, or transformation. In transitoriness he sees not evanescence, but metamorphosis, continuation, survival.

It is no coincidence that Luce first appears in his own house, surrounded by the "joyous *galopade*" of half a dozen children. Caressing the head of one of his boys, he addresses to Barois these words, simple but deeply felt: "Life is so beautiful. . . ." Throughout the novel, he affirms, explicitly or implicitly, the intrinsic value of life. His large, healthy family symbolizes the beauty of procreation. He himself has preserved a childlike capacity to take delight in small things and to face daily events with a "loving curiosity." A "beautiful life" seems to him as valid as a beautiful work, for even vitality requires conscious human participation. It is with pride that he shows his garden: the tree carries its own fruit, but first the gardener's work had to be accomplished. Life thus appears as a real obligation, an act not of submission, but of collaboration. Our very *awareness* of life implies a duty to live. But that duty is neither an abstract task nor a mechanical compulsion. It is enough to give the best of oneself, to sow the seed generously. Then others must take our place. The coming generation is, for Luce, a source not of bitterness but of

[18] Clément Borgal, *Roger Martin du Gard* p. 53.

faith. There is a symbolic significance to his last words: "How beautiful they are, my children."

The eternal renewal, the ever recurring cycle which so much distressed Barois, provides Luce with a basic argument for hope. He thus appears as the force which challenges the defeatist, suicidal tendencies of the main character. His generous conception of History casts a sunny light on determinism. His relativistic outlook serves to protect his idealism. "Let us remember," he advises his friends, "that the Dreyfus case will only be a tiny episode in the struggle between reason and blinding human passions; that it will merely be a moment, and no more, of this slow and marvelous evolution. . . ." This represents his permanent attitude: every act, every event—victory or defeat—is but a stage; each generation must perform its duty, but has no right to be discouraged. This faith in universal movement has several important implications. On the one hand, it negates the meaninglessness of individual suffering by relating every act to a metaphysical global effort: life arises out of death, energy from pain, harmony from chaos. Nothing is lost; the seed will grow. An individual defeat can never be equated with the defeat of life. But, on the other hand, Luce's hopeful determinism points to a cult of Time which not only redeems the death of the individual through the vision of a collective future, but tends to replace God himself by History.[19]

The divinization of History is no doubt too strong a term to apply to Luce. His is, after all, primarily a feeling of pride in belonging to an important historical moment and in having lived up to its exacting demands. "Future generations will say 'The Affair' the way we say 'The Revolution.' . . . What a century which begins with such a victory!" The emphasis on the future is nonetheless symptomatic of a general tendency of our time to think along the lines of Hegelian dialectics and apply to History the logic of becoming.[20] Luce's answer involves a subtle interplay between the

---

[19] Gaëtan Picon writes: "If humanity has no future, everything falls into absurdity: our duty has no foundation. In other words, God can really be replaced only by History" ("Portrait et situation de Roger Martin du Gard," Mercure de France, September, 1958, pp. 5-25).

[20] Pierre-Henri Simon has very ably shown, in L'Esprit et l'Histoire, how the twentieth-century mind tends to view history no longer as an archeological exercise, but an immersion of the individual (the être-dans-l'histoire) in a tragic current.

individual and collective determinism which is reminiscent of the theological tension between predestination and free will.[21]

¶ IV. *A "roman engagé"*

THE PROFOUND ORIGINALITY of *Jean Barois* as a novel of ideas becomes even more striking if measured against Anatole France's *Les Dieux ont soif* which appeared less than a year earlier. Contemporary readers, especially the younger ones, felt the impact immediately. Many, like René Lalou, discovered the novel on the eve of the World War, and were deeply moved to find that it reflected the problems which tormented their minds and sensibilities.[22] No "aesthetic" reasons could account for its success. Martin du Gard never sought to be a creator of new forms or a virtuoso at aesthetic thrills. Though he became their friend, his temperament was altogether alien to the group of the *Nouvelle Revue Française*. This is not to deny his technical boldness. His handling of the novel in dialogue form is unique and masterful. It is, moreover, perfectly appropriate to the dialectical tone and to the themes of the work. "The dialogue form," according to Renan, "is in the present state of man, the only one which suits the exposition of philosophical ideas." [23]

The true achievement of the work is to be found, however, in the scope and vision with which the author handles a complex of subjects. The multiplicity of dramatic themes is impressive. None of them is treated as a mere digression, as is so often the case with Anatole France. Martin du Gard does not indulge in intellectual pyrotechnics. All his themes are firmly rooted in the basic question that gnaws at Jean Barois: "What is the meaning of this life and of man's presence on earth? What is the purpose of so much suffering?"

---

[21] The meaningfulness of this question for our time is summed up by Kyo in *La Condition humaine:* "There is in Marxism a sense of fatality as well as the exaltation of human will." Heresy sets in as soon as the one wins out over the other.

[22] See René Lalou, *Roger Martin du Gard*, pp. 8-9. Other testimonies point to the same enthusiasm on the part of the young intelligentsia. Jean Guéhenno and Philippe van Tieghem recall with nostalgia their gratitude to an author who spoke to them with such moral and intellectual intensity. They were tired of psychological, sentimental or purely narrative fiction. "Finally we were discovering the novel of an intellectual. . . ." (See "Hommage à Roger Martin du Gard," *Nouvelle Revue Française*, December, 1958, pp. 1037-1067.)

[23] See the preface to *Le Prêtre de Némi.*

It is because he remains so well rooted in the psychological anguish of a single consciousness that Martin du Gard can also raise with impunity the abstract issues of Religion and Politics, Faith and Reason, and dramatize a conflict of ideals. Writing neither a case history nor a work of propaganda, Martin du Gard situates his novel at the confines of the concrete and the abstract. No literary work belies more flagrantly Ortega y Gasset's pronouncement that every novel inspired by transcendental intentions is still-born.[24]

The existential foundations of the novel have much to do with the author's own commitments. In the first place, there is Martin du Gard's commitment to his literary work, his determination to write a *summa* into which he could pour without reticence all that was authentically meaningful to him. But, as Gaëtan Picon points out, Martin du Gard's fictional world itself is *engagé* to the extent that it takes the individual's relation to History as the measure of man.[25] The acceptance of a collective struggle and a collective predicament, the discovery that no man lives and dies alone, make of Luce a true prophet of the existential credo. Like Dubreuilh, in Simone de Beauvoir's *Les Mandarins*, he knows that private ethics and individual salvation are impossible.

The intellectual's fascination with the myth of History is also, beyond a doubt, a form of Romanticism. Other writers—Malraux, for instance, like Barrès before him—have in our time echoed Napoleon's pronouncement that modern poets would seek in politics a sense of fatum no less despotic than that which inspired the Greek tragedians. The generation of 1930, for instance, fully exploited such a concept of destiny—at times with apocalyptic fervor. But already in *Jean Barois* Martin du Gard reacts against the unheroic hero of the nineteenth century by presenting, as one of the rare forms of heroism still possible, the intellectual's lucid and self-willed submissiveness to a historical necessity.

In time, the mystical marriage between man and History lent itself to a new type of histrionic pose. But Luce and the group of *Le Semeur* are not corrupted yet by fads and fashions. Their ardor is pure. As intellectuals, they view their intervention in politics, not as a self-seeking and self-glorifying adventure, but as a unique occasion to translate ethical concepts into action. A similar dream

[24] *The Dehumanization of Art and Notes on the Novel,* p. 92.
[25] "Portrait et situation de Roger Martin du Gard," *op. cit.*

inspired the generation which, thirty years later, fought in the Resistance movement and hailed the Liberation of France as the beginning of a new era. The story of their bitter disappointments—symbolized by the failure of Sartre's Rassemblement Démocratique Populaire—has been recorded in Simone de Beauvoir's *Les Mandarins*. The generation of Jean Barois and that of Dubreuilh and Perron are indeed not unrelated cultural phenomena. They are part of that same crisis of European civilization which, in the words of the philosopher Brice Parain, has "rejected God from its thinking." [26] For Nietzsche's cry that God is dead was not really the cry of a lonely prophet. It was immediately understood and repeated. Its prolonged, ominous reverberation accounts to a large degree for the philosophical preoccupations of our "era of responsibility." [27] Private tensions are no doubt at the heart of the non-religious metaphysical consciousness that pervades *Jean Barois* and makes of it both an original and a representative work. Yet Martin du Gard's tensions, though perhaps unresolved, still permit a harmonious, quasi-serene outlook. Bitterness has not yet contaminated Martin du Gard's intellectual. He has not yet reached that tragic impasse in which the rebellious and suicidal hero of Guilloux's generation will soon find himself.

[26] *L'Embarras du choix*, p. 111.
[27] The expression is used by R. M. Albérès in his extremely stimulating *Portrait de notre héros*, p. 87. Albérès compares the modern hero to a Cornelian character for whom love and death are a matter of free choice. "Every one of us, before committing himself, repeats the Cid's stanzas." Corneille, one might add, enjoyed unusual prestige during the dark days of the Occupation.

7

Louis Guilloux and the Myth of Cripure

"HE WAS THE LAUGHINGSTOCK OF THE town," says Guilloux of his hero in *Le Sang noir* (1935). It is easy to see why Professor Cripure provokes such hilarity among the inhabitants of this small Breton community. His gigantic silhouette has become as legendary as a grotesque landmark. Generations of lycée students have taken delight in sabotaging his classes and in mocking this man afflicted with the physique of a paralyzed orang-outang. Generations of worthy citizens have been amused and scandalized by this philosophy teacher, an acromegalic giant, whose comical deformity is further heightened by his grease-stained jacket, his pathetic short-sightedness and his huge flatboat feet. To passers-by, meeting him on his way to school, this figure walking like a drowsy tight-rope dancer, lashing the air behind him with his cane, appears indeed both comical and nightmarish.

One of the weirdest figures in French fiction, Cripure has been symbolically robbed of his real name. For Cripure (rhyming unpleasantly with *pelure* and *ordure*: peel and garbage) is really a nickname Monsieur Merlin acquired the day an inventive student decided that the oft-quoted title of Kant's "immortal masterpiece" should really be *La Cripure de la Raison Tique!* The nickname, together with legends of past ridicule, now clings to him like an open invitation to laughter and indiscipline. This persecuted thinker who is busy writing a *Chrestomathy of Despair*, and who seeks refuge in Anjou wine when the feeling of moral asphyxia becomes too unbearable (he then indulges in contemptuous dialogues with himself: "Philosophia, jokologia, hypocritologia . . ."), is indeed not only weary of his tormentors, but nauseated by the duplicity and the compromises that corrode even the loftiest thought. Now living with an illiterate peasant whore, he can remember more glorious days when, after the publication of his work on the Medes, he

119

acquired a certain notoriety in the literary circles of the capital. But that was long ago. Since then the Sorbonne has rejected his thesis on the philosopher Turnier who committed suicide over an unhappy love affair, in the same town where Cripure, now in his last year before retirement, leads the existence of a grotesque *raté*. He too has been in love and even married, but was betrayed and had not the courage to fight a duel with the handsome officer-seducer. His dreams of protest thus go hand in hand with lucid and unflattering self-appraisal. The ultimate irony of a life poisoned by persecutions and abdications is that it comes abruptly to an end when Cripure, after a pathetic last scene (his beloved dogs have chewed to bits the manuscript of his *Chrestomathy of Despair*), shoots himself because, for a second time, he has not had the courage to fight. But that is only the superficial cause of his death. His suicide symbolizes a larger bankruptcy.

Three experiences have been important in determining Guilloux's outlook and the climate of his work. The first goes back to his childhood. Born of poor working-class parents, he early came in contact with militant socialism. Books such as *La Maison du peuple* (1927), *Compagnons* (1931), *Hyménée* (1932) echo the pre-war socialist idealism of the French working class. *La Maison du peuple* is in large part an autobiographical novel, and describes with effective simplicity the struggle and the dreams of enlightened small-town craftsmen. The second and obviously more significant experience was the war of 1914-1918, at the outbreak of which Guilloux was fifteen years old, and consequently most impressionable. He has never been able to forget these wartime memories: the extinction of all pacifist dreams, the anguish of departures and notifications of death on the *champ d'honneur*, long trains filled with wounded men, camps crowded with prisoners of war—but, worst of all, the Great Lie of official propaganda and professional patriots (*mensonge* is one of his key words), the absurdity of chauvinism, and the willful betrayal of human values. Romain Rolland was one of his early intellectual heroes. *Dossier confidentiel* (1930) is entirely colored by this atmosphere of war and frustrated idealism.

The third experience—the immediate catalyst for *Le Sang noir*—was the suicide of the philosopher Georges Palante, who taught in the lycée of Guilloux's home town, Saint-Brieuc. This tragic death of a man he loved made a profound impression on Guilloux, and later compelled him to write some very moving pages about him. The memory of this lonely figure became for him a permanent source of revery. "To Palante's protest, I have added my own. Our hatreds have met in a poetic creation."[1]

The action of Le Sang noir takes place within twenty-four hours. We are at the beginning of 1918, the last year of the war, on the day the wife of Député Faurel is to be officially decorated for her services as army nurse. Preparations for festivities at the lycée are taking place; speeches are being rehearsed—and all this while the mayor is busy running from house to house "distributing the dead" to unsuspecting families. Patriotic pronouncements are cruelly situated in the contrapuntal context of bitter anti-militarism as soldiers riot at the local railroad station. The lycée, with its sullen struggles between students and teachers, its jealousies and petty intrigues among the faculty, its hierarchical obsessions, stands at the center of the action. It is here that, enveloped in traditional school odors, the lie of chauvinism prospers in the form of cultural intolerance or smug, pseudo-lyrical outbursts about the war dead.[2] It is this atmosphere that asphyxiates the intellectual as he takes stock of the varieties of moral cowardice and of his own compromise with turpitude.

Much of Le Sang noir is in the form of a one-day chronicle of a small town (one is at times reminded of Joyce) in which, without any real plot line, a number of individual destinies cross paths or run ironically parallel. There is Professor Babinot who collects weapons (his dream is to own a German flag!), writes patriotic verse, gets slapped by angry soldiers on furlough, invents stories about German spies, while the mayor is about to inform him that his son has died at the front. There is the drama of the school principal, M. Marchandeau, who, on the very day of the patriotic festivities, has learned that his son is to be shot for mutiny. There is Simone Point who steals money from her father, an abhorrent,

---

[1] See Frédéric Lefèvre's interview with the author, "Une heure avec M. Louis Guilloux," Les Nouvelles Littéraires, December 15, 1935.

[2] For instance Professor Nabucet's quatrain composed for the decoration ceremony: "Dormez grands morts dans vos tranchées / Fécondez les épis nouveaux / Moisson d'or plus jamais fauchée / La France veille à vos berceaux." ("Sleep, honored dead, in your trenches / Make fruitful the new grain / A golden harvest which will not be mown again / France watches over your cradles.")

greedy notary, and escapes with one Kaminsky, a cynical, pleasure-seeking but wonderfully intelligent "Slav" (in fact a Polish Jew) who is in turn responsible for the suicide of an over-ripe mythomaniacal landlady whose boarding-house seems to come straight out of Balzac. And of course, there is Lucien Bourcier, Cripure's former student, whose boat leaves for England just about the time Cripure shoots himself, and who is there to remind the reader that not all is an answer of despair.

Teachers and students, fathers and sons—the novel seems to concern itself with the gap between two generations. The inhabitants of the town are indeed judged by their offspring. Simone Point and Lucien Bourcier view their parents without a trace of pity. The fathers themselves, when finally made lucid by suffering, stare obsessively into their guilt. One of the most gripping scenes takes place when, after the departure of the military convoy, Marchandeau and Couturier meet under a streetlight. Their despairing handshake is an avowal that they are united in remorse. But Guilloux is not interested merely in the traditional misunderstanding between two generations. His theme is both more precise and more unsettling. It is the drama of a supposedly *betrayed* generation—a drama in which the teacher becomes symbolic of all moral hypocrisy.

It would seem that the two world wars have raised this theme to the level of a common experience. Erich Maria Remarque's soldiers, after they discover the mud of the trenches and the stench of the dead, find themselves impelled to insult their former teachers. Similarly, after World War II, the "visitor" in Jean Tardieu's *La Politesse inutile* brutally slaps the sententious Professor. In *Le Sang noir* there are, of course, real slaps and real insults; but there are also more articulate protests, such as Francis Montfort's anarchic, anti-militaristic verse:

> *Vous m'avez trompé*
> *Menti*
> *Vestons*
> *Binocles*
> *Souliers vernis*
> *Chapeaux melons*
> *Qui le preniez de si haut!*
> *Montrez voir un peu votre âme immortelle?*
> *A présent*

Rien que le vent
Qui tombe
Sur cent mille cadavres.[3]

Cripure's tragedy is that he finds himself caught: deceiver and deceived in one; rebellious teacher who yet plays the game of those against whom he rebels. "Faker" and "crook" (*escroc!*) is what a disappointed former disciple calls him after he discovers that Cripure, who is bitter and honest enough to know that one cannot always be faithful to oneself, has begun to debunk his own dreams. Lucien Bourcier is more charitable. He knows that Cripure is a bankrupt thinker who now has only his bankruptcy left to cherish. But he also knows that Cripure has been his master, his "initiator." He has adored and cursed him. He has understood him. And yet he cannot *justify* him.

The hero of this novel is thus accuser and accused, victim and culprit—a contradictory though paradoxically "pure" figure who symbolically broke off with his colleagues, but did not have the courage to follow the disciples whose minds he had aroused to rebellion.[4] Cripure's purity is largely due to his loneliness, no doubt. His conscience is a private theater into which we are allowed glimpses as a moral crisis is about to ripen into tragedy. On the surface, however, this is a day like any other day. Nothing of particular significance seems to happen to Cripure. He makes casual love to his Maïa, thereupon insults her as usual, finds out that some students have unscrewed the bolts on his bicycle, whips himself into a titanic rage, carries on a clumsy conversation with his bastard son home on a furlough from the front, has a frustrating interview with a disciple, goes to the bank, teaches a class, gets drunk in the Café Machin, jots down a few notes for his *Chrestomathy of Despair*, remembers his former love and his cowardice, watches the wife of a Deputy being decorated, witnesses soldiers rioting at the railroad station, slaps his old foe and colleague Professor Nabucet. This slap, long overdue, is the only real *act* of his day. Yet it too is less an act than a clumsy parody of all the acts he never had the courage

---

[3] "You have deceived me / Lied / Coats / Eyeglasses / Polished shoes / Derby hats / Putting on big airs! / Let's see that immortal soul of yours! / Now / Nothing but the wind / Falls / Over a hundred thousand corpses."

[4] Readers who delight in toying with the symbolic meaning of names may be tempted to interpret Cripure as *cri pur* ("pure cry").

to carry out. His suicide in the dawn of the following day is equally casual, absurd, and superfluous. It is the caricature of a noble death.

Guilloux, as a matter of fact, insists on the elements of caricature. Cripure, we are told, is different from others (*"un homme à part"*) by reason of his very deformity, a *"difformité . . . caricaturale."* Cripure's feet are so enormous that a local shoemaker proudly exhibited his shoes side by side with those of an itinerant circus giant (Cripure won). Who can help laughing when he walks by, talking aloud to himself in schoolboy slang? Or when he rides by on his bicycle, his cloth hat held fast by an elastic band and his penny whistle dangling about his neck by a string? Even his death and the procession to the lycée are viewed in a buffoonish light. And so are his relations with his one faithful disciple, the *pion* Moka (a half-witted, sentimental, mystical, blundering character not unworthy of Gogol or Dostoevski) whose affection and respect for his "beloved master" are that of a clownish famulus for a burlesque Faust.

To understand Guilloux's Cripure as a literary phenomenon, it is indeed necessary first to replace him in a tradition of intellectual caricature which combines satire, pathos, hostility and admiration. The French novel of ideas, ever since the beginning of the nineteenth century, has repeatedly tapped this tradition. Balzac probably set the tone in his *Etudes philosophiques*, which exploited the atmosphere of the supernatural tale (Hoffmann's works had only recently been translated) in order to toy with metaphysical themes and to present his views on the relationship between action, thought and will. The inept doctors and scientists in *La Peau de chagrin*, the "diabolical" painter Frenhofer in *Le Chef-d'oeuvre inconnu*, the mad chemist (or alchemist) in *La Recherche de l'absolu*, the maniacal composer Gambara—Promethean intellects afflicted with the disease of genius—are all situated in a demonic climate by means of the most hackneyed tricks of caricature.

Cripure once more raises the old question of this particular type of comic distortion. What are its sources, what are its deeper themes? Obviously, we have here another version of the absent-minded, dreaming, self-contained thinker, the *zerstreute Professor*—one of the many echoes of the old fable of the astrologer falling into a well. But Cripure's is not simply a pedantic one-track-mindedness which Bergson might classify under the comfortable rubric of "the mechanical imposed upon the living." Idealism is also a form of obstinacy. In this sense Don Quixote embodies the "intellectual," the man who has read too much and now wishes to impose his dreams and his abstractions upon a shifting and recalcitrant reality. Bergson was of course perfectly right about one thing: behind this kind of mockery one can usually detect the uneasiness of the pedestrian mind in the face of the extraordinary, the instinctive fear which any atrophy or hypertrophy is bound to provoke. Predestined victim of his own supposed unbalance, the man of superior intellect also appears as a frightening phenomenon. Horror films and science fiction have found a steady source of inspiration in the supposed "madness" and inhumanity of all genius.

"*Tout bon raisonnement offense*," said Stendhal. It is difficult to conceive of a terser formula to describe the basic divorce between intellectualism and the vulgar mind. Julien Benda, truly obsessed by this conflict, pointed out that when the vulgus laughs at the cleric (calling him an astrologer!), he is in fact mocking all "idealism" and thus corroborating Socrates' remark, in the *Theaetetus*, that the philosopher will forever be the jest of the common herd.[5] All through Western history, it is indeed possible to trace a recurrent fear of the intellectual elite. Renan, who called for some such elite, but who also foresaw some of the reactions this call was to provoke, sadly observed in *L'Avenir de la Science* that philosophers irritate the people who are perhaps willing to forgive the gold of the nobleman but never intellectual superiority. "*Le peuple aime l'ignorance*," asserted Vigny, who was saddened by this unremitting friction between the *homme esprit* and the *homme matière*.

This friction and this conflict pervade every page of *Le Sang noir*. When Mme Bourcier curses the "abominable" influence Cripure has exerted on her son Lucien and thinks of him as a "Professor of Discord," an enemy of the family and of society, a "public menace"—she obviously expresses the age-old view of the intellectual as subversive. Guilloux unquestionably wishes to raise his characters and his situation to a symbolic level. The small town, enemy of all intelligence, becomes a microcosm in which the clumsy giant-thinker is slowly asphyxiated. *Le Sang noir* describes the ache of awareness, the pain of being alive beyond mere physical existence. The very walk and stature of Cripure are pathetically meaningful. The brain and the limbs, utterly unsynchronized, are out of gear.

[5] *La Fin de l'éternel*, pp. 26-28.

The feet do not obey: heavy, invalid, they keep the philosopher rooted in the mire. For the difficulty lies not only in the clash with the outside world of which Nabucet, Cripure's private enemy and symbol of all turpitude, is the incarnation. The enemy is also within, an invading, corrupting, paralyzing Fifth Column of doubt and disgust. Thoroughly inebriated, Cripure confides to his Doppel-gänger this sense of nausea which philosophy now provokes. "What an idea to ramble through life carrying this slop jar!"

The disease of thinking! The suffering of the intellect! As he thinks of his own death (the thought occurs to him as early as page three), Cripure must admit that all that will be lost is that "little thing" in his head, so futile and so "piercingly painful," which he ironically calls his thought. And yet he is proud of it, too: it is all he has. At times, he views himself as a lucid mirror of this world, enjoying the comedy of the absurd ("Priceless! . . . can't be bored . . . the sublunar isn't half bad!"); at others, he feels that there is greatness in despair, that there is courage and dignity in facing the existential absurdity with an unmuddled mind, even if it means the rather futile courage of "a lucid man stifled by his grief." He com-poses his *Chrestomathy of Despair*, taking a malicious, perhaps maso-chistic pleasure in misanthropic hair-splittings. His ambition now is to evolve a "philosophy of contradiction and of grief." The trouble is that he remains lucid enough to be aware that even this exaltation of suffering is only cant—a pretentious illusion, "a deadly idiocy"! He discovers that even contempt is no longer possible, except for himself. There is no way of escaping that thinking machine which generates only self-deprecation. "No way of escape, not even in wine! Always his own spectator." He invents for himself an inter-locutor (the mythical "Monsieur" of the Café Machin), but it is only to learn that he will die alone. Cripure's real tragedy, how-ever, is not his loneliness. It is the bitter negation of intelligence by his own intellect. That is the meaning of his suicide which fol-lows the destruction of his *Chrestomathy of Despair*.

The disease of the intellect may appear as a private form of an-guish—a pathology in a vacuum. In reality, however, this mental anguish is closely bound up with Cripure's horror of his environ-ment as symbolized by concrete beings, objects and expressions. Nabucet is of course the prime living embodiment of all that de-serves to be slapped—just as Cripure's slap is an expression of global contempt. There are days, no doubt, when Cripure yearns for a brotherhood to compensate for that "poignant feeling of common tragedy"; but his hatred is never given time to disarm. There is always another Nabucet to see to it that he rediscovers a hatred keener than the one before. For the Nabucets have many faces. There are the cowardly students, the revolting bourgeois (the "dead souls" of this "Deathgorod"), Basquin the concessionaire at the prisoner-of-war camp with whom Maïa cuckolds the philosopher —and, ironic last touch at the close of the novel, the policemen on bicycles, the "black angels," symbols of a social order Cripure despised, who clear the way for the creaking, dilapidated "troïka" in which Cripure lies dying. And there are objects, too, which symbolize moral ugliness: arrogant top hats and fur-collared overcoats, family portraits of worthy colonels or prefects—a world of objects which prefigures Sartre's *La Nausée* with its dominical procession of patrician hats, the statue of Gustave Impétraz as solid as the solid narrow ideas of the townspeople, and the room in the museum filled with portraits of the local great men, the smug race of *salauds*.[6] Even images and expressions, like musical phrases or leitmotifs, punctuate the bitterness and provide a steady commentary on this Nabucetian world: *bande de vendus, jeu de cache-cache, moyen de tricher;* official speeches made under umbrellas; Chopin's funeral march exploited for patriotic purposes. One image, however, sums up all the moral sordidness: the *cloporte,* or common woodlouse, the dictionary definition of which Cripure recites to himself whenever he feels the need to define the inhabitants of his town. "Popular name given undiscriminatingly to crustacean isopods . . . Essentially terrestrial (temperate zones), these animals live on the seashore, under stones or in the clefts of rocks, sometimes in moist, obscure places, such as caves and cellars. . . . Some of them have the faculty of rolling up into a ball at the slightest sign of danger." Cripure's vision is at times nightmarish. The streets are metamorphosed into breeding grounds of *cloportes,* passersby become "furtive silhouettes" of large *cloportes,* the sight of which makes him shudder with uncontrollable anguish.

---

[6] This tendency to situate a personal sense of "nausea" outside the self, within concrete objects, is of course characteristic of Sartre's novel: "Nausea is not in me: I feel it *there,* on the wall, on the suspenders, everywhere around me. It is one with the coffee."

The image of the woodlouse brings to mind Flaubert who at one time, before he developed a secret liking for his two characters, thought of entitling *Bouvard et Pécuchet: Histoire de deux cloportes*. More directly, the image points forward, once again, to Sartre's *La Nausée* (1938). The inhabitants of Bouville also have insect legs and mandibles. The "old woman" is in fact called *"vieille cloporte"* and her hobbling walk seems to echo the haunting step of the old woman in *Le Sang noir*. Bouville (Mud-Town or Bovine Town)—Sartre's name for Le Havre—is not without resemblance to Guilloux's Boeufgorod. (*Bov*ary, *Bouv*ard: Flaubert was also haunted by the bovine image.) *La Nausée*, to be sure, is a more extreme, more philosophically "consistent" work. By the same token, it is a less lyrical, less charitable, less compassionate book than Guilloux's. Yet one can easily point to parallels. The populations of Boeufgorod and Bouville are really interchangeable. The sense of nausea in the two novels is closely connected with the urban landscape. Both works make use of concrete symbols to suggest or provoke a sense of metaphysical disgust. The central character in each is, or has been, composing a biography of another figure and both experience a similar loss of faith as they discover that the biographer's idea of a human destiny is a lie, that the meaning of the life they have so painfully constructed is beginning to disintegrate. Both Cripure and Roquentin are tragically alone in the crowd (Sartre insists more heavily, perhaps, on this willful exclusion: "It was their Sunday and not mine"!). Roquentin, no less than Cripure, is obsessed by the sensation of being superfluous—which is, in fact, one of Sartre's main themes: *je suis de trop!* (Guilloux's hero is convinced that the students who unscrew the bolts of his bicycle and the chauffeur who nearly runs him over are part of a larger plan to *rid* the world of the monstrous superfluity named Cripure.) Even Roquentin's hostility to his own intellect recalls Cripure's image of the slop jar. The same bitterness against "leaders" and "big shots" pervades both works. The surrealist passage in *La Nausée* (the town begins to "palpitate," rags are transformed into rotten meat, pimples into cyclopean eyes, tongues into enormous centipedes) has its counterpart in Guilloux's dance of the *cloporte* and the hallucinating vision of the church as a giant Ox, with towers in the form of massive horns—the fitting artifact of a bovine society creating everything in the image of the Quadruped. Finally, even

the existentialist note, that sense of original contingency, that *sin
of existing*, as Sartre puts it—can be clearly felt in *Le Sang noir*.
Cripure knows that man was "not necessary." He is aware that the
universe is "absurd," and that all the greatness and all the integrity
of man consists in "knowing this absurdity." Prophet of existentialist clichés, Guilloux has one of his representative characters say:
"The question is not what meaning this life may have. . . . The
only question is: what can we make of this life?"

Yet neither the intellectual themes nor the metaphysical "anguish"
can account for the boldness and brilliance of *Le Sang noir*. Eleanor
Clark admires Guilloux's talent—seldom equaled, according to her,
in American writing—of manipulating ideas in the novel without
"smothering" the characters under a *parti pris*.[7] The texture, the
color, the movement of Guilloux's work are indeed such that instead
of being crushed by "ideas," the novel endows them with a density
that inevitably brings to mind some of the great Russian models.
Guilloux himself, an early admirer of Gogol and Gorki, is fully
aware of this. Kaminsky, one of the lucid observers in *Le Sang
noir*, has the following to say of the other characters in the book:

> . . . generally speaking, socially and psychologically, we might be in
> the midst of imperial Russia, my good friends. Your petty Christian
> bourgeoisie is Tolstoy's bourgeoisie. And your peasants are real
> moujiks. . . . The most successful characters of Chekhov, for in-
> stance,—well, I found them right here, trait for trait, except for the
> samovar.

And not only Chekhov and Tolstoy are thus invoked, but Gogol
too, whose "dead souls" seem to differ from the inhabitants of
Boeufgorod only in so far as the vilest of them is endowed with
a grain of redeeming madness.

There are other reasons why Guilloux's novel is not smothered
by ideas. The most obvious is that, unlike many of the cerebral
works of fiction written during the same period, *Le Sang noir* is
not situated in a sophisticated, cosmopolitan, intellectual setting, but
in a provincial atmosphere where words adhere to objects, and
where sounds, smells and daily habits remain disturbingly familiar.
This is not a matter of literary strategy. Writing about the world
of Saint-Brieuc is as natural for Guilloux as it is for Mauriac, Bern-

---

[7] "Death of a Thinker: A Note on the French Novel, 1925-1940," *The
Kenyon Review*, Summer, 1941, pp. 322-334.

anos or Giono to situate their myths in a particular physical and moral landscape. It is undeniable that such a particularization is responsible for much of the vigor, simplicity and lyrical vehemence of these works. Louis Guilloux is without question a novelist of ideas, but he is also a poet-novelist: the nocturnal dance of the giggling hunchback and the steel-footed woodlouse under a street light is a piece worthy of any prose anthology. And he is also capable of great technical virtuosity, particularly in his handling of time. *Le Sang noir* is a most successful attempt at temporal condensation. In *Jeu de patience* (1949) Guilloux is even more daring: chronological time duration is utterly abolished, several layers of the past are telescoped—a subversion of time which, as Nelly Cormeau reminds us, is bound up with Guilloux's vision of the "indefatigable renewal of man's madness and suffering." [8]

BUT WHAT ABOUT GUILLOUX'S ATTITUDE toward his hero? Certainly he does not strive for a pseudo-olympian objectivity. It is easy enough to sense a permanent intrusion on the part of the author, a permanent sentimental involvement. Is it simple pity, however? On one level, Cripure is quite evidently an objectively *pitiful* character. A chronic victim of triviality (whether he drops his glasses in the street or is terrified by his students), he seems predestined to a "derisive fate." There is of course a deeper pathos: his love for Toinette whose picture is there to remind him of his grief, his thesis on Turnier (he had hoped that Toinette would read it and that the broken bond would be renewed), his other secret hope that the blond officer would die. Instead—again that "derisive fate!"—he learns about the death of his Toinette. . . .

Quite obviously, however, the author's attitude, at least on the surface, remains ambiguous to the very end. His pity, strongly tinged with irritation and disappointment, implies a condemnation. Cripure is weak. He is afflicted with a strong dose of cowardice. Guilloux even hints at a certain masochism responsible for Cripure's distress. Did he not "collaborate" with his own destiny? Did he not secretly will, from the very first, that Toinette should deceive him? Had he not done all in his power to bring it about? Cripure thus cheats with himself. Even when he is honest, this honesty only leads

8 "Révolte contre le temps chez les romanciers d'aujourd'hui," *L'Age Nouveau,* May, 1951, pp. 37-44.

to further abdications. He then negates and betrays his own value, as he negates and betrays his thesis on Turnier. He is a "submissive Rousseau" who may have known the courage of despair but never had the nerve to liberate himself and to rebel openly. He has "seen the lie" all about him, but has never put up a fight. He knows this and consequently judges himself without mercy. As he is about to order another glass of Anjou wine, he surveys the café scene, casts a somber glance at the card players, and concludes: "I'm nobody at all. . . . Just one of them." Thus he expresses not his solidarity, but his guilt and the pathos of acquiescence.

Just one of them . . . This weakness of consent is also a form of treason. At least, that is what his former disciple Lucien Bourcier means when he associates Cripure with his parents' standards, calling him "one of their kind." Indeed, Cripure is not only a true *fils de bourgeois* (his father was a ruined businessman, he himself believes in prudent investments), but he has repeatedly betrayed the clerical values by a lowly submission to "bovine" ethics. He too has made patriotic speeches. He too, while his former students are being torn to bits by shell explosions, rubs his hands when his bonds bring in dividends. Guilloux thus denounces Cripure's complicity with the hated bourgeoisie. Sartre's attitude toward his intellectual heroes will be equally ambivalent: they too will be guilty of compromises with the world of the *salauds*. An "ashamed bourgeois" is what Jacques Delarue calls his brother Mathieu in *L'Age de raison*.

"I do not deny that I have written this book with passion, with anger; I do not deny that I have written it with hatred; but I would like the reader to discover also the love that I have put into this book." [9] The general tone of Guilloux's novel comes indeed closer to love than to reprobation—a love which seems to grow stronger with every failing and every frailty of Cripure. Though Lucien Bourcier does not mince words in assessing the moral situation of his former master, his remarks have a tender panegyric warmth that borders on resigned hopelessness. "We can do nothing for him, just as he can do nothing for us." The sobs of the illiterate Maïa, the wails of the half-wit Moka, the whimpers and whines of the faithful dogs constitute the uninhibited dirge that accompanies the dying Cripure through the crowd of the self-righteous. But this quasi-animalistic attachment is not the only form of affectionate fidelity

[9] Louis Guilloux, "Notes sur le roman," *Europe*, January 15, 1936, pp. 5-9.

to Cripure. Well before the fatal pistol shot, Guilloux lavishes his affection vicariously. When Député Faurel explains that he is "deeply fond" of Cripure, Lucien, who is visibly moved, answers: "And what about me? Don't you think that I love him? . . . My poor old Cripure!"

Pauvre vieux Cripure . . . And yet, in spite of all the reprobation, pathos and ridicule, Cripure does emerge as a character endowed with dignity and even with grandeur. Beyond the tenderness, beyond the pity, there is an unmistakable note of admiration. Neither his grotesque appearance nor his extravagant manners prove to be incompatible with a certain fierce nobility. Guilloux's work is of course not the first one in which caricature is paradoxically close to the tragic view. Much of Balzac's work shows how caricature can be placed at the service of a demonic atmosphere that exalts the tragic fate of the thinker. In *Le Sang noir* this exaltation is stated explicitly. The great event for successive generations of lycée students has been their year of philosophy with Cripure. "He has been my master in the loftiest sense of the word," explains Lucien. As for Député Faurel, always mildly rhetorical, even when he happens to be sincere: "Permit me to tell you that Monsieur Merlin, in our eyes, stands for, incarnates all that is noblest in this world: the Human Spirit, if you will allow me to make use of so high-sounding a word."

But it is the *implicit* glorification which clearly reveals that Guilloux is out to vindicate Cripure and to transform him into a noble figure. His stature is that of the tragically predestined victim. Like Turnier, the philosopher whose biography he has written and in whom he no doubt saw an alter ego, Cripure is a "marked man"—a figure condemned to defeat. The comparison with Rousseau is not fortuitous. It emphasizes his clumsiness, his lack of elegance and savoir-faire, his *esprit d'escalier*—but also the obsessions of a tragic temperament: his misanthropy and his persecution mania. Morally, his stature is that of the fundamentally incorruptible man—the prophet in the wilderness (though perhaps an ailing prophet)—refusing to play the social game. According to young Etienne, he is the only *clean* person (*"le seul pur"*) in the midst of corruption and butchery. It is difficult to be a human being determined to remain human in a town which—like all of Europe—is blind with hypocrisy and drunken with the urge of self-destruction. Cripure's own definition of a decent human being is that he cannot be "one of the herd." It is this painful and tragic lucidity which gives Cripure the right to say to his imaginary interlocutor in the Café Machin: "Intellectually, *we* are not cowards. . . ."

A clumsy but grandiose repository of important truths, Cripure continued to haunt the imagination of the author. In *Jeu de patience*, his name is repeatedly mentioned. The various characters are all tempted to consult him. "Cripure alone would understand. . . ." His understanding is, however, a haughty, lonely and bitter experience. "I do not want to forgive," Cripure explains to Moka. This refusal, as global as the slap that lands on Nabucet's face, is symbolic of the rebellion of the mind which makes of *Le Sang noir* one of the most stirring cries of intellectual revolt in recent literature. But it is an ironic cry. Cripure is a laughable Prometheus. The final irony of the novel is that the soldiers who stand at attention while Cripure dies are honoring an intellectual hero whose message they cannot possibly understand.

PART II: *The Tragic Impasse*

8

1930-1950: The Age of Guilt

An intelligentsia is born to be unhappy.

—ARNOLD TOYNBEE

¶ I. *Politics as tragedy*

THE NOTION OF *engagement* is neither the invention nor the monopoly of the Existentialist writers. It represents the prevalent climate of an era rudely awakened to its own political tragedy. The nineteen-thirties are indeed a point of cleavage and a time of crisis. Unemployment, the growth of fascism, the Spanish Civil War, the concentration camps—all serve to explain the political orientation of literature following a period of introspection and poetical escapism. As the postwar euphoria comes to an end, the thirties brutally thrust the writer into the nightmare of History. Ominous problems loom. The values of a traditional humanism seem, for the first time, to be seriously questioned. A literature given over to analysis no longer appears satisfactory at a time when the individual recognizes the priority of collective issues.

Europe's dark hours are thus responsible for the emergence of a generation that feels *"située"* and responsible in the face of history—a generation whipped on by the urge to transmute its anguish into action. "Anguish," "action," and "solidarity" are indeed among the key words used by intellectuals during these years. Assessing his own generation (he significantly groups himself with Malraux and Saint-Exupéry), Sartre has shown how the awareness of death, the threatened subjection to torture and the systematic will to degrade brought writers to the extreme frontiers of the human condition and inspired them with a jansenist concern for moral issues.[1]

There is indeed something militant about the literature of this period. In their resolve to take a stand, in their contempt for the

[1] *Situations II*, pp. 245-251.

smugness and aesthetic detachment of the previous generation—the *"Eglise triomphante,"* as Claude-Edmonde Magny ironically calls it [2] —the contemporaries of Malraux deliberately turn their backs on literature as a form of dilettantism. Even their elders are caught up in the political fever. François Mauriac recalls how the emotional impact of the Spanish Civil War first drew him away from the dream world of *pure* literature. "The horror of the real world exiled me from fiction." [3] Bernanos, likewise, took sides in the ideological conflict, explaining—with a play on nuances—that he was giving up his *métier* for his *profession.* But particularly the younger writers regarded themselves as committed to the role of witnesses and denouncers, and saw in the art of writing a prophetic vocation. The very style of French letters has been affected by these dynamics of commitment. A new "intellectual" prose, tense, abstract and highly dialectical, has already created a storehouse of new clichés. In his provocative *Le Degré zéro de l'écriture* (1953), Roland Barthes goes so far as to proclaim the emergence of a new type of *scripteur,* halfway between the man of action and the writer, whose style reflects the conflicting vocations of creative artist and militant thinker.

¶ II. *The prestige of the Left*

No LESS SIGNIFICANT than this "politicization" of the spirit which a self-righteous Benda denounced in a series of books,[4] is the steadily growing prestige of Leftist and extreme Leftist ideologies. Alain, who influenced some of the best minds of his time, was wont to say that the intellectual hero *"est de gauche"*—belongs to the Left. *"Intellectuel de droite"* is indeed a special expression describing the unusual, the rare bird. The attraction to the Left was already strong in artistic circles well before the 1930's. Romain Rolland, who in a sense embodied the ideas as well as the sentimentality of the turn-of-the-century socialism, explained in *Jean-Christophe* that an artist must needs take sides against the monstrous social system.[5] The Dreyfus

---

[2] *Histoire du roman français depuis 1918,* p. 58.
[3] "Le métier d'écrivain," *L'Express,* April 5, 1957.
[4] *Dialogues à Byzance,* 1920; *La Trahison des clercs,* 1927; *La Fin de l'éternel,* 1928.
[5] *Le Buisson ardent,* p. 67.

case, of course, enhanced the moral luster of "*la Gauche*" by dramatically confirming its dedication to Truth and Justice.

Literature, ever since Romanticism, has been a fertile ground for the myth of Revolution. When Sartre writes that "literature is, by its very essence, the subjectivity of a society in permanent revolution," [6] he echoes—consciously, no doubt—the literary views which, from Rimbaud to Surrealism, see writing as an eminently explosive activity. With time, however—and this is what distinguishes Sartre's generation—subversion ceased being a pure, gratuitous gesture of global rebellion, and instead came to serve precise ideologies, though at times reluctantly, with infinite scruples and hesitations, and with the uneasy awareness that this subversive role could ultimately turn against the writer and the culture he represents.

Karl Marx optimistically prophesied, in the *Communist Manifesto*, that at the decisive hour of the class struggle, the intellectuals of the bourgeois world would rally to the cause of the Proletarian Revolution, much as, in the eighteenth century, the enlightened elements of the nobility took sides with the bourgeoisie. Certainly no single ideology or spiritual force in the twentieth century has come close to rivaling the prestige of Marxism among European intellectuals. The important Catholic revival in French letters—in part a reaction against the sterilizing religion of science—remains a significant but nonetheless isolated phenomenon which presents none of the symptoms of a collective obsession. Moreover, the Catholic writers themselves did not escape the attraction of the Left. Péguy attempted all his life to reconcile his religious fervor with his socialist mystique. Even outspoken foes of revolutionary ideologies could not entirely escape the fascination of Marxist dialectics.

Few French intellectuals, particularly after 1930, managed to remain aloof; those who did were soon made to feel they had lost touch with their time. Even the most unlikely men of letters (a Gide, for instance, who otherwise believed in never getting "involved") flirted for a while with extreme Leftist beliefs. Marxism thus became the touchstone as well as the center of the debate. It became impossible to deal with important issues without thoroughly examining the criteria of social-revolutionary thinking. Writers themselves were fully aware of this. Roger Stéphane explains that while each preceding generation strove to define itself in relation to Christi-

[6] *Situations II*, p. 196.

anity or to bourgeois society, "ours will have been the first which attempted to define itself in relation to socialism." [7]

A political hypnosis of this magnitude was bound to produce alarm. Raymond Aron, in *L'Opium des intellectuels* (1955), seems to suggest that the fateful hour announced by Marx has arrived; that the intellectuals of France consider themselves destined to guide the workers; that they are seduced by the historic mission of the proletariat which, like a new Messiah, will through suffering bring about the redemption of the universe. Pointing to the utopian nature of French political thinking in general, Aron notes that three words seem to have become sacred because they correspond to the basic myths of the new religion: the myth of the Left, the myth of the Revolution and the myth of the Proletariat. One may take issue with some of Aron's hostile simplifications. Politics, for the intellectual, is not merely a form of entertainment, an avant-garde fad or an opportunity for moral non-conformity. But not all Aron's analyses are equally peripheral. He has shrewdly diagnosed the intellectual's quest for an ethics of global responsibility, though one suspects that he interprets this "proud will to think for all mankind" as a particularly noxious form of arrogance.

¶ III. *The ethics of responsibility*

THE NOTION OF A MORAL AND POLITICAL involvement in the suffering of others is, quite clearly, not an invention of the twentieth-century mandarins. Nothing is more unfair than Rousseau's petulant assertions concerning the indifference of the *philosophes* to the problems of ordinary humanity. The "encyclopedic" literature of the eighteenth century is not merely haunted by the *idée fixe* of public weal and very courageously immersed in social and political action, but consistently (and sometimes stubbornly) refuses to transcend immediate issues for fear of betraying its vocation of solidarity. "The philosopher is not an exile in this world. . . ." Points of contact are not lacking between the ideals of the *Encyclopédie* and the program of Sartre's *Les Temps Modernes*. It is no coincidence that Sartre, in "Qu'est-ce que la littérature?," has credited the eighteenth-century writer with the discovery of a new moral dimension, the Present, no

---

[7] Jean Kanapa very appropriately utilized this statement as an epigraph to his *Situation de l'intellectuel* (1957).

longer viewed as a figuration of the Eternal, but as a contingent and absolute reality which allows no withdrawal and transforms even silence into an act.

In the nineteenth century, this sense of social responsibility, coupled with lyrical effusions, becomes the predominant note in humanitarian thinking. *Le Peuple*, the title of one of Michelet's most characteristic works, can be considered a key term, charged with emotional appeal. The humanitarian declamations of George Sand, the grandiloquent pity of Hugo, the utopian socialism of Zola all proclaim the eminent dignity of the poor. The very misery of the working classes seemed to lend them a tragic, even a messianic grandeur. Hugo's "Les Pauvres Gens," which exalts the sense of sacrifice and solidarity among the destitute, is probably the most significant "modern" poem in the epic cycle of *La Légende des siècles*.

In part, this movement toward the people, this glorification of the proletariat, can be attributed to a growing belief among writers that a new mass public, mystically regenerative, would permit them to assume the longed-for function of spiritual guide. This yearning for a prophetic mission coincides with the ferment of idealism which spreads among the young intelligentsia of the eighteen-thirties and the eighteen-forties. Saint-Simon, Fourier, Proudhon, Lamennais are only a few on a long roster of idealists, social reformers and political dreamers. Saint-Simonism, in particular, was influential in literary circles. The pamphlet *Aux Artistes* (1830) exhorted artists to become the "*précepteurs de l'humanité*," the high priests of the new social religion. The *peuple* and the *poète* were henceforth to march side by side; art was to express the needs and hopes of an "indefatigable humanity"; it was to be the "prophetic organ" of the human epic.[8]

Important social factors and social changes are implicit in these prophetic effusions. The very concept of a proletariat was a recent one. The uprisings of the Lyons textile workers in 1831 did much to create a public awareness of the existence of a suffering working class as a social reality, and focused attention on the responsibilities

8 Balzac's series of articles "Des Artistes" (published in *La Silhouette*, February 25, March 11 and April 22, 1830), which casts the thinker in the role of prophet, clearly is inspired by Saint-Simonian ideology. The critic Sainte-Beuve also expounded a thorough Saint-Simonian conception of the artist in an important article, "Espoir et voeu du mouvement littéraire et poétique après la Révolution de 1830," published in *Le Globe* (October 11, 1830).

of the bourgeoisie. Raymond Giraud, in his lively study of the writer
and the bourgeoisie in nineteenth-century France, points to the
early 1830's as a pivotal date, when intellectuals—even those who did
not subscribe to the hopes of the republicans—felt humiliated by the
behavior of their own social class.[9] It is indeed significant that even
Stendhal, who otherwise (in spite of professed liberal views) felt
little sympathy for the lower classes, devotes some of his most biting
pages, in *Lucien Leuwen*, to the police action of Louis-Philippe's
army against striking workers, and almost falls into a most un-Bey-
liste sentimentality. Certainly, the spirit of rebellion that set so many
children of the bourgeoisie against the values of their own class is
symptomatic of a deep moral uneasiness. This gradual process of
desertion and quest for *déclassement* assumes many forms, ranging
from aesthetic contempt to positive political commitment. By 1848,
the attitude of the intelligentsia toward the bourgeoisie has become
definitely hostile.

Finally, the prestige of the very word "revolution" must be taken
into account—a prestige so great that even the foes of the Revolution have adopted a revolutionary vocabulary. This attachment to
an event of the past is not merely a form of political memory or
nostalgia. The effort at perpetuation is closely bound up with an
almost mystical concept of reincarnation according to which the
Revolution is on one level an historic event, and on the other a
perpetual celebration which re-enacts an original "Passion." It is not
enough to say, as Raymond Aron does, that the phraseology and the
notion of revolution appeal to the writer for literary reasons. It is
true that rebellion appears to many minds as exciting and "poetic,"
that moral non-conformism and the hatred of the philistine became
a literary theme and one of the commonplaces of art. But though the
fecundity of upheavals is an idea with which many a Romantic and
post-Romantic mind has toyed, it cannot be summarily dismissed as a
form of aesthetic dilettantism. Deeper ties bind French Romanticism to the principles and consequences of revolutionary thinking.
Even a Lamartine could convince himself that the "bloody abyss"
of revolutions was a sign of an eternal *becoming* that justified suffering and death.

These social, literary and ideological factors must be kept in mind.

---

[9] *The Unheroic Hero*, p. 6.

They are rooted in the history of the eighteenth and nineteenth centuries. But only in our own time have these ethics of guilt and responsibility assumed truly obsessive proportions and influenced French literature so deeply as to create a new type of tragedy and a new type of hero. Put in its simplest terms, this hero's dilemma stems from the feeling of being trapped between his bourgeois culture and his idealization of the Proletariat, while aware that he can neither deny the one nor quite espouse the other. A certain "romantic" self-consciousness and self-pity no doubt colors the dilemma: the perennial complaint of having been born too early or too late. But what distinguishes the more recent spirit of rebellion from nineteenth-century anti-bourgeois feeling is that the writers of our time, particularly those who reached the age of reason around 1930, have suffered from a near-pathological guilt complex, and are haunted by what Paul Nizan has called the "social original sin." [10] As early as 1929, Emmanuel Berl partially diagnosed the moral disease in *Mort de la pensée bourgeoise*, where he asseverated that the contemporary intellectual betrays his own social class because, in bourgeois society, he smells the odor of death. Indeed, the very sons of the bourgeoisie, like Hugo-Raskolnikov in Sartre's *Les Mains sales*, suffer from the stench, deny their family ties and set out to forge for themselves a fresh virginity.

A deep sense of shame, private and collective, seems to be at the root of this epidemic of defection. The one French word which perhaps most adequately expresses the nature of this shame is *"tare,"* which frequently recurs in this context, and which suggests a slowly corroding congenital malady. It is no doubt this kind of incurable corruption that Sartre has in mind when he refers to the *"tare originelle"* of the modern intellectual. Contemporary fiction is thickly peopled with characters who—like Roger Vailland's hero in the excellent Resistance novel *Drôle de jeu* (1945)—fight against their social class with fanatical perseverance while fully aware that they have "inherited its vices." In this quest for atonement, the amateur psychologist might well be tempted to detect a manifestation of father-hate. Arthur Koestler, in *Arrival and Departure* (1943), went so far as to explain his hero's yearning for social martyrdom as a

[10] See *La Conspiration* (1938), which depicts the rebellious spirit and moral rootlessness of sensitive bourgeois adolescents.

form of guilt toward his father ("I felt cheated of my punishment"). Without indulging in the facile simplifications to which such a literary psychoanalysis can lead, one must not take Koestler's basic insight too lightly. Unquestionably, a revolt against paternal morality is one of the mainsprings of the intellectual's craving for a new allegiance. For this craving symbolizes a revolt against the liberal-Humanist tradition which, for more than a century, has been the ideal but also the defense of the bourgeoisie, and which ultimately became a pretext for "paternal" smugness. Even a Camus, despite his personal acquaintance with poverty, is painfully aware of the weight of this "humanist" heritage. Jean-Baptiste Clamence, in *La Chute*, despises himself because he has come to realize that it was not out of love or charity that he defended the widow and the orphan, but so as to have the right to despise them. In the works of Sartre and Simone de Beauvoir the reaction is even more violent. It is precisely for their complacent myth of "paternal" rights and duties that the civic leaders in *La Nausée* are called "*salauds.*" In a similar manner, Perron, in *Les Mandarins*, tersely declares that humanism has become contemptible and individualism a "*saloperie.*" This vocabulary of filth calls for attention. It is not enough for the modern intellectual to become the gravedigger of his class; he feels the desperate need to cleanse himself of his origins.

This obsession with guilt (as something to be borne but also to be cultivated), this sense of imaginary debts and of impending punishment are of course not unrelated to political developments. The policy of non-intervention in Spain, the Munich agreements which led to the dismemberment of Czechoslovakia, gave many thinking Frenchmen the uneasy feeling that something fundamental had been betrayed and that they had been tacit accomplices. Men most opposed to war could thus, paradoxically, feel most guilty when war finally broke out. Simone de Beauvoir's Dubreuilh is in this sense representative: ". . . because he had failed, he judged himself guilty."

Most often, however, the sense of guilt is infinitely more vague. It is an all-pervasive, generic, subjective, largely unaccountable feeling of culpability presenting all the symptoms of a new *mal du siècle.* "If I haven't been guilty of this, then I've been guilty of something else," says one of the key characters in Louis Guilloux's *Jeu de patience* (1949). Nor is this merely the sort of decent embarrassment about one's own good fortune which made a Voltaire write "I am ashamed to be so happy." [11] Such a moral, fully rational sense of remorse in the face of the less privileged has little in common with the *idée fixe* that personal happiness is a nemesis.[12] With certain twentieth-century writers, the sense of shame assumes metaphysical dimensions: it is the shame of being alive. Brice Parain, in his moving *La Mort de Jean Madec* (1945) has shown how this *honte de vivre* goes hand in hand with a mystical attraction to misery and a desire for self-mutilation. If one adds to this the ascetic denial of pleasure, the steady search for a cross to bear and the conviction that every day is a day of judgment, one comes close to attitudes which, paradoxically, echo basic Christian sentiments. Only here, suffering is not only the central motif; it has become the sole virtue, and *not to have suffered enough* the one cardinal sin. For the intellectual's guilt exists specifically in relation to the suffering of others. Anne Dubreuilh, in *Les Mandarins*, sums it all up (the novel is indeed a central document concerning the psychology of the French intellectual): "I was ashamed; ashamed because I had not suffered enough."

But the sufferer is here, at first, less a redeemer than a tragically unattainable *other*. It is no coincidence that Malraux, and later the Existentialist writers, all haunted by the loneliness of the self (the *solitude des consciences*), should have been obsessed with the reality of pain and torture. Malraux's work is filled with atrocities: prisoners into whose shoulders nails are driven, dead bodies discovered with their mouths slit to the ears, political prisoners burned alive in the boiler of a locomotive. As for Sartre, he is literally fascinated by physical suffering. "Blood, sweat, pain, death are not mere ideas," he writes, as though this were not a truism but a revelation.[13] Nazi atrocities at Dachau, Auschwitz, Oradour are for him not merely a cause for moral indignation, but a constant stimulus for the imagination. He likes to remember an atmosphere ominously charged with terror and guilt: men were tortured, during the Occupation, while others were eating or sleeping or making love; he likes to indulge in

[11] Letter of May 27, 1756.
[12] Loys Masson's novel *Le Requis civil* (1945) offers a perceptive analysis of this particular type of *idée fixe*. Pierre Josmat, the hero, is obsessed with the "fear of happiness."
[13] "Matérialisme et Révolution," in *Situations III*, p. 220.

nightmarish, almost erotic images of human degradation.[14] But at the back of his mind there is always the one question which reveals his fear of estrangement: "If I were tortured, what would I do?" For the reaction of the victim cannot be grasped by another's experience: pain suffices to create an abyss between two human beings. Few writers have suggested fear of pain in bolder pages than Sartre; yet even in those works where the theme of fear is treated in the starkest, most aggressive fashion (*Le Mur, Morts sans sépulture*), it is less fear as such that appears to inspire him than an undefinable longing for a privileged state of suffering of which, it would seem, not everyone is worthy. "Don't you understand that I am more unhappy than all of you," laments the one character in *Morts sans sépulture* who has not been tortured. He has learned, through no fault of his, what it means to feel excluded from a human community. Hence his pathetic question: "Must my nails be torn out so that I may again become your friend?"

This obsession with torture is, understandably, a trait common to much of the literature of the thirties and forties. It is, however, not a simple reaction of horror in the face of political events. Nor is it the mere anxiety of wondering what one's own reactions might be. The core of the obsession is the tragic awareness that the suffering of another human being remains beyond reach, that one is guilty no matter what one does. Even singing other men's courage is a form of dishonesty. "Deserve your song; undergo what those whom you praise have undergone." [15] But how can one? "One cannot suffer for what one wants to," Mathieu bitterly remarks in *Les Chemins de la liberté*. Such an exile from suffering deprives one, it would seem, of the very right to speak up, and can lead to a reticence which comes close to Christian humility. This is the moral lesson taught by Brice Parain's schoolmasters. "On your knees . . . You will ask forgiveness of all those who do not own a handkerchief. . . . You will ask for-

---

[14] Characteristically, Sartre views torture not only as a kind of Black Mass in which both the torturer and the tortured commune in the destruction of humanity, but as a sexual relationship: ". . . this moaning, sweating and polluted creature begging for mercy and surrendering with a swooned consent . . ." (*Situations II*, p. 247). This fascination with torture is again apparent in his latest play, *Les Séquestrés d'Altona* (1960).

[15] Loys Masson, *Le Requis civil* (1945), p. 50. Many Resistance writers, though taking great risks themselves, have experienced a similar sense of guilt.

giveness for not being like them." [16] But even more important than humility is the nostalgia for a mystical communion to which this exile from suffering has given birth. "If only one could share the suffering of others, experience it, if not in their stead, at least as much as they," sighs the nun in Jean David's *Passes du silence* (1954). Though expressing a Christian view, the nun symbolizes here the intellectual's thirst for idealism, his deep need to transcend private concerns and merge again with a larger identity. This surrender to a *whole* (a surrender which at times implies an abdication) is what the Polish writer Czeslaw Milosz had in mind when discussing, in *The Captive Mind* (1953), the modern intellectual's yearning to lose himself in the masses. This is precisely what Beauvoir's Perron experiences: the desire to find his lost "brothers." If one cannot join through suffering, if one cannot suffer for what one wants to, one can at least establish a bond with humanity through guilt.

Symbolically—though it may seem a paradox—such guilt is bound to increase in direct proportion to the distance of the suffering. The further removed the scene of human anguish, the greater the self-reproach, and the more persistent the feeling of responsibility. Global involvement thus goes hand in hand with a "geographic" awareness. "When my comrades were deported to Siberia, I was in Vienna; others were murdered in Vienna by the brown-shirts, and I was in Paris; and when Paris was occupied, I was in New York." [17] In the work of Simone de Beauvoir and Sartre, a catalogue of cities often suffices to evoke or provoke this sense of guilt. In *Le Sang des autres* (1945), Blomart, walking in the soft Parisian twilight, is painfully aware that at the same moment men in besieged Madrid or in a Nazi concentration camp are entitled to think of him as a *salaud*—a bastard. In Sartre's novels, particularly at the beginning of *Le Sursis* (1945), the theme of geographic simultaneity seems to result in sheer technical virtuosity. But evidently this fascination with the *elsewhere* is related to fundamental existentialist concerns: the separation of conscience and its objects; the tendency to humanize the latter and objectivize the former; the dynamics of shame dependent on the fear

---

[16] *La Mort de Jean Madec* (1945), pp. 91-92. In *L'Embarras du choix* (1946), p. 130, Brice Parain has analyzed the modern "rebellion" in the face of death and suffering. He quotes the following sentence from Sartre's *Les Mouches* as symptomatic: "Forgive us for living while you are dead."
[17] Scriassine in *Les Mandarins*.

of another consciousness.[18] But again, it would be shortsighted to attribute these themes exclusively to the Existentialist writers. One could find countless illustrations of similar attitudes and reactions in the literature of the past twenty-five years. The hero of Lucette Finas' *L'Echec* (1958) sums up what at first may seem like a romantic sense of frustration ("Wherever there was some misfortune, I was not there"), but which in reality is an expression of global responsibility assuming nightmarish proportions.

This sense of "global" responsibility can easily be ridiculed. In a symposium organized by *Partisan Review* (February-May, 1950), James Agee mockingly describes these poor people who have been badgered half out of their minds by "the daily obligation to stay aware of, hep to, worked-up over, guilty towards, active about, the sufferings of people at a great distance for whom one can do nothing whatever." He scornfully refers to this acute sense of social responsibility as a sort of playing-at-God (He being in exile) over every little accident or incident, with the sense of virtue increasing in ratio to the distance. On occasion, the fictional characters themselves display their impatience. Hélène, in *Le Sang des autres*, reminds Blomart that he has not created the world. The guilt-ridden intellectual hero himself at times finds his guilt tedious. Perron—who to some extent portrays Camus' attachment to the simple, palpable joys of life—rebels against what he considers a morbid delectation in distant catastrophes.

It is possible to deprecate such attitudes, or inveigh ironically against the lack of true love and charity in men whose moral presbyopia sometimes prevents them from seeing the puddle of blood at their very feet.[19] Even as objective a mind as Raymond Aron smiles disparagingly at what he considers the somewhat pompous illusion of worrying at a great distance about the peasants of India who do not eat enough, the mistreated Negroes of South Africa, the worker-priests affected by the Papal decision or the ex-Communists pursued by McCarthy.[20] But what writers such as Aron and Agee seem to forget: condemned to watch from the sidelines, the intellectual also wishes to be a martyr. And this cannot be taken lightly. It is not with

[18] Frederic Jameson brilliantly analyzes these themes as reflected in the style of Sartre in his forthcoming *A Reading of Jean-Paul Sartre*.

[19] Jean-Louis Curtis indulges in such rather pungent attacks in *Les Justes Causes* (1954).

[20] *L'Opium des intellectuels*, p. 304.

impunity that our century, echoing the cry of Nietzsche, has proclaimed the bankruptcy of Christian beliefs. Since God is in exile, who remains to give an account of human destiny? The ultimate paradox is that hand in hand with sincere scruples and an authentic humility goes the modern intellectual's hybris. But perhaps it is this very pride—the pride of suffering and the pride of persecution—that explains, better than any other single fact, the undeniable attraction of the millenaristic dream-theories of Marxism, and the belief in the immanent sacredness of the Proletariat. The intellectual rediscovers the antique myth of the redemption of the universe through suffering.

¶ IV. *The prestige of an ideology*

"FOR US MARXISM IS NOT MERELY A PHILOSOPHY; it is the very climate of our ideas." With these words, Sartre stresses the cultural significance of Marxist ideology for his generation.[21] In one of his autobiographic moods, he recalls how a "tragic sense of life" (the very expression attests to the influence of Unamuno) alienated him and his friends from "idealistic" philosophies, how this alienation and the notion of the "absurdity" of existence prepared them for the "irresistible attraction of Marxism."[22] The "friends" Sartre mentions are no doubt a modest way of speaking about his own intellectual development; but they are also a convenient symbol representing an entire generation. "It is not exaggerated to say," writes Pierre Emmanuel, "that the best representatives of contemporary thought have all, more or less, been brought up in the school of Marxism."[23]

[21] "Le Réformisme et les fétiches," *Les Temps Modernes*, February, 1956, pp. 1153-1164. We cannot trace here Sartre's political evolution, so rich in nuances, scruples, ambiguities and frustrations. It is only fair to recall, however, that far from being the darling of the Communists, Sartre has been a steady bugbear to them. *L'Humanité* denounced his *Les Mains sales* as a "dirty play." As early as "Qu'est-ce que la littérature," Sartre proclaimed the incompatibility of Stalinist communism and "honest" writing; in his essay "Matérialisme et Révolution" (*Situations III*) he rejected dialectical materialism as a "doctrine which betrays thought." After the Hungarian revolt, he denounced the Communist Party as "monstrous" (*L'Express*, November 9, 1956).

[22] "Questions de méthode," *Les Temps Modernes*, September, 1957, pp. 338-417.

[23] "Ordre et désordre de la France, 1939-1949," in a special issue of *La Nef* ("Réflexions sur la littérature moderne"), December, 1949-January, 1950, pp. 196-202.

An important distinction, however, has to be drawn between the philosophical seduction of an ideology, on the one hand, and on the other, the romantic appeal of revolutionary action. Ideological commitment and nostalgia for heroic rebellion may at times coincide; they express, however, totally different needs. This is not to belittle the importance of a literature of Revolt. The Surrealist attempt to liberate man from utilitarian constrictions by means of a dynamics of violence is certainly one of the most significant cultural phenomena of the past fifty years. In addition, political events, such as the war in Spain, provided a new opportunity for a poetry of action. But it must be said that the Surrealist experiment, primarily aesthetic (in spite of pseudo-philosophical aims), viewed rebellion and violence as ends in themselves, so that the pleasure of negation finally annulled literature itself. As for the Spanish Civil War, it marked an awakening of consciousness for those intellectuals who were there (perhaps even more for those who yearned to be there)—a period of intense hope and lyrical exaltation which Malraux has appropriately called the "Exercise of the Apocalypse." Ideological issues were, for many, far less important than the poetry of insurrection and the pathos of defeat.

Malraux himself is, of course, the most outstanding embodiment of the mystique of revolutionary action. His very concept of man as being what he *does* (and not what he hides), as well as his romantic belief that man's true fatherland is courage, would account for his expressed notion that everything that falls short of revolution is worse than revolution. It will not do to dismiss these attitudes as the pose of an adventurer flirting with history and guilty of heroic parasitism. It is true that the very technique of his novels betrays a dream of ubiquity; that his heroes, following the example of Garine, in *Les Conquérants* (1928), are essentially *gamblers* who despise the outcome of the game. His work expresses, however, deeper urges: the need to inflict a "scar" on the world, a power complex with erotic undertones, the obsessive belief that one can only possess that which one changes. Malraux's very language is one of will and choice. But although he understood, as Gaëtan Picon reminds us, that the struggle of the twentieth century is essentially a struggle between myths,[24] Malraux is not really concerned with ideology. It is perhaps a trifle excessive to suggest that his heroes are men of contemplation

[24] *André Malraux*, p. 19.

who do not think; nevertheless one has to agree with Irving Howe that Malraux is often impatient with ideas, that he tends to view them as façades for irrational compulsions and is concerned with Revolution primarily as an "arithmetic of emotion." [25] The dialogue between Kyo and Vologuine in *La Condition humaine* clearly reveals that Malraux prefers the revolutionary fighter to the revolutionary thinker or party official, much as he would always prefer the saint or the mystic to the theologian. Malraux in fact never endowed any party or ideology with mystic appeal. If he is fond of the notion of the *sacré*, this term always refers to man's ability to create an artistic image of himself and of the universe.

It is here, perhaps, that Malraux most differs from those writers for whom political ideologies, and particularly the myth of Revolution and Marxism, hold out a quasi-religious fascination. It is not enough to suggest in a derogatory fashion that the bourgeois intellectuals, driven on by personal ambition or by the dream of "sophocracy," discover a vocation for "guiding the workers," that they view themselves as a new elite, or—as Marcel Aymé nastily proposes—that they are merely in search of new aesthetic thrills.[26] Nor will it do to explain these numerous conversions by the attraction which rationalism or pseudo-rationalism exercised on scientifically inclined minds. It is true that certain conventional types in fiction, such as Professor Mirambeau in Vercors' *Colères*, equate science with Revolution in a manner strongly reminiscent of Zola's intellectual heroes. But such an attitude is primarily sentimental and echoes, in a somewhat stilted fashion, the idealistic dreams of nineteenth-century socialism. Certainly neither the sentimentally "scientific" nor the purely philanthropic interpretation can account for the extraordinary wave of conversions or near-conversions during the period 1917-1939. The very term "conversion," which so often recurs in this context during those years, appropriately points to an intellectual or spiritual crisis. *The God that Failed* (1949), a collection of essays by re-converted ex-converts, amply demonstrates how, in various countries, men like Arthur Koestler, Ignazio Silone, Richard Wright, André Gide, Stephen Spender attempted to transcend their despair or cure them-

[25] *Politics and the Novel*, pp. 207-211.
[26] *Le Confort intellectuel*, p. 72. Barrès, in *Les Déracinés* (1897), had described young intellectuals who saw in socialism a lever for their private ambitions: *"un rôle à prendre."*

selves of a powerful sense of social guilt by espousing an ideology which, in addition to a myth of history with its accompanying millenaristic dreams, offered them a complete theory of social injustice. The Russian Revolution, interpreted as the incarnation of an ideology ("the soul of the world had found its body" [27]), often paradoxically made its deepest impression where religious sensibility was keenest.

It is easy, no doubt, to ridicule this tragic or mystical appeal. Jean-Louis Curtis, in one of the most caustic passages of *Les Justes Causes*, has brilliantly satirized the intellectuals' *valse-hésitation*, their desire to merge with the "current of History," their "veneration" of the working class as a mysterious entity, their "reverential compunction," their scruples and permanent fear of *"lèse-Prolétariat."* But the very satire is an implicit tribute to the hold of the Marxist myth over the French intellectual, and points to its most meaningful attractions: a solid dogma, a theory of incarnation and an eschatological account of redemption.

The need for discipline or dogma, the age-old search for the solid Rock, proved indeed a determining factor for many disoriented minds in search of absolutes. Marat, the hero of Vailland's *Drôle de jeu*, learns that many of his more "puritanical" companions have come to the Party the way one enters into Holy Orders, because they could find in it "a doctrine as precise as a Dogma" and thus satisfy their need for an ascetic discipline. Fiction, in this case, accurately mirrors reality. The English socialist Richard Crossman even goes so far as to suggest that the appeal of Marxist dogma was particularly strong in Catholic countries.[28] Perhaps the disease of knowledge already diagnosed by Flaubert—modern man's fear of becoming the victim of his own intellect—is at least partially responsible for this renewed thirst for absolutes. Scientific relativism indeed created a nostalgia for Truths which Christianity no longer seemed able to satisfy. The taste for ideological constraints, compulsions and repressions thus betrayed a sense of psychological and intellectual uprootedness from which few intellectuals, even those who experienced

[27] Brice Parain, *La Mort de Jean Madec*, p. 59.
[28] See his introduction to *The God that Failed*. Raymond Aron, in *L'Opium des intellectuels*, suggests that France was a particularly fertile ground for a "replacement religion" in which the intellectuals would play the role of a new secular clergy preaching and defending substitute dogmas.

no social or economic tensions, escaped. "Let us fear our future infidelities," proclaims a character in Paul Nizan's *La Conspiration*, one of the key novels of the thirties. "We must invent the constraints which will make fickleness impossible." The "fickleness" in question is of course political: only a *total* surrender to an ideological discipline seems sufficient warranty of the irreversible nature of "engagement." Even a Perron, though Simone de Beauvoir describes him as strongly solicited by the dream of personal happiness, is fully aware of the promises held out by a "religious" abnegation. "To lose oneself in a great Party, to fuse one's will with an enormous collective will: what peace and what strength!"

But this abstract collective will is not merely a reassuring, supposedly unequivocal voice leaving no room for hesitation or despair. Its real power is closely bound up with the conviction that it is embodied in a concrete reality: the working class. If a Sartre repeatedly insisted that the contemporary writer had to tie his destiny to that of the working class, it is primarily because he felt that this class incarnates some deeply meaningful myth of suffering, and that in its emancipation lies the general "salvation of mankind." [29] Ultimately, this messianic theory of incarnation leads back to ideology; it is in turn the Party which *incarnates* the will of the workers—thus producing a chain of incarnations responsible for the vicious circle that forced a Sartre to defend positions which, philosophically, he knew to be untenable. Some critics have alluded to Sartre's "religious complex." [30] It is certain that in his writings one can find traces of a theological vocabulary, as well as the theological notions of Free Will, the Fall, Original Sin and the doctrine of Redemption. But the phenomenon has broader historical and philosophical implications; it cannot merely be attributed to the Marxist version of the Judeo-Christian concept of salvation through suffering. Kenneth Douglas, speaking of the general climate of ideas in modern Europe, has suggested that it is one of the characteristics of our time that non-Chris-

[29] "Matérialisme et Révolution," *Situations III*, pp. 172-173.
[30] For instance Maurice Nadeau in "Sartre et l'Affaire Hervé," *Les Lettres Nouvelles*, April, 1956, pp. 591-597. Sartre himself, in his recent preface to Paul Nizan's *Aden Arabie* (p. 33), makes this revealing statement: "He and I kept for a long time the Christian vocabulary: though atheists, we did not doubt that we had been placed in this world in order to save ourselves and, with some luck, to save others."

tian philosophers, and even avowed atheists, come up with answers paradoxically akin to those of Christian orthodoxy.[31]

This theological vocabulary in a secular context is, however, at best rather muddled, and frequently degenerates into sheer logomachy. Words such as "redemption," "incarnation," "salvation" are impressive, but tend to be used loosely when applied to the doctrines of political responsibility. Nevertheless, their recurrence is extremely important in evaluating the intellectual's attraction to the Marxist myth, and helps bring into focus a number of basic attitudes: (1) a characteristic, nearly pathological *humility* in the face of the Proletariat (Koestler describes the cult of the "prolo," this obsession of all Communist intellectuals: how they attempted to imitate the archetypal, broad-shouldered, square-jawed worker of the Putilov factories, gave up wearing ties, made sure their nails were dirty and did their utmost to castrate their thinking); (2) the belief that the bourgeois intellectual can save his soul only by sharing the suffering of the working class and by imitating its "Passion" (Silone, in *The God that Failed*, speaks of the sacrifices that were to bring about a "common redemption"; Roger Vailland, in *Drôle de jeu*, describes the typical young intellectual who wants to "save his soul"); (3) the conviction that any present sacrifices, even self-destruction, will be eschatologically justified; that the intellectual's duty is to prepare the future, and that this future will justify everything, including the intellectual's betrayal of intellect; (4) the concomitant quest for holiness by means of martyrdom. Czeslaw Milosz compares this to the attraction of the butterfly to the flame: the intellectual throws himself into the fire, and burns to death for the greater glory of mankind. Arthur Koestler, more succinctly, quotes from Donne:

> . . . for Oh, to some
> Not to be martyrs, is a martyrdome.[32]

¶ v. *An unhappy marriage*

THE SAME ARTHUR KOESTLER REMINDS US, however, that the mystical marriage between the intellectual and the extreme Left is far from a successful one. In recalling his own associations with the Party, he

[31] "The French Intellectuals: Situation and Outlook" in *Modern France* (1951), ed. Edward Mead Earle, p. 76.

[32] Koestler uses these lines from Donne's "The Martyrs" (*The Litanie*, x) as the epigraph for *Arrival and Departure*.

describes with great vividness the atmosphere of suspicion that reigned in Party cells, and the mental tortures undergone by him and his fellow intellectuals. Barely tolerated, their position was somewhat akin to that of the "Useful Jews" during the Hitler regime, who were permitted to survive and wore special armbands to prevent their being sent to the gas chamber by mistake.

The attitude is not a new one, though it may appear somewhat paradoxical in view of the fact that it is the intellectuals who, for more than half a century, had led the European socialist movements. It is very characteristic that a Proudhon, one of the rare radical theorists to have come from the lower classes (though Marx called him a petit-bourgeois socialist), resented all his life being considered a thinker. Blanqui and his followers appeared to many workers as ruthless seekers of power. No less significant was the attitude of the French delegates to the First Congress of the Workers International in Geneva (1866): pointing to the danger of the organization's being invaded and undermined by unscrupulous, ambitious and privileged schemers, they asked for the exclusion of all intellectuals. Far from accepting them, the revolutionary Left tended to consider them as enemies or as subversives. Did not Lenin—though he knew better than anyone that socialism had come from outside the working class —refer to the intellectuals as cowardly menials of the counter-Revolution, as self-satisfied narcissi enamored of the dung-heaps that surround them? (Gorki was later to call them "arrogant pimps."[33])

The violence of Lenin's tone corresponds, it is true, to the blackest phase of the reaction after the ruthless crushing of the 1905 insurrection. Nevertheless, the bitterness toward the intellectuals remains a constant fact. They are accused of plotting to use the ignorant proletariat as an instrument for selfish gains. Machajski is tireless in pointing to the *knows* as a rising privileged class.[34] Bakunin repeatedly affirms the impossibility of converting to honest socialism the "aristocrats of the intellect," and finally resigns from the International (. . . "I am nothing but a bourgeois"). Karl Kautsky advises the Party to protect itself against the intellectual success-hunters. Hubert Lagardelle, in a speech delivered to a group of socialist students in 1900, refers to the intelligentsia as a "floating" group,

---

[33] *On Guard for the Soviet Union* (1933), p. 138.

[34] For a succinct exposé of Machajski's ideas, see Max Nomad, *Rebels and Renegades* (1932), pp. 206-207.

with bourgeois sympathies and contempt for the workers, who should only be used as *phonographs* to propagate the wishes and decisions of the proletarian movement. Paul Lafargue goes even further, and in *Le Socialisme et les intellectuels* (1900) bluntly states that the intellectuals possess neither a sense of solidarity nor civic courage, that they are merely fit to be the clownish entertainers of a paying clientele. In 1912, after some resounding articles in *La Bataille Syndicaliste*, Georges Yvetot decided to exclude the intellectuals from the C.G.T. (Confédération Générale du Travail) under the pretext that they belong to secondary professions, display no group interest, and *"have not suffered enough."* More recently, the polemics that raged around Pierre Hervé's exclusion from the Party after he published *La Révolution et les fétiches* (1956) showed very clearly how widespread the notion was, in Leftist and extreme Leftist circles, that the intelligentsia felt in reality totally alien to the class struggle, that it was merely exploiting Marxism for literary or prestige reasons, that it was a traitor group dreaming of a new priesthood and filled with contempt for the working man.[35]

To be sure, the danger of fascism, and in particular the Spanish Civil War, had changed the tune considerably. Real efforts were made to convince the intellectuals that there was no such a thing as an innate bourgeois blemish, that intellectual self-mutilation was an aberration, and that the Party considered "plebeianism" and the abasement of Reason a "deviation." In 1936, Paul Vaillant-Couturier wrote a special report for the Central Committee of the Party which reads like an official appeal to the French intelligentsia.[36]

[35] The following articles, all related to the *"Affaire Hervé,"* deal with the different aspects of this question: Sartre, "Le réformisme et les fétiches," *Les Temps Modernes*, February 10, 1956, pp. 1153-1164; "Réponse à Pierre Naville," *Les Temps Modernes*, March-April, 1956, pp. 1510-1525; Pierre Naville, "Les mésaventures de Nekrassov," *France-Observateur*, March 8, 1956; "Les nouvelles mésaventures de J.-P. Sartre," *France-Observateur*, April 19, 1956; "L'Intellectuel communiste," *Les Lettres Nouvelles*, June, 1956, pp. 871-886, and July-August, 1956, pp. 60-79; Maurice Nadeau, "Sartre et l' 'Affaire Hervé,' " *op. cit.*, Gilles Martinet, "La politique et le roman," *France-Observateur*, April 19, 1956; Jean Duvignaud, "Le marxisme est-il arrêté?," *Les Lettres Nouvelles*, May, 1956, pp. 746-752.

[36] *Au Service de l'Esprit* ("Pour la convocation des Etats Généraux de l'Intelligence Française"), 1936. Some of these themes were broached again, and for the same reasons, by Laurent Casanova in *Le Parti communiste et la nation*, 1949. After World War II, the French Communist Party sought to exploit the prestige it had achieved in the eyes of the intellectuals through its role in the Resistance.

But it was difficult for this intelligentsia to forget the sharp criticism leveled at them by Communists and Socialists alike, for these accusations (and self-accusations) rankled in their conscience. Considered faithless, arrogant, ready for compromise, they continue to suffer from the contempt in which they are held or in which they hold themselves. In the words of Sartre's hero Mathieu, they feel "innocent and guilty, too severe and too indulgent, powerless and responsible, bound up with everyone and rejected by all." Is Brunet not there to remind him that he is only a watchdog for the bourgeoisie? But strangely enough, even Brunet, the Communist, feels uneasy: "*Intellectuel. Bourgeois*," he mutters to himself. "*Separated for ever.* Try as I may, we will never have the same memories." "You are not one of us," similarly says the Communist Gaigneux to his Party comrade, young Professor Jourdan (in Marcel Aymé's *Uranus*).

The French novel, ever since Vallès broached the theme of the misunderstanding between the intellectual and the revolutionary, has repeatedly echoed these accusations and laments. Vallès himself, it is worth recalling, was posthumously reprimanded by the Communist leader Marcel Cachin for being an isolated intellectual rebel rather than a disciplined member of an ideological movement. It is of course perfectly consistent for a militant Communist to make such an accusation. Thus it is not surprising to find in Aragon's *Les Communistes* a portrait of the cowardly and treacherous journalist-intellectual. What is more astonishing—and also far more significant— is that writers with such completely divergent techniques, preoccupations and themes as Romain Rolland, Martin du Gard, Malraux, Louis Guilloux, Brice Parain, Paul Nizan and Sartre, should all have been haunted by this divorce between the intellectual and the causes he yearns to espouse. Jean-Christophe's friend, the *normalien* Olivier Jeannin, wants to be part of the social movement, but "the current rejected him." He wants to help the destitute, but is received with suspicion. Symbolically, he dies—an innocent victim—in a popular riot, while attempting to save a boy's life. The hero of Romain Rolland's war novel *Clerambault* (1920) also suffers from the workers' and revolutionaries' animosity toward an intelligentsia they consider morally bankrupt. Jacques, in Martin du Gard's *Les Thibault*, is accused by his socialist friend of being a bourgeois intellectual, filled with typical intellectual "scruples," unfit for revolutionary action, critical but faithless, at best a "sympathizer," but *"pas des leurs"* ("not one of them"): "You'll never be a real revolutionary, my comrade." In one of his early works, *La Maison du peuple* (1927), Louis Guilloux describes the hard life and socialist dreams of enlightened small-town craftsmen who feel betrayed by their "intellectual" leaders ("they want to flatter us and use us"; they have "nothing to lose"; they are *"arrivistes"*). The conclusion: "Let's believe only in ourselves." On a different level, Nicolaieff, in Malraux's *Les Conquérants*, explains that there is no room in a revolutionary party for the individual who "wants to be himself." But it is probably Brice Parain who, with characteristic restraint, has best summed up, in what amounts to a parable, the *impossibility* of assuming another's situation or burden. The philosophy teacher in *La Mort de Jean Madec* explains to the idealistic student who, out of humility, has decided to sabotage his own work and become the last of the class, that one cannot alter the natural order of things; that his action is not only dishonest, but reveals a particularly refined form of pride. "You would preserve the advantage of a brilliant reputation without assuming the weight of an authentic situation." Such self-mutilation must, under all circumstances, remain suspect.

¶ VI. *The suicidal tendencies*

OF ALL THE TEMPTATIONS, the intellectual's impulse to mutilate or destroy himself is indeed the most disquieting. This abdication of intelligence assumes tragic proportions, not merely because of its consequences, but because of the drama of lucidity, self-accusation and self-punishment it implies. "The tragedy of the contemporary intellectual is that he wants to be a revolutionary, and yet cannot succeed in becoming one." [37] Emmanuel Berl's analysis, though it dates back to 1929, casts much light on the nature of Sartre's political despair, on his chronic envy of men who were never in a position to *choose freely*. Such an exile from "social fatality" is doubly anguishing, since it involves an insoluble philosophical dilemma. For Sartre believes that man is condemned to freedom, yet he envies the hypothetical "proletarian" bound to an authenticity he cannot alter. Even an absolute form of heroism, Sartre knows, cannot change the fact that the intellectual exploits other men's struggles to justify a death

[37] Emmanuel Berl, *Mort de la pensée bourgeoise*, pp. 136-137.

which he has seen fit to choose.[38] Like Madec's brilliant young boy who wants to be the last in his class, like the hero in Vailland's *Drôle de jeu* who sees himself as a lonely *promeneur*—the "engaged" intellectual, suffering from a subjective guilt that no allegiance can cure, is haunted by the conviction that he is the superfluous man. "What am I doing here?" Professor Mirambeau asks himself in Vercors' *Colères;* he feels *"de trop,"* out of place, unneeded and unnecessary.[39] It is perfectly consistent (and not at all simple modesty) that even when he does participate in a common action, the intellectual should consider his contribution inadequate. Thus Rousseaux and Sartre disparaged their own Resistance work. "I was often ashamed of it," writes Sartre in "Qu'est-ce que la littérature?," referring to his comparative security. But this shame reveals an even broader sense of inadequacy: the tragic awareness of the futility of Thought. Charles Moeller, in reviewing *Les Mandarins*, very appropriately recalls Edouard Mounier's conviction that the intellectual was facing a wall of impossibilities.[40] Indeed, the central tragic theme of Simone de Beauvoir's novel is the obsessive fear that the intellectual has no function whatsoever—the "lucid awareness of his ineptitude."

The intellectual, paralyzed by the very shame of being an intellectual, thus feels compelled to deny himself the right to speak up. "I do not claim that the Party is above criticism; I do claim that one has to deserve the right to criticize." Readers of *Les Temps Modernes* may remember Sartre's ironic answer to Camus during the polemical and insulting exchange of open letters in the summer of 1952. The importance of such a statement reaches far beyond the personal relationship of a Sartre and a Camus, or their divergent assessments of a particular ideology, or even the underlying complex of "not having suffered enough." It symbolizes a peculiar form of self-exclusion and self-punishment: the deliberate abdication of the

[38] See Sartre's preface to Roger Stéphane's *Portrait de l'aventurier* (1950). In it, Sartre analyzes the fundamental difference between the man of action ("the adventurer") and the revolutionary masses. Sartre's text turns around one central idea: it is not the function of a revolutionary party to cure the intellectuals of their "guilt."

[39] It is hardly necessary to point to the importance of this concept of superfluity in Sartre's philosophical scheme. The awareness of being *"de trop"* is at the very core of Roquentin's experience in *La Nausée.*

[40] *La Revue Nouvelle,* February 15, 1955, pp. 181-185.

critical intellect. Thus a Dubreuilh-Sartre sacrifices his intellectual prerogatives to a sense of political *duty*, while aware that the doctrines of materialism and historical determinism "kill Thought." [41] And it is precisely this awareness which makes for tragedy: as unalterably as Madec's young student who dreams of destroying his mind, the intellectual is condemned to his intelligence. Without respite, he sees himself trapped in an impasse, while yearning for that *suprême volupté* Barrès has described—the superior joy of renouncing one's most cherished possessions. And the temptation is not merely to "kill Thought," but art and literature as well. Scriassine (no doubt a fictional portrait of Koestler) explains in *Les Mandarins* that moral scruples have driven the French intellectuals to the secret conviction that whatever they have to say is unimportant or harmful, that they no longer have anything to contribute to art or thought. "In the country of Diderot, Victor Hugo and Jaurès it is assumed that culture and politics go hand in hand. For a long time Paris took itself for Athens. Athens no longer exists, that's finished. . . ." Somewhere in the back of Perron's and Dubreuilh's minds, hidden like an unspeakable desire, there still lurks the love of gratuitous literature; but the very presence of such a nostalgia makes for a renewed sense of guilt. Of course, Scriassine (and Simone de Beauvoir) tend somewhat to amplify this literary and artistic suicide. The situation, however, is grave enough for a Roland Barthes to observe, in *Le Degré zéro de l'écriture*, that the intelligentsia, tormented by political pressures, not only insist on "militant" writing, but have begun to "question the validity of Literature itself."

One could easily show, of course, that this suicidal impulse has, in many cases, been translated dramatically and artistically into powerful literature. Ever since Balzac, and even more so since Flaubert, the drama of intelligence and the obsessive death-wish of the thinker have been fertile literary themes. But the suicidal impulse is not limited, it would seem, to this abstract level of critical Reason and artistic creativity. The intellectual of the "engaged" years comes dangerously close to wishing for the death of his entire group. Romain Rolland, who was one of the first to sense the tragic gap between the thinker and the revolutionary proletariat, observed in *Clerambault* that some intellectuals were among those most ardent in

[41] See "Matérialisme et Révolution," in *Situations III*.

calling for the humiliation of their "guild." [42] This tendency toward group suicide has been made manifest even more explicitly in our own time. A character in Koestler's *Arrival and Departure* explains that the revolutionary intelligentsia are committing "hara-kiri," that contemporary intellectuals are the "suicide squads" of their own class or group. Perhaps it is the fundamental tragedy of the modern revolutionary intellectual that he desires and prepares a world in which he knows there will be no place for him. Raymond Aron discusses with irony those who are fated to be the first to people any concentration camp. Sartre himself is aware that for the militant intellectual the moment of victory will be the beginning of defeat, that he is destined to be a "grave-digger" even at the risk of burying himself. [43] It is possible that all of this points to a more general failure of our culture, so unsure of itself, or so taken with the myth of heterogeneity, as to have lost the desire or the ability to defend its own values. Roger Ikor, in his provocative essay *Mise au net* (1957), describes with alarm a peculiarly self-destructive form of cultural "exoticism" which he associates with self-betrayal, masochism and suicide. (Scriassine also attributes the perennial dream of intellectual dictatorship to a "masochism characteristic of all intellectuals.") E. M. Cioran, who specializes in articles even more challenging and paradoxical than those of Roger Ikor, suggests that the intellectual, seduced by the very force that crushes him, longs for his tormenter and executioner, invokes History with the hope of becoming its chosen victim—thus making himself, in the most prodigious bankruptcy since antiquity, the sacrificer of his own intellect. [44]

The very same masochistic abdication of the intellect has inspired Camus to write one of his most powerful parables. "L'Esprit confus," which later appeared under the title "Le Renégat" in *L'Exil et le Royaume*, is a hallucinating allegory of the missionary-intellectual who believes that he is out to convert the barbarians, but who in fact seeks tyranny in order to submit to it. Brutalized, tortured, humili-

---

[42] According to Micheline Tison-Braun (*La Crise de l'Humanisme*, I, pp. 488-489), Romain Rolland intuits the bourgeois socialist's "unconscious need to hasten his own destruction." One might add that, at times, this need is quite outspoken: "*Il était remarquable que quelques intellectuels fussent parmi les plus ardents à réclamer cet abaissement de la confrérie*" (Clerambault, p. 283).

[43] See the preface to Roger Stéphane's *Portrait de l'aventurier*, p. 22, and *Situations II*, p. 276.

[44] "Sur une civilisation essoufflée," *Nouvelle Nouvelle Revue Française*, May, 1956, pp. 799-816.

ated in his flesh and in his spirit, he adores his torturers and proclaims the omnipotence of the evil Fetish. The symbolism of his quest and of his punishment—his tongue is cut out, his mouth filled with salt —are quite transparent. But it is interesting to note that he feels betrayed by his own culture ("my teachers have deceived me"), that even in his original desire to convert others there was the desire for "absolute power," that in fact he adores the Fetish long before he sets out on his journey. By means of a dazzling imagery of heat, sun, sterility, silence and inhuman tension, Camus succeeds in creating an atmosphere of primitive ritual, of sexual hypnosis which only dramatizes the extent of the intellectual surrender. (See Appendix B.)

In the face of such disastrous temptations, writers have sought varying answers and adopted different attitudes. Camus himself, spokesman for a new Humanism, has steadily rejected all transcendent "kingdoms," whether religious or political, and sung instead with pagan accents the "implacable grandeur" of a life in which all the idols had feet of clay. Though at one time he spoke the unbending language of intellectuals, Camus is—as Germaine Brée reminds us—"suspicious of all absolutes."[45] His books, whose very titles announce the theme of alienation and exile, assert the need to rediscover a lost birthright and to cling desperately to one's most precious virtue: the "generous exigence of happiness." Happiness and love are indeed key words in Camus' vocabulary. But above all, he has reaffirmed in lyric fashion the need to return to the modest "mortal" condition. His intellectual pilgrimage evokes the journey of Ulysses; it is a return from the world of monsters back to the world of men.

This struggle against abstractions, this concern for the stark realities of the "human condition," have made of Camus—so at least it seemed—the heir of the best in Malraux. But similarities can be deceptive. Though Camus no doubt greatly admired Malraux (one of his first theatrical ventures was an adaptation of *Le Temps du mépris*), his writings often sound like a reply to Malraux's work, and appear to challenge the latter's basic themes and attitudes. In *La Peste*, Camus may seem ironical when he proposes Grand as the

---

[45] *Camus*, p. 168. This fear of absolutes may help explain why there are in fact few authentic intellectuals among Camus' protagonists. Neither Meursault, nor Rieux, nor Tarrou, nor Jean-Baptiste Clamence are "intellectuals" in the sense that Cripure, Vincent Berger or Roquentin are intellectuals. Perhaps one can call them intellectuals in disguise?

"hero" of his story. But the irony is not at the expense of the character, for this "insignificant hero," with his kind heart and "apparently ridiculous ideal," proves, as it were, that there are humble virtues more precious than heroism. The simple humanity of Camus' characters thus stands in direct contrast to the haughty, strident, somewhat aristocratic tone of Malraux's "heroic" heroes. If Malraux's work is the Iliad of our time, Camus' is our Odyssey.

Contrary to both Malraux and Camus, who sought an answer in either transcendent action or human solidarity, Sartre (though attracted simultaneously to both of these attitudes) preferred to remain the victim of a philosophical dilemma. Indulging in dialectical debates with his own conscience, he views the Marxist myth primarily in terms of a philosophical drama: the tragedy of the intellectual caught between conflicting allegiances. With a measure of self-inflicted cruelty, he condemns himself to the "authenticity" of a tragic impasse from which he has no moral and no intellectual right to escape. "He has lived until the very end his *impossible* condition," Sartre wrote of the bourgeois intellectual who chose the Revolution while fully aware that he remained the prisoner of his solitude.[46] Of Sartre, too, it could be said that he always felt attracted to impossibilities, to situations that offered no hope of solution.

It is perhaps his essay "Matérialisme et Révolution" (first published in Les Temps Modernes in 1946) which brings most sharply into focus the nature of the philosophical dilemma: "To betray the proletariat in order to serve Truth, or to betray Truth in the name of the Proletariat?" Here indeed lies the paradox: the doctrine of historical determinism which, Sartre feels, negates human freedom on the metaphysical level, has become, on the political level, the instrument of man's liberation. Dialectical materialism may be a metaphysics that annihilates itself, an "unseizable Proteus," a doctrine which destroys thought—yet on the other hand, it constitutes, in Sartre's opinion, the only myth that can satisfy the Revolutionary needs. Answering some objections raised by George Lukacs in *Existentialisme ou Marxisme*, Sartre sums up the nature of the dilemma:

We were convinced *simultaneously* that historical materialism supplied the only valid interpretation of history and that existentialism remained the only concrete approach to reality. I do not pretend to

[46] Preface to Roger Stéphane's *Portrait de l'aventurier*, p. 26.

deny the contradiction in this attitude. . . . Many intellectuals, many students have experienced and are still experiencing the tension of this double exigency.[47]

This tension can be felt throughout the entire work of Sartre. Put in its simplest terms, it is the conflict between a moral and emotional commitment, on the one hand; and on the other, the austere demands of a philosophical mind. On the philosophical level, Sartre feels committed to a *choice;* but on the social, political and sentimental level, he believes in the value and beauty of necessity, in the intrinsic merit and dignity of those who suffer not because they have chosen to suffer, but because suffering was granted them like a grace.

This basic contradiction, symptomatic of a tragic uneasiness, is reflected in much of the best writing of the past two decades. The intellectual hero appears increasingly paralyzed by the conflicting demands of passion and of intellect. But the paralysis and accompanying despair were gradual. For a while, it seemed as if these demands could be reconciled in a dynamic synthesis. The work of André Malraux is an outstanding example of this effort to find an equilibrium.[48] How long and how successfully such an equilibrium could be maintained remains another question. By the time World War II came to an end, the voice of Malraux already sounded to many like a voice from a Golden Past, when the choice between good and evil had been a relatively simple matter.

[47] "Questions de méthode," *Les Temps Modernes,* September, 1957, pp. 338-417.

[48] In this equilibrium—or tension—W. M. Frohock finds one of the main sources of Malraux's literary power. (See "André Malraux: The Intellectual as Novelist," *Yale French Studies,* No. 8, 1951, pp. 26-37.)

9

Malraux: Passion and Intellect

Qu'est-ce que tu veux que me fasse ta pensée, si tu ne peux pas penser mon drame?
—Garcia in *L'Espoir*

¶ 1. *"Death to intelligence!"*

WHAT GOOD IS YOUR THINKING . . . ? Bitter words with which Garcia, a spokesman for the besieged city, reproves Miguel de Unamuno, the philosopher who preferred absolute truths to political commitment. What are absolute truths in the face of Madrid's heroism? What common measure is there between academic meditations and an apocalypse? Just as inadequate as words in the presence of a shell-torn body, so the intellect itself appears defeated before it can even begin to account for man's instinctive choice of tragedy, for his *amor fati.*

We cannot avoid the question: does Garcia's exclamation, which ironically echoes the far more brutal outcries of the Salamanca Falangists ("death to Unamuno," "death to the intellectuals," "death to intelligence," "long live death"), mark the bankruptcy of reason? Certainly this is a key question not only for Malraux and his readers, but for an entire generation haunted by the conflict between thought and action. Malraux himself, according to Emmanuel Mounier (*L'Espoir des désespérés*), was no more motivated by ideas or by an idea when he sided with Gaullism after the war than when he espoused the cause of communism in the thirties. "He has little esteem for ideas," writes Mounier. But can we agree that Malraux really feels or ever felt that ideas only serve to evade or betray decisions, and that at best they set up fake dialogues between individuals or cultural groups who, in fact, have nothing to tell each other?

A convincing case (but how honest?) could no doubt be made to prove that Malraux does indeed hold a skeptical view of intelligence as such. His novels are all clearly in rebellion against the long tradition of clinical analysis on which the French novel prides itself from Mme de Lafayette to Gide and Proust. Few writers—and certainly few novelists—are more remote from the atmosphere of the salon conversation. His early novels (*Les Conquérants, La Voie royale*) are perhaps even a little excessive in their lyrical praise of the adventurer. No wonder Gaëtan Picon calls him and his generation romantic. But even in his later and more mature works, he consciously shuns the analytical novel, both introspective and retrospective. His is a literature of the present, a literature of "extreme situations," as Sartre calls it; a literature of war and death, in which evil, as represented by the sadistic will to degrade, remains pure and consequently unredeemable. In the revealing preface to *Le Temps du mépris*, Malraux fervently takes issue with the cerebral (and pathologically impartial) kind of novelist who, obsessed by the notion of individualism and individual antagonisms, forever explores the "inner world" of his characters, but neglects what alone in man is great: his ability to take sides and to find solidarity in common action.

For the lack of such a sense of solidarity Unamuno, in *L'Espoir*, is called "immoral"; he has turned his back on a just war because no armies can be just. He has refused action. If the word *intellectual*—which occurs so often in the work of the author—has pejorative connotations, it is precisely because of this separatist tendency, this unwillingness to *be with*. Few characters in his novels come so close to being thoroughly hateful as the scientist in *Les Noyers de l'Altenburg* who arrives at the Russian front with his bottles of phosgene gas to supervise their utilization and observe the results. He has so completely divested himself of any *human* quality that even the most hardened German officer considers him an "enemy" who, with all his impersonal talk of phosgene, mucous membrane and respiratory tracts, seems to have appeared at the front to destroy the very notion of courage. But Professor Hoffmann is a caricature—and an exception. Most often, the scholars in Malraux's novels are merely incapable of action or ineffective. Unamuno retires to a kind of cell, lies in bed, bitter and sullen, surrounded by books. In *Les Conquérants*, Tcheng-Dai—the Chinese Gandhi—prefers the role of advisor to that of leader. Tired old Gisors, in *La Condition humaine*, although he has formed revolutionary disciples, is obsessed by the thought of death ("his memories were full of tombs"), refuses to participate in the action and withdraws into the world of art and opium while his son dies in a hopeless struggle.[1] In *L'Espoir*, Alvear, professor of history of art and father of the blinded aviator (the sons are decidedly more committed than the fathers), reads, drinks and recites a sonnet by Quevedo while passively waiting for death in his Madrid apartment. The intellectuals who meet for a symposium in *Les Noyers de l'Altenburg* perorate endlessly on the concept of man to the accompaniment of the "idiotic cackle" of hens coming from the outside. As to the ethnologist, Möllberg, he denies the very concept of man, and symbolically destroys the manuscript of his work, *Civilization as Conquest and as Destiny*, the sun-scorched pages of which probably hang scattered on branches between Zanzibar and the Sahara.

Without indulging in hostile caricature (he does not share Edouard Berth's views—*Les Méfaits des intellectuels*, 1914—that intellectuals represent a morality of cowardice), Malraux nevertheless seems to intimate that professional thinkers tend to be incorrigible dreamers. "Intellectuals are like women, my dear! soldiers make them dream," says one of the characters in *Les Noyers de l'Altenburg*. Dreamers who also suffer because they are the first to believe (although they would not admit it, even to themselves) that thought is inferior to action. When, exceptionally, one of them turns out to be an adventurer of the T. E. Lawrence type, all the others inspect him with curiosity and admiration. More revealing still: when such an adventurer-intellectual delivers a series of lectures, it is on "The Philosophy of Action." Needless to add that this emancipated individual (is there a faint memory of the Michel of Gide's *L'Immoraliste?*) has become far more interested in action than in philosophy. As for the others—those who have remained faithful to their books, and to the glib and oily art of learned colloquies—they are condemned to dreams and talk: *"les intellectuels sont bavards . . ."*

Throughout Malraux's work—from *La Tentation de l'Occident* to his recent studies on art—there seems to be a tendency to devaluate the intellect which finds its most succinct formulation, in *Les Noyers de l'Altenburg*, at the moment of greatest revelation: "thought" is but a "monstrous fraud." Kyo knows that his father

---

[1] W. M. Frohock puts it very well: "[Gisors] is powerless against his own paralysis. The physician cannot save himself" (*André Malraux and the Tragic Imagination*, p. 78).

deludes himself, that action seldom stems from thought and that one cannot use one's *knowledge* of the "inner life" of others to make them act: "what is deepest in a man can rarely be used to make him act." Moreno, in *L'Espoir*, has learned that neither thoughts nor deep truths exist when shells begin to fall. The most damning commentary on the Altenburg symposium is that it remains exclusively a dialogue with culture, not with life (or death). "An idea never grew from a fact, but always from another idea."

Unable to give birth to action, or to account for it, the intellect, especially in its analytical function, seems moreover to possess disturbing powers of corrosion. Recently, in an irritating though challenging article on our "exhausted" civilization, E. M. Cioran has again blamed our lucidity, and shown the danger of unmasking the fictions which alone can make us bold.[2] The idea is not a new one: Sartre, in the preface to the first issue of *Les Temps Modernes* (1945), called for the death of the analytical mind: "We are convinced that the spirit of analysis has outlived itself and that its only remaining function is to disturb the revolutionary consciousness and to isolate men. . . ." But Malraux had already pointed to the same dangers. Kyo in the presence of his father (symbol of absolute intelligence) always feels that his will to action softens or even disintegrates. "As soon as Kyo came into his presence, his will to action was transformed into intelligence, and he found this rather disturbing." It is again Vincent Berger who puts it most tersely when he tells von Bülow's envoy that dreams corrupt action.

All the values most prized by Malraux and his heroes—courage, audacity, love (?) and fraternity—seem, at first sight, to be at odds with intellectual prowess. Kyo discovers that to judge others is less beautiful than to love them, and that virile fraternity is a more exalting refuge than the mind. Ch'en, the terrorist, knows that death is greater than the meditation on death. Similarly, the behavior of the peasant-soldiers in *Les Noyers de l'Altenburg* convinces Berger that it is the common man, not the intellectual, who perpetuates life.

This tendency to humble the mind—like most of Malraux's themes —is already present in his earliest writings. *La Tentation de l'Occident* (1926) questions the very "intelligence" of Europe which, according to Ling, the Chinese observer, suffers from the myth of

2 "Sur une civilisation essoufflée," *Nouvelle Nouvelle Revue Française*, May, 1956, pp. 799-816.

order (a confusion of order and civilization), from a chaotic sensibility (where order would be required), but most of all from a disease diagnosed as the *maladie de la pensée:* the mind turning in a vacuum, like a beautiful machine spotted with blood. A. D., Ling's French correspondent, compares European culture to a self-contemplating madness, while Ling is even more contemptuous as he calls the intellect an evil ornament (a *"néfaste parure"*).

Finally—and this is perhaps the most devastating criticism leveled at the mind—Malraux seems to make it very clear that the truly fundamental experiences of man are not known but perceived. The body is frequently a more adequate means of communication than language. Desperate (but eloquent) clutchings of hands! Visceral participation in a human communion of suffering and pity! "What these men were doing, my father now understood: not with his mind, but with his body. . . ." This is how Malraux describes the moment of revelation during the gas attack on the Russian front when the German assault wave is metamorphosed into an "assault of pity," and every German soldier returns to his lines carrying a Russian victim. And *revelation* is no doubt the proper word here. Germaine Brée and Margaret Guiton put it very well: according to Malraux, the fundamental aspects of human experience are "mysteries that cannot be elucidated but only revealed."[3] Malraux himself refers to the insight into "a mystery which did not give away its secret but only its presence." And when the meaning of this mystery is revealed to Berger, he can only find one telling word to evoke his former cerebral search for philosophical significations: *crétin!*

¶ II. *Scholars in action*

Crétin . . . AND YET. And yet, as someone has observed (was it Gide?), idiots are conspicuously absent in Malraux's work. The educated, the articulate, and even the erudite occupy a privileged position in his novels. In spite of their ineffectiveness, Malraux does not truly disavow the intellectuals of the Gisors-Alvear type. They all are, in one way or another, the repositories of some important truth. Alvear, for instance, knows that at best man can involve in an action only a very limited part of himself. And as for Gisors, it would seem that Malraux, far from disavowing him, has placed him

[3] *An Age of Fiction*, p. 189.

at the very center of the novel: radiating tenderness and understanding, he is simultaneously outside the action and at the heart of the meaning of the novel. Kyo, Ch'en, Ferral—all come to consult him. He is the mirror where all action reflects itself, a conscience where all thought finds an echo and a prolongation. He is a beginning (after all, he formed a generation of revolutionaries), but he is also the one who outlives tragedy, for he remains alive after Kyo and his comrades have died: his suffering, his consciousness—above all his meditations—constitute the novel's epilogue.

And what about the myth of the intellectuals' ineffectiveness? Paradoxically, all of Malraux's heroes (the most adventurous, the most competent, the most violent, the most "heroic") are precisely intellectuals. The list is quite impressive. Garine, in *Les Conquérants*, has studied literature, directed the translation department of a Zurich publishing house and meditates on Saint-Just. Claude Vanec, in *La Voie royale*, has studied Far Eastern languages and published articles on Oriental art. To be sure, Kassner, the militant communist, in *Le Temps du mépris*, who undergoes torture in a German prison, is the son of a coal miner; but he too has had an intellectual formation: a scholarship student at the university, he later organized a workers' theater, became a writer and the colorful reporter on the Siberian civil war. The main characters in *La Condition humaine* are even more clearly "intellectuals": Kyo is the son of a university professor; Ch'en is the former disciple of Gisors at the University of Pekin; and even Katow—the hero of several revolutions and survivor of a White Army firing squad—has studied medicine in Odessa. But it is no doubt in *L'Espoir* that we meet with the greatest concentration of intellectuals in action: the aviator Scali, who was professor of the history of art in Italy and has published the most important study on Piero della Francesca; Garcia, one of Spain's foremost ethnologists, and now one of the heads of the Loyalists' military intelligence; Magnin who, like Malraux himself, organized and leads one of the air squadrons, and whose gestures (the way, for instance, he takes off his glasses) betray "*la marque complexe de l'intellectuel.*" Three generations of Bergers have devoted their energies to books and ideas. And not only the major characters, but also the figures in the background would, under less dramatic circumstances, feel not at all out of place in a writers' or artists' conference: Gérard, in *Les Conquérants*, has been professor at the Hanoi lycée.

Pei, in *La Condition humaine*, writes for Chinese magazines and prepares an apologia of terrorism. Shade, the journalist, and Lopez, the sculptor, discuss the problems of contemporary art in *L'Espoir*. As for Guernico, the deeply moving leader of the Madrid ambulance corps, he is one of Spain's well-known Catholic writers, now walking through the nightmarish streets of a besieged city in search of the living presence of Christ. Even characters not unduly afflicted with idealism have not escaped the contamination of books: the power-crazy erotomaniac Ferral, president of a super-capitalistic consortium, is the son of a learned jurist, obtained an *agrégation* in history, and directed, at the age of twenty-nine, the first collective history of France!

Malraux is not the only writer who has taken the scholar out of his study and placed him in the midst of a struggle; he is not the only one who has transformed his peaceful and slightly ironic contemplation of life into a scorching meditation, a dialogue, a battle of ideas—and promoted him to the rank of tragic victim or hero. The contemporary French novel is peopled with artists, journalists and teachers who think, discuss, analyze and accuse—and above all who indulge in what Henri Peyre calls a new-romantic *mal du siècle:* the sense of metaphysical anguish.[4] According to Emmanuel Mounier, all of Malraux's characters are *"métapracticiens"* [5]: neither pragmatists obsessed by the notion of efficiency nor hysterics in search of thrills, but "explorers of the unknown" by means of action. Mounier has diagnosed them well. For Malraux's characters are not merely concerned with solving the problems of their time or suffering from their own sense of inadequacy. Theirs is not the mire of shame and guilt through which flounder the victimized professor-martyr Cripure or Sartre's scruple-ridden Mathieu Delarue. They are about the only intellectuals in the recent French novel to get involved in action out of a clear choice, with a clear faith and an unmuddled sense of destiny. (Roger Vailland's Resistance heroes in *Drôle de jeu* are either priggish political fanatics like young Frédéric, or ironic and somewhat Stendhalian picaresque figures like Marat.) The heroes in the world of Malraux may be the heirs to the same ironic culture which finds its culmination in the arrogance and disincarnation of a Monsieur Teste, but they are also willing to sacri-

[4] *The Contemporary French Novel*, p. 183.
[5] *L'Espoir des déséspérés*, p. 28.

fice momentarily such a culture if that is the price they have to pay so as not to betray. Only the elder generation of intellectuals, those who belong to the Alvear type (Roger Stéphane has shown that for them the idea of Revolution is inseparable from a systematic skepticism [6]), are unwilling to make such a sacrifice and consequently are doomed to succumb without hope and without faith, superannuated representatives of an epoch whose moral criteria no longer apply. Dr. Neubourg, as he leaves a sullen Unamuno in his room, has the impression "of taking leave of the nineteenth century."

Dramatically (given the themes and concerns of his novels), the presence of intellectuals is a force indispensable to Malraux: they heighten the artistic and moral consciousness within the novel. The ordinary peasant-soldiers may be the key to the problem of the unity of man—but it is after all Berger, not a peasant-soldier, who discovers and formulates this eternal unity. Moreover, in order to give the *common* man an aura of eternity, Berger (or rather Malraux) has recourse to artistic allusions and metaphors: a soldier's mention of Bamberg suggests the "German Chartres"; peasant faces recall Gothic statuary (the scene takes place in Chartres); joyful gestures bring to mind medieval farces or scenes painted by Breughel. This technique is not unlike that used by Proust for ironic and poetic effects when he compares a maid to a Giotto "charity," a courtesan to a figure by Botticelli and an old servant to the statue of a saint in her niche. But the most important function of the intellectuals in the novels of Malraux is that they discuss the very problem of intelligence and incarnate the central conflict between passion and intellect. It is Garcia, after all—an ethnologist, an "intellectual"—, who finds Unamuno immoral.

¶ III. *Being and doing*

THE AWARENESS OF THIS CONFLICT between passion and intellect, between vitality and lucidity, permeates nearly every page of Malraux. And not only of this particular conflict, but of any dialogue: contradictory myths which demand the allegiance of man, alternating voices of hope and of doubt, clashes between thinking and doing which become particularly dramatic in times of revolution. At every

6 *Portrait de l'aventurier*, p. 120.

moment, man has to *choose*, caught—as Claude Mauriac has shown[7] —between two treasons. No matter how unworthy it may be of man—and Garcia is the first to suffer from it—the world man faces is Manichaean. But to be able to choose is also beautiful: through choice alone man becomes a hero. The Greek knew it: "Of my own will I shot the arrow that fell short, of my own will," declares Prometheus to the Chorus. Similarly, Vincent Berger proudly declares that the home of any man who can *choose* is where the darkest clouds accumulate. For a Stendhal, this would be Cornelian *"espagnolisme"*; for a Sartre, it is only "heroic parasitism" (the hero demanding of fighters who have not chosen their fight to legitimatize a death which he, the hero, has chosen)—but in any case the choice, and the desire for the choice stem from a sense of the heroic.

If Malraux is a romantic, it is primarily through this awareness of fundamental antitheses—an awareness which manifests itself on the artistic level through antithetical images: the Loyalist prostitute carrying a rifle is contrasted with the perfumed Fascist women who round out the pleasures of a banquet by going to watch the execution of prisoners; homeless children are asleep beneath giant floats of Mickey Mouse and Donald Duck while Franco's flotilla bombards the nearby port; Manuel evokes his first lesson in the military art with toy soldiers while all around him the living or dead flesh of real soldiers is carried on litters. One of the most unforgettable scenes in *Les Noyers de l'Altenburg* is Walter Berger's description of Nietzsche's mad, but sublime chant, in the obscurity of the St. Gotthard tunnel, to the accompaniment of the rhythmical clatter of the train's wheels and the mechanical pecking of a chicken belonging to a peasant traveling in the same compartment. Malraux is a master of dramatic contrasts and of grandiose images: the growing shadow of Katow as he walks to his death; men with wounded arms in plaster casts gliding by like spectral statues of violinists pushed through the corridors of the hospital; ghostlike figures building barricades during a misty night—all these create an effect of enlargement and of tenseness.

Ever since *La Tentation de l'Occident* (there is an astonishing unity to his work), Malraux has been obsessed by the "hopeless conflict" between man and that which man creates, between the thinker and his thought. This tragic cleavage takes many forms. Ling dis-

[7] *Malraux ou le mal du héros*, p. 208.

covers that in Europe the man of passions (*"l'homme passionné"*) finds himself in disharmony with the very culture he has forged, that the erotic pursuit is nothing but a desperate attempt to be at the same time oneself and *the other*, that thought and emotion are forever divorced. A. D. quite agrees: "with a calm sense of anguish, we become aware of the opposition between our actions and our inner life." In *Les Noyers de l'Altenburg* (written some fifteen years later), Malraux is still concerned with the many shapes of this same conflict: knowing and living; action and talk ("In Tripolitania, my father had acted; here, he was talking"); the very problem of the definition of man. Is man what he *hides*, or is he what he *does?*

It is in *L'Espoir*, however, that this sense of conflict between being and doing, between the intellect and the passionate commitment to action finds its clearest and most artistic formulation. Critics have not always been fair to this very beautiful book, the greatest unquestionably to come out of the Spanish Civil War. Claude Mauriac complains that the characters are too numerous and not sufficiently individualized. Others have deplored the excessively rapid shifting of scenes and the consequent impossibility for the reader to remember them. Yet there are many unforgettable scenes in *L'Espoir*: Colonel Jimenez limping across the Barcelona square to give the signal for the final attack on the Hotel Colon; the machine-gunned fireman on a ladder fighting off the enemy planes with his water hose; the distribution of cigarettes and razor blades to the besieged Falangist officers in front of the Toledo Alcazar; the execution of Hernandez; the spontaneously heroic defense of Madrid—without mentioning the famous airplane scene (with the peasant) over the Teruel front and the extraordinary descent of the wounded aviators from the mountain. Nearly constantly lyrical, no novel of Malraux so clearly elicits our enthusiasm, nor gives us such a powerful feeling of participation. What reader has not, for a moment at least, imagined that he was there, with Siry and Kogan, on that foggy November morning, when the International Brigade in Madrid's West Park halted Franco's Moors? Some of this enthusiasm and nostalgia is due, no doubt, to the prestige which, from the very first, the Spanish War acquired in the eyes of many European intellectuals—a prestige which is well summed up by the hero of Roger Vailland's *Drôle de jeu*: "Everybody knew immediately what side to take; it was the purest of recent wars, the one in which dying came most easily." It is perhaps because so many of the characters in *L'Espoir* have chosen freely to die that the readers, whose common destination is also death, can—as Malraux has said in relation to another work of art—"contemplate with envy characters who for a moment are the masters of their destiny." [8]

The antithesis passion-intellect is worked out on several levels in *L'Espoir*. On the most "sentimental "one, passion takes on its etymological significance (*passio:* to suffer), and ideas are shown as thoroughly inadequate in the face of physical anguish. Magnin knows it: "What is the weight of an idea when two legs have to be amputated?" Scali knows it too, after having seen works of art besmeared with human blood. "Paintings . . . lose their force."—"Art is weak in the face of suffering; unfortunately, no painting can stand up against a pool of blood."

It is, however, on the level of politics (much more so than on the level of sentiment or psychology) that the dialogue between thought and action is most cogently developed. This dialogue centers around three key problems: (1) *Being versus doing* (or political purity versus political efficacy). A whole section of the novel is entitled *"Etre et Faire."* Garcia knows that a revolution has to be "organized" even though the very discipline endangers the ideas of the revolution. Manuel, the apprentice-leader, learns first of all to be more concerned with what people *do* than with what they *are*. But not all agree (Hernandez, for instance) that the justice of the instrument depends exclusively upon the justice of the cause. (2) *Can an intellectual take sides?* To what extent does an intellectual ("the man of the nuance, of quality, of truth as such, of complexity") betray the values of culture by taking sides in what is necessarily a grossly oversimplified Manichaean concept of a world sharply split between total good and total evil? Alvear and Unamuno refuse the sacrifice and the betrayal. But is not this refusal an even worse spiritual treason? (3) *A nostalgia for a synthesis*, perhaps most clearly felt and expressed by Garcia. Asked by Scali what is man's noblest effort, Garcia answers: "To convert as wide a range of experience as possible into conscious thought."

These discussions and these formulas, when lifted out of their dynamic context of shell explosions and battle reports, may sound

[8] "Laclos" in *Tableaux de la littérature française, XVIIe, XVIIIe siècles*, pp. 417-428.

unbearably abstract. But if the novel is successful, it is precisely because Malraux has given these discussions life by placing them in the midst of action and moreover used the very structure of the novel to lend concrete meaning to the dialectics of thought and passion. And this is no doubt the reason for the multiplicity of characters which has so much disturbed some critics. For it becomes obvious, as the novel progresses, that Malraux alternates scenes of war with philosophical and political conversations, and that to do so, without falling into monotony, he had to vary the couples. There are altogether fifteen major conversations in *L'Espoir*, each one separated from the other by scenes of action, each one centering on a different topic and shuffling the participants: Ximenes–Puig, 25-28 (courage, anarchism, religion); Shade–Lopez, 34-39 (the new art); Ramos–Manuel, 64-67 (the function of the Spanish army); Manuel–Barca, 69-72 (the impossibility of neutrality); Garcia–Magnin, 81-87 (revolution and the problem of discipline); Magnin–Enrique, 112-115 (the Communist Party); Manuel–Alba, 122-125 (the problem of leadership and trust); Ximenes–Manuel, 125-128 (the problem of leadership); Garcia–Hernandez, 153-156 (the need to organize the Apocalypse); Hernandez–Moreno, 162-166 (experience of prison and awareness of the absurd); Garcia–Guernico, 221-227 (churches, faith, Christ and Spain); Scali–Alvear, 228-235 (man, war, art and the intellect); Garcia–Dr. Neuburg, 272-275 (Unamuno); Garcia–Scali, 281-286 (intellect versus action); Garcia–Magnin, 359-361 (communism and the Communist Party).[9]

Even a cursory inventory of these conversations reveals that they are more or less evenly distributed, that they are all of about the same length (on the average, four pages) and that there is considerable variety in the combination of participants (Garcia, with six conversations, seems to be the most talkative). Moreover, it is interesting to note that half of these conversations take place *in movement*. "Ximenes liked to talk as he walked." All the characters seem to share this taste for the somewhat nervous promenade-conversation-meditation when both body and mind are pressing forward. Ramos and Manuel are "walking on the embankment" on the Sierra front; Magnin and the Commissar Enrique are pacing up and down the Loyalist airfield; Manuel and Alba "walk among the rocks" in the direction of the Fascist lines; Ximenes and Manuel "walk toward

[9] Pages refer to the Gallimard edition, 1937.

San-Isidro"; Garcia and Hernandez deambulate through the death-infested streets of Toledo; Garcia and Guernico cross foggy unreal Madrid where groups of shadows seem to participate in a tragic nocturnal ballet; Garcia and Scali walk through the "black streets" in the direction of the Prado—so that, within the "conversational" pages, the contrast between action and thought continues to be felt, just as it is felt through the very structure of the novel. The book closes on a meditation-promenade among the shambles of a liberated town.[10] Neither the characters nor the reader are ever permitted to forget the world in which men hope, act and die. As they walk and talk, the intellectual heroes symbolically stumble against loose stones or are interrupted by the sound of a passing ambulance. Even when the abstract dialogues take place in an apparently secluded apartment, the outside world continues to impose its presence: cars shifting gears, the smell of a burning perfume factory, or—more ironically—the voice of a blind man singing the words of hope of the *Internationale*.

Dramatically indispensable, given the central themes of his work, the intellectual also appears as fully endowed with tragic attributes. Malraux's novels (perhaps this is true of all great novels) represent simultaneously an action and a commentary on that action, a sequence of tragic events and a meditation on tragedy. But the intellectual is not merely the commentator, he is also the victim. There is sometimes pathos in this sense of victimhood, in the meek acceptance of one's condemnation: "Guernico would not fight; he would be killed." Yet there is also a hard lucidity (the very kind of lucidity which impels the tragic hero to stare into the unadorned face of his destiny): the lucid inventory of despair. And there is also the more resilient feeling of justification which comes from the awareness that thought means suffering ("each one suffers because he thinks"), and from the Pascalian pride in this ability of man to *comprehend* and consequently to rise above the forces that crush him: the victory of being "the only animal who knows that he must die." But above all, there is a quest for wisdom, that wisdom which—as the chorus in Greek tragedy knows—comes only through suffering. All of Mal-

---

[10] Malraux's technique is not unique. James Joyce also likes to promenade his characters. Harry Levin writes: "It should be noted that the principal action of the *Portrait of the Artist*, whether in conversation or revery, is walking" (*James Joyce*, p. 43).

raux's heroes—he first of all—seem to discover and announce some fundamental truth. Like Dostoevski and Goya (on whom he wrote an admirable study), they speak the "obscure and pressing language" of modern prophets.[11]

¶ IV. Toward a synthesis

"THE BASIC PROBLEM lies in the conflict between two systems of thought: the one which questions man and the universe—the other which suppresses all questions by a series of actions." Malraux wrote these words, in 1933, in a letter to Gaëtan Picon.[12] But is the conflict really so hopeless, and has not Malraux himself attempted to resolve it? Does not all of European literature in the past twenty-five years, while keenly aware of precisely such a divorce, yearn for a new synthesis? Armand Hoog—at a time when most critics were baffled by Malraux's Gaullism (some even accused him of having surrendered to Fascist pessimism)—very perspicaciously affirmed that the author of Les Noyers de l'Altenburg was striving to bring out of chaos a new and *justified* man.[13] Sartre (in "Qu'est-ce que la littérature?") defines the new "metaphysical" literature not as a sterile discussion of abstract ideas, but as a dynamic effort to apprehend *from within* the human condition in its totality. And is it not highly revealing that Les Noyers de l'Altenburg, the first part of La Lutte avec l'Ange whose biblical title suggests a metaphysical struggle, ends on a note of total harmony between man and the universe?

Without going in search of metaphysical unity, it is clear that Malraux has become increasingly concerned with the unity of the individual. He admires Laclos for having created the *"personnage significatif,"* but he too has given life to what might be called *representative* characters—so representative indeed that they sometimes lose their individuality. (What do we really know of Kyo, Katow or Gracia?) Above all, he has striven to represent *complete* man. That is why he so repeatedly returns to the savage in man, and insists on erotic sadism and torture: not to analyze hidden complexes,

---

[11] *Saturne,* p. 113.
[12] *André Malraux,* p. 81.
[13] "André Malraux et la validité du monde," *La Nef,* March, 1947, pp. 121-126.

but because he is determined to leave nothing outside the human. Because he does not want it to be said: here man ceases to be man. In the preface to *Le Temps du mépris*, he accuses nineteenth-century literature of having sacrificed the will to create *"l'homme complet"* to a fanatical taste for subtle psychological differences.

The unity of the individual depends moreover on the very unity of culture. To prove—or to affirm—the interrelation, or even the interdependence, of all civilizations has been one of Malraux's most constant efforts in recent years. In a speech delivered in the Salle Pleyel, in March, 1948, he put it very firmly: "There are irreducible political conflicts: but it is absolutely false to say that cultural conflicts are irreducible by definition." [14] In this light, the entire *Noyers de l'Altenburg* is a refutation of Dr. Möllberg's pessimistic view that civilizations are separated by hermetically sealed cultural barriers, that a dialogue is as impossible between them as between the caterpillar and the butterfly and that consequently the concept of Man is devoid of any kind of permanent reality.

It is not surprising that Malraux has turned (or rather returned) to studies on art: they carry his arguments for a possible unity and synthesis more convincingly than his novels, although, in a sense, they may properly be considered as a logical sequel to his fictional work. Kama, the painter in *La Condition humaine*, already knows that art is a weapon against loneliness, a means of communion with life . . . but also with death. It is he, really, who seems to answer Reverend Smithson's question: what faith, other than Christianity, can account for the world's suffering or conquer death? More than any other of his novels, however, *Les Noyers de l'Altenburg* proclaims this faith in art. First of all the setting: the Chartres cathedral, an Alsatian abbey. But even more the conviction of the characters that salvation comes from art: "The first sculpture which represented a human face, simply a human face; liberated from the monsters . . . from death . . . from the gods. That day, man formed man of the dust of the ground." For Walter Berger, the first work of art was the first victory over the absurdity of the universe, the first and most lasting defiance of death. Through art, man escapes his condition ("our art seems to be a correction of the world"), and is delivered from space and time. Obviously, Alvear, on that gloomy

14 "Adresse aux intellectuels," *Le Cheval de Troie*, July, 1948, p. 977.

night in his Madrid apartment, was in possession of some important truth.

Faith, salvation—these words suggest the need for a religion. Will Malraux convert to Christianity? It is certain that he is aware of the synthesizing virtues of the Christian religion. In *La Tentation de l'Occident*, he has Ling remark that Christians reach out toward God by "ordering" violent emotions, and that Christianity teaches a communion with the world through an "exalted consciousness of its fundamental chaos." Vincent Berger believes that the *coup d'état* of Christianity is to have installed fate *within* man and that it is consequently necessary to *know* man in order to fight the demon. His entire work is an effort at reconciliation and unification. Clearly, if ever Malraux is converted, it will be out of a cerebral quest for a synthesis between passion and the intellect. In the meantime, however, his intellectual heroes remain the indispensable witnesses of man's only possible grandeur in a meaningless universe: they know that we ourselves must create the concepts and the images which can "negate our nothingness."

10

Sartre and the Existentialist Novel: The Intellectual as "Impossible" Hero

> *Un esprit négatif, un intellectuel.*
> —Brunet in *La Mort dans l'Ame*

¶ 1. *The Sartrean climate*

THE FOLLOWING PASSAGE plunges the reader into a typical Sartrean atmosphere:

> Must become his buddy, Mathieu said to himself. No contact. 'Tellectual for life. Separated for all eternity. Texier would look him over with a calm contempt. "It's you, Delarue?" he would say. "The guy who uses them high-falutin' words?" Mathieu would feel that he was getting red all the way up to his eyebrows. My good intentions forever useless, he thought bitterly. He was *superfluous*.[1]

It does not matter that Sartre is not the author of these lines. A skillful pastiche not only reproduces the climate of the original, it constitutes an eloquent critical commentary. What Jean-Louis Curtis successfully points up in this amusing army scene is the technique of the interior monologue used to project a self-conscious consciousness into frustrating awareness of superfluity. The typical Sartrean character is the intellectual; his characteristic mood is one of shame and guilt.[2]

The presence of the intellectual is obviously useful in a fictional work which not merely evokes man's sense of loss and exile, but discusses it in abstract terms. Roquentin, in *La Nausée*, serves a func-

---

[1] Jean-Louis Curtis, *Haute-Ecole*, p. 210.

[2] Sartre's earliest fictional venture, which appeared in the short-lived student magazine *La Revue Sans Titre* (1923), already centers around pitiful intellectuals whose life is a fiasco. Gaillard and Laubré, the "professors" in *L'Ange du morbide* and in the unfinished *Jésus la Chouette, professeur de province,* possess many a trait that will be shared by Roquentin and Mathieu Delarue. (See Jean Gaulmier, "Quand Jean-Paul Sartre avait dix-huit ans . . . ," *Le Figaro Littéraire,* July 5, 1958, p. 5.)

tion which only an intellectual could fulfill. For *La Nausée*, a poetic fiction about the visceral experience of alienation and absurdity, is also an ascetic exercise in methodical doubt leading to the discovery that life is not justifiable, that existence is a scandal and that the absence of essence condemns man to freedom. The hero, sickened by the tasteless taste of living, keeps us in intellectual suspense as he slowly glides toward fear. The very hum of his brain suggests, hallucinatingly, the drama of thought that makes of him both a hero and a victim:

> I exist. I think that I exist . . . I do not want to think . . . I think that I do not want to think. I must not think that I don't want to think. For that too is a thought. Won't there ever be an end?

Or again:

> I am, I exist, I think therefore I am; I am because I think; why do I think? I no longer want to think; I am because I think that I do not want to be; I think that I . . . because . . . pouah!

This sense of disgust, this sense of terror even, becomes most intense during the almost mystic illumination, the ecstasy of horror which, in the public garden scene, reveals the gratuity and contingency of life. But it is significant that all these revelations, fully *lived*, are also intellectually *translated*. The sin of existence is perceived ontologically; but this basic experience is soon transmuted by the protagonist himself into philosophical conclusions formulated in typical philosophical language. "The discourse of a madman is absurd in relation to his situation but not in relation to his madness." "The world of explanations and of reasons is not the world of existence." "Existence is not necessity."

¶ II. *War on Humanism*

"*Sale intellectuel*," THINKS BRUNET. This unflattering opinion echoes throughout the novels and plays of Sartre. The intellectual fulfills a philosophical function; but he is also, from the very start, an object of sarcasm and animosity. The Autodidact, a spiritual child of Bouvard and Pécuchet, is cruelly exposed as a shabby, pathetically unintelligent sentimentalist. In *Les Mouches* the Tutor is a coward, a former slave proud of the skepticism à la Pangloss with which he looks down on the people of Argos. "You are a heap of dung," says Jupiter in an explosion of disgust. "You stink!"

The Autodidact and the Tutor are of course essentially comic figures; the same type of comic vision lies behind some of the most felicitous descriptions in *La Nausée:* the statue of Gustave Impétraz, the Chaplinesque choreography of hats during the Sunday promenade, the portraits of the *salauds* in the art gallery. But comic inventiveness does not explain the permanent hostile current. For even the "serious" intellectuals are presented in an unflattering light. Roquentin lives in selfish loneliness. "Their" Sunday—that of the humble employees as well as of the smug bourgeois—is not his Sunday! The public library and the café are his refuge, his hiding place from life. He has no ties: neither a home, nor wife, nor parents, nor children, nor friends. He no longer even has a mistress: his sexual activities are nothing more than an hygienic exercise.

Mathieu Delarue, despite his less theoretical situation, is also presented in a pejorative fashion. This self-styled "free" man is highly ineffectual in his relationships with others. "Neither fish nor fowl," is Lola's acrid comment. "He always makes people ill at ease." But this is not all. He abandons his mistress without having the courage to admit that this is what he wants to do. He gets involved in a hesitant flirtation with a young girl. He steals money, but even this he does half-heartedly. Politically, also, he does not seem to have grown up. This thirty-four-year-old professor of philosophy, who tries to live out in petty-bourgeois comfort an adolescent resolve "to be free," appears to others as an "irresponsible aging student" living in eternal parentheses. This guilt-ridden self-denouncer blames himself for not participating in the Spanish Civil War (one is of course not "free" to suffer for what one wants!), yet even in France he does not bother to vote. Throughout the novel, the reactions of the other characters as well as his own relentless self-accusations point up his flaws. Mathieu knows that he is never *"dans le coup,"* that he has never truly bitten into life, that he has in fact led a toothless existence, *"une vie édentée."* Even his indignation against himself is empty rhetoric. His self-accusations are a form of self-indulgence.

Behind this caricature of the intellectual lies a more general attack on the traditional values of Humanism. Through the Autodidact Sartre mocks a certain brand of conventionally sentimental ethics as well as a certain type of culture. This Self-taught Man is a *collector* of knowledge. His alphabetical approach to culture is symptomatic of an essential *indifference*. All appears equally interesting and equally valuable. The most exotic tribes dance a disordered choreography in his mind. They eat their aged fathers, commit incest, castrate themselves, pierce their lips. The Autodidact catalogues their customs just as he files away all other knowledge. But more irritating than this taste for inventories is the Autodidact's notion of anonymous brotherhood, the mildly lachrymose manner with which he refers to the concept of "Man." "There is man, sir; there is an aim. There is man." Roquentin, exasperated, recalls with distaste the even more eloquent Parisian "humanists" who pronounce magic formulas concerning the existence of "Man" with still greater talent. There is for instance Virgan:

> Virgan was unsurpassable. He would take off his glasses, as though to show himself in his nakedness, in his human flesh; he would stare at me with his moving eyes, with a heavy tired look as though to undress me in order to capture my human essence; and then he would murmur melodiously: "There is man, old chap, there is man," while pronouncing "There is" with a sort of clumsy power, as though his love for men, perpetually fresh and surprised, got entangled in its giant wings.

Roquentin evokes the various types of humanists he has known: the Liberal, the Communist, the Catholic, the Philosopher—those who love man as he is and those who love him as he ought to be, those who would save him with all his qualities and those who would save him against his own will. There can be no doubt: *La Nausée* is in part a satire on Humanism, and surprisingly also a caricature of the very notion of *engagement* which the Autodidact propounds with ludicrous pomposity.

This attack against the basic tenets and attitudes of Humanism is a permanent feature of Existentialist literature. When Perron, in *Les Mandarins*, remarks that Humanism is "laughable," he merely echoes what has become an underlying assumption. All through the forties a guerrilla war against Humanism was being waged. At a time when pacifism has been politically discredited, it is the incurable fuzziness of humanistic optimism that is brought to task. The figure of Philippe, the pacifist in *Le Sursis*, is in part the caricature of such ineffectual dreams. As Simone de Beauvoir reminds her readers in *Pyrrhus et Cinéas,* "one always has to work with some men *against* some others."

"False" culture—the kind taught by the Tutor in *Les Mouches*—is judged as particularly pernicious because of the impersonal values (or absence of values) such a culture implies. To count the number of steps on the temple at Ephesus, to caress stones and statues, to observe with supercilious curiosity the quaint mores of the natives, may be agreeable pastimes for a detached dilettante, but—as Orestes points out—such philosophical tourism has done sufficient harm already. The archeological data filling the mind of the Tutor are as *weightless* as the anthropological curiosities collected by the Auto-didact. The ruins of the past as well as the multiplicity of tribal customs are symbolic here of a moral exoticism, an attempted escape from the need to create values.

And with false culture goes false freedom. It is significant that the Tutor is a former slave who has retained a cowardly slave mentality. He can at best conceive a freedom-not-to-do, a negative freedom, but not the freedom of choice and action.[3] Similarly Mathieu Dela-rue, in *Les Chemins de la liberté,* is told by the other characters who are his witnesses that his life is one of missed opportunities, that he is avoiding risks, that he is "floating," "abstract" and "absent."

This false culture and false freedom further lead to a false sense of altitude. The typical Humanist is in a sense not unlike Erostrate, in *Le Mur,* whose favorite pastime is to stand near the window of his sixth-floor apartment and look down on people. The *"perspective plongeante"* reduces man in size and humiliates him. Erostrate laughs as he "bends over" the window ledge. The French word for bending or leaning over is *se pencher,* and Sartre plays with the double mean-ing of this word. For *se pencher* also means to examine with benign though distant solicitude (*"se pencher sur une question"*), and Sartre, in the editorial manifesto of *Les Temps Modernes,* vigorously de-nounced the kind of writer who claims that it is his obligation to *"se pencher"* on a social problem or a social group. (*"Il se penchait! Où était-il donc? En l'air?"*)

This cultural heritage of elegant and noncommittal "understand-ing" can lead to the most criminal aberrations. Sartre and Simone de

---

[3] Robert Champigny defines the Tutor's apparent freedom of mind as a "freedom-from." See his excellent chapter "Tragedy and Freedom" in *Stages on Sartre's Way.*

Beauvoir cannot find terms strong enough to denounce the kind of "broad view" of History which makes itself the accomplice and the legalizer of any *fait accompli*. The lover of historical studies, the intellectual tourist through time and space, witnesses the rise and fall of civilizations with aesthetic detachment. But it is also possible, as Simone de Beauvoir reminds us in *Pour une morale de l'ambiguïté*, to strike a tourist pose in relation to the here and now. Many "intellectuals" were thus tempted, during the Occupation, to remain "above" the events, while some others, undermined by the "intellectual disease called historicism," were led to justify and even to ratify the political crimes of their day, and thus quite logically became "collaborators" while indulging in a peculiarly refined form of escapism.[4]

If Humanism is, as Merleau-Ponty suggests, the religion of man as a natural species, the religion of "completed man" (*"la religion de l'homme achevé"*[5]), then only the smallest of distances separates the representative humanist from Sartre's *salaud*. For this humanist, like the patricians of Bouville, lives on inherited values which he treats with as much reverence and self-righteousness as the capitalist his acquired capital. The "spirit of seriousness" which Sartre and Simone de Beauvoir hate with equal intensity is nothing but this permanent belief that values *are* in the world, and that man only needs to pluck them like pretty flowers which providence placed in a garden for his delight. Good and bad, existing as an objective reality, thus could be learned from infallible paternal lips. The very outspoken father-hate in all of Sartre's work must be, in part, assessed in this light. It is with bitterness that Hugo recalls his father's complacent advice ("I too, in my own day, I belonged to a revolutionary group. . . . You'll get over it"). Adults, in the works of Sartre and Simone de Beauvoir, are shown at their most sickening as they talk down to children and pose as the depositories of wisdom. M. Darbédat in *La Chambre* and M. Fleurier in *L'Enfance d'un chef*—both of them secure in a world of values seemingly designed to justify and protect them—are the great practitioners of the patronizing tone. The presence of this type of father in the work of Sartre casts light on the implicit yearning of so many of his characters to be their own cause,

---

[4] See Sartre's important essay "Qu'est-ce qu'un collaborateur?," in *Situations III*, pp. 43-61.
[5] *Sens et non-sens*, p. 91.

their own foundation, to be self-possessed and in a sense self-born—
a yearning to which corresponds on the philosophical level (see
L'Etre et le Néant) man's urge to be his own beginning, *ens causa
sui*.[6]

Sartre thus levels his criticism not only at the smugness of tradi- ✕
tional Humanism, but at its hypocritical recourse to transcendent
authority in the form of dogmas inherited from the past. For in his
eyes the absolute is constantly being smuggled in through the back
door. Supposedly alien concepts are being stolen and surreptitiously
imported all the time. Sartre is of course not the only one to be
disturbed by this moral contraband. The 1930's, rudely jarred by
discordant notes, woke up to the awareness that humanistic optimism
is based on a misunderstanding or on a hoax. Summing up the new
insights gained in these bitter years, Pierre-Henri Simon convincingly shows, in *L'Esprit et l'Histoire*, that humanist thinking was
constantly forced to turn to transcendent values in order to save its
optimistic credo. It is no doubt in reaction to such philosophical
"cheating" that a character in *Le Diable et le Bon Dieu* proclaims as
an axiom that one can only love on this earth, and *against* God.

The intellectual hostility to Humanism ironically also implies a
critique of the intellectual *qua* intellectual. Even though he be a
declared enemy of the Darbédats of this world, the intellectual can
also be guilty of the solemn *esprit de sérieux*. Two contradictory
and equally powerful temptations assail him. On the one hand, he
chronically thirsts for the absolute. The murderous action of Erostrate is only an extreme form of Hugo's dream of purity. Hugo
wants to kill for an abstraction. But as Hoederer reminds him, this
monklike idea of action only brings about inhuman deeds ("You
don't like human beings, Hugo, you only like principles") and turns
out to be the intellectual's alibi for inaction. This temptation of the
inhuman absolute can be diagnosed in Hugo, as well as in Orestes
and Goetz. But the disease—Sartre seems to treat it as such—becomes
progressively worse. Francis Jeanson quite rightly points to this evolution: Orestes needs the entire city of Argos as witness; but Hugo is
concerned with abstract humanity and Goetz is satisfied with noth-

---

[6] Kenneth Douglas ("Sartre and the Self-inflicted Wound," *Yale French
Studies*, No. 9, pp. 123-131) brilliantly demonstrates how this dream of reach-
ing self-identity clashes with the desire to remain sufficiently separate from
this self, and conscious of it.

ing short of the "most absolute" glance of God.[7] A progression which logically culminates in a clash with a hypothetical supreme divinity and in the mad dream of replacing him.

The other temptation of the intellectual is that of self-indulgent soul-searchings which constitute another, and subtler, form of de-solidarization. For narcissism, even of a cerebral type, is a way of reducing the other to the role of mirror, a way of negating the very witness. Sartre repeatedly suggests that meditation, deliberation and analysis are perfidious forms of separatism. In *L'Etre et le Néant* he goes so far as to qualify deliberation as always dishonest (*"la délibération est toujours truquée"*—p. 527). Elsewhere, he calls for the death of the analytic spirit because it has outlived its "cultural" function, and now only serves to disturb the revolutionary consciousness and to isolate men.

¶ III. *Self-hatred*

WHAT BEGAN AS A SEEMINGLY OBJECTIVE critique of Humanism turns out to be an attack directed by the intellectual against himself. This self-accusing bias reveals itself fully in Sartre's most developed fictional character, Mathieu Delarue. Despite endearing traits (he is friendly, open, honest—even tender at times) Mathieu is not only *shown* to us in a cruel light, but *seen* in a cruel light by the other characters, above all by himself. He inspects himself through the eyes of Ivich, and finds himself "horrible." But it is a welcome horror: he derives satisfaction from this indirect self-contempt. Mathieu is "pleased" to hear the unpleasant truths Brunet has to tell him. He even asks for them ("I would like you to tell me what you think"). Similarly, he experiences a "belligerent" need to hear his brother's opinions.

The Sartrean intellectual wants to be judged. Like Stendhal's characters who know that the eye cannot see itself, he is forever in search of a witness-judge. Only he is far more determined to find the most unflattering image of himself. Sartre generously satisfies this thirst for condemnation. At the very beginning of *L'Âge de raison*, we learn that Marcelle is Mathieu's *lucidity:* "his companion, his adviser, his judge." But she is not his only judge. Mathieu is literally encircled by judges. Structurally, the novel presents itself as a series

[7] *Sartre par lui-même*, p. 57.

of scenes or interviews during which Mathieu is exposed to hostile judgments. There is Ivich, a capricious, petulant girl who belongs to that curious Existentialist type (other versions are Xavière in *L'Invitée* and Nadine in *Les Mandarins*) whose function seems to be to complicate life and tell unpleasant truths. She nettles Mathieu into an awareness of his intellectual comfort, pedestrian Sunday excursions into art, and bureaucratic security. There is Jacques, his brother, who points out the inconsistencies of his petty-bourgeois rebellion against a background which he is ashamed of, but too cowardly to repudiate ("Your life is a perpetual compromise"). There is his old friend Brunet, who found salvation in political action and who, jokingly (but he means it!), calls Mathieu a *social-traître* living in shabby loneliness, deluded by false freedom and a critical intelligence that provides him with an alibi for irresponsibility. Even absent crowds pass judgment on him. He imagines that he can hear the survivors of the Valencia bombings mutter: *salaud*. Later, in *La Mort dans l'âme*, such group feelings will become a reality. Longin, a fellow soldier, explains to Mathieu with plebeian candor that the entire company dislikes him ("Even when you get drunk, it's not like us"). Conversely, the group itself (of which the intellectual is the most lucid member) can be condemned from the outside. In what amounts to a verbal orgy of judgment and condemnation, the defeated soldiers are "judged, measured, explained, accused, excused, condemned, imprisoned" by the imagined collective eye of France, the already indifferent stare of History focused on dead people and dead events.

This perpetual presence of the other as judging and invading consciousness is clearly bound up with Sartre's philosophic views. "It's always interesting to hear someone explain how he sees you," thinks Boris. Interesting? Unavoidable, Sartre would suggest. For we are surrounded by mirrors, walled in by contradictory images of ourselves. Repeatedly, Sartre describes this awareness of the other's consciousness that accompanies his characters when they are seemingly most alone with themselves. Mathieu, walking in the street, suddenly stops—transfixed. "He was not alone; Marcelle had not let him go. She was thinking of him. She was thinking: dirty bastard. . . . The consciousness of Marcelle remained somewhere out there. . . . It was unbearable to be thus judged, hated. . . ." Or this other street scene: "Behind him, in a green room, a little consciousness filled with hate was rejecting him. . . ." The consciousness of the other hangs fluttering, like a permanent threat, over the head of the protagonist. "Above his life, a pure consciousness began to hover . . . it hovered and watched the false bohemian, the petty bourgeois clinging to his comfort, this failure of an intellectual, this abstract dreamer in the midst of his flaccid life." It is in fact the other who decides what Mathieu is. "Brunet has decided: he thinks I am a bastard. Jacques also. They have all decided that I am a bastard. Poor Mathieu, he's finished, he's a bastard. And what can I do against them all?" This helplessness points to the ambiguous and tragic nature of the Sartrean *pour-autrui*. For the awareness that others have of oneself is not only a hard fact and a desired mirror, but a trap, a form of imprisonment and even a form of death. "*L'enfer c'est les autres,*" concludes a character in *Huis-clos.*

But this hell is also a self-willed hell. The deprecation by the other turns out to be a technique for self-deprecation. Mathieu accepts being a "bastard" in the eyes of his witnesses because he is ready to accept his own hell. The Sartrean hero is alone with his image. His dialogue is self-directed. Roquentin's observation ("With the Auto-didact one is two only in appearance") applies to every Sartrean character. His is a loneliness shared with himself, a perverted form of mental narcissism which impels him to search for his most unflattering image. The many "couples" in Sartre's work (Roquentin-Autodidact; Orestes-Tutor; Hugo-Hoederer; Mathieu-Brunet) are symptomatic. They suggest the extent to which the Sartrean intellectual needs the other in order to feel the contempt for himself he *wants* to feel. The other exists also as pretext and confirmation.

Mathieu's self-denunciation is aimed primarily against his "hobby" of freedom, his private pact, his connivance with himself which permits him to cultivate, in his secret little garden, an anesthetized happiness and dreams of individual salvation. Obliquely, it is his own illusion of liberty he ridicules through his judges. The critique thus involves the basic philosophic themes of the novel. What is questioned is the fundamental ideal of the Sartrean intellectual: "To be free. To be the cause of oneself. To be able to say: I am because I want to be. To be my own beginning." But the words, as Mathieu realizes, are pompous and empty.

Self-condemnation leads to true orgies of shame. Mathieu seems to collect reasons, specific as well as vague, for feeling guilty: his remoteness and cozy non-involvement, his shame of being afraid ("*j'ai eu les foies*") and shame of a non-tragic existence, and, to top it all, his hypocrisy. For he knows that he would not want things to change. Shame is indeed the leitmotif as well as the key word in Mathieu's mode of living. For him, the "sin of existing" (described by Roquentin in *La Nausée*) is a permanent reality. His stealthy visits to Marcelle's room and his equally furtive departures (slipping noiselessly through the half-open door, sliding by with his shoes in his hands) are symbolic gestures. At every point, he feels "vaguely guilty." And "vaguely" has, in this context, an all-pervasive meaning. When Brunet, in *La Mort dans l'âme*, also begins to feel "vaguely guilty," Sartre explains: "Guilty of being alone, guilty of thinking and living. Guilty of not being dead."

"He was ready for every remorse"—a remark in *Le Sursis* which could be an epigraph for the entire *Chemins de la liberté*. On the very first page of the trilogy, remorse presents itself in the form of a drunken beggar who, out of gratitude for Mathieu's generosity, gives him a token present: a stamp from a letter mailed in Madrid. The meaning is quite clear. The stamp and the letter remind the beggar and Mathieu of a war in which they have both chosen not to participate, and thus establish between them a complicity of guilt. As the novel progresses, Mathieu feels increasingly haunted by the image of the beggar with his stamp, until this memory simply merges with a permanent, debilitating feeling of shame. The image of Spain itself is ultimately also just another symbolic reminder of his non-commitment and superfluity: he is not "*dans le coup.*"

The beggar is a symbol of shame in still another sense. His very presence as he accosts Mathieu places the latter—whether he chooses to give or not to give—in a position of false superiority. It is no coincidence that Sartre introduces this figure on the first page of his novel. For this beggar-motif will run through the entire work. Mathieu "gives" to the beggar (a way of getting rid of him), he protects him from a policeman (thus assuming a "superior" role) and finally denies him solidarity by refusing to have a drink with him. This refusal of the proffered drink foreshadows Mathieu's refusal, in *La Mort dans l'âme*, to get drunk with his fellow soldiers. Only here the sense of shame becomes explicit. ("He was ashamed: who gave me the right to be so severe?") He knows that his refusal to share in their drunkenness is also a refusal to share in their misery.

The loathsome pan filled with wine disgusts him, but at the same time he blames himself for feeling such disgust. He is "ashamed" of the sense of superiority which, against his desire, this refusal bestows upon him: "Who am I to refuse to drink when my buddies are drunk?" But even this will not appease the demon of shame. Detecting pride in his very contrition, Mathieu denounces his self-accusations as a particularly refined way of opting out. "Indulgent for everybody, severe for myself: another ruse of pride."

¶ iv. *Collective guilt, or the blood of others*

IT IS PARTLY BY SUCH DEVIOUS, involuted roads that the Sartrean hero comes to view *collective* guilt as a road to personal salvation. A basic paradox underlies his itinerary. The *others* appear simultaneously as a *judging* consciousness and as a *guilty* group with which the private guilt is invited to merge. Mathieu, in *La Mort dans l'âme*, discovers a fresh sense of release as he assumes the weight of the collective shame of defeat. "It was a heavy group shame. It was not at all unpleasant." Already in *L'Age de raison*, he half hopes that the impending personal tragedy will merge with an imminent collective disaster:

> "It'll end badly," Mathieu thought. He didn't quite know what would end badly: this stormy day, this business of abortion, his affair with Marcelle? No, it was something vaguer: his life, Europe, this insipid and sinister peace.

Orestes' desire to win the name of "guilt stealer" should be assessed in this light. In his case, also, the attitude remains ambiguous. For Orestes envies the very crowds for whom he feels contempt. He feels this contempt for their diseased sense of shame ("Forgive us for living while you are dead"). But what he envies them is the sense of belonging to a particular community, manifested in this morbid way. The people of Argos love their disease and do not care to be cured. Orestes dreams of curing them by taking upon himself the guilt of the fly-infested city. He knows that he must commit a crime in order really to "exist" in the community. But he also knows that it is not the crime that attracts him, but the possibility of genuinely exerting his freedom by committing an irrevocable act. This explains, no doubt, why Orestes leaves his city when he becomes its king. Yet there remains the uneasy feeling that, at the moment he seems most concerned with a collective destiny, the Sartrean intellectual is in reality most taken with his own. Sartre prefers always to present involvement as a *fact*. The cause, the human motivations remain elusive. Is solidarity the attempt to attain a social solution (as an aloof Humanism demonstrably failed to be)—or is it only a compulsion, a private therapy?

Le Sang des autres ("The Blood of Others") is not merely the title of one of Simone de Beauvoir's most significant works; it is a permanent dramatic theme with the writers of the Existentialist generation. Man is condemned to be free, Sartre declared in *L'Etre et le Néant*. But this freedom implies man's obligation to carry the weight of the entire world on his shoulders. "He is responsible for the world." [8] Any event is *his* event, any war is *his* war. One of Brice Parain's characters puts it tersely: "The truth is that everything that happens is our fault." [9] Sartre himself tried to give this notion an aesthetic equivalent; hence the technique of dramatic simultaneity in *Le Sursis*. But it is Simone de Beauvoir who gave this theme its neatest formulation. In her essay, *Pyrrhus et Cinéas*, she explicitly states that only through the myth of solidarity could Humanity take on reality. Man needs the *other* (the child needs approval as much as, if not more than his toys); conversely, the World as a concept can exist only if Candide extends the boundaries of his garden beyond the limits of his private world. Those only are his brothers for whom he can cry. Thoughts such as these are not merely an intellectual pose, they correspond to certain forms of the imagination. Simone de Beauvoir recalls the emotion with which she learned that Simone Weil, then a fellow student at the Sorbonne, had broken down in sobs when told about the famine in China. "I envied a heart that could beat across the entire world." [10]

Her novel, *Le Sang des autres* (see Appendix C), communicates this anguish, or thirst for anguish, with full impact. But it also conveys a series of ambiguities that lead to the tragic impasse in which the Existentialist intellectual hero remains trapped. For the doctrine of global responsibility implied in the epigraph from Dostoevski ("Everybody is responsible to everybody for everything") presents

[8] *L'Etre et le Néant*, p. 639.
[9] *La Mort de Jean Madec*, p. 209.
[10] *Mémoires d'une jeune fille rangée*, p. 237.

itself on one level as the only possible answer to the "curse of existing," that lurking remorse which assails Jean Blomart. But neither communion through group action, nor the exalted awareness that it is man who creates values, can cure Blomart of his sense of alienation or cleanse him of his guilt. The "fault of being another" becomes the *curse* of being another. He discovers that no matter how deeply he involves others in his life, or his life in theirs, he will forever remain separated from them. His escape from solipsism only leads back to loneliness. But his "passion" (Simone de Beauvoir uses the word in its etymological meaning, "suffering") has not been useless. Though he remains his own prisoner, he has learned to bear this burden with courage, and to find in this courage his only possible freedom.

This tragic and paradoxical loneliness of Existentialist freedom (paradoxical, because it leads to *engagement*, yet finds no cure in it) has been summed up by Sartre in *L'Etre et le Néant* (p. 641): "I carry all by myself the weight of the world without there being anything or anyone that can lighten the burden." But is the burden desired or inflicted? This too remains ambiguous. The Sartrean obsession with the idea of shared suffering no doubt also betrays a form of psychological "exoticism": the desire to break through the walled-in consciousness. Even pain seems more tolerable than the stale, insipid awareness of the self—this *fadeur* which is the tasteless taste of ourselves and which accompanies us like an incipient anxiety. But the breakthrough is not feasible. The "blood of others" remains a psychological obsession. The intellectual hero is left struggling with himself.

¶ v. *The mirror and the knife*

THROWN BACK WITHIN HIS OWN LIMITS, Sartre's intellectual knows the full insipidity of his existence. For *existence*, he discovers, is precisely this: to be one's own taste, to drink oneself without thirst. He feels walled in, surrounded, isolated and rejected. *Le Mur, La Chambre, Intimité, Huis-Clos*—so many of Sartre's titles betray metaphorically the feeling of alienation within a prison, an exile within oneself. Mathieu sees himself "surrounded" by his own life. Lucidity only serves to immobilize him in this confinement. The more sharply he perceives the clash between his view of himself and the mirror-perspective of others, the more inescapably he locks himself up in his own consciousness, living out his "latent solitude" to the point of impossibility.[11]

The search for an exit carries its own paradox: one cannot break through a mirror. Sartre's characters are in need of the mirror, but they also live in dread of it. The "I" and the "other" remain locked in a hopeless, unresolved choreography. More powerful even than the desire to be seen is the fear of the condemning glance, the terror of the intruding stare. Yet this is no Stendhalian game of hide and seek. A Fabrice experiences keen pleasure on top of the Blanès tower because he can see without being seen. His poetic excitement is unquestionably bound up with a characteristic fear of self-revelation. Mathieu, on top of the church tower, also can see the German soldiers without himself being detected. But Mathieu's action leads, symbolically, not to beauty, or memory, but to death.

Daniel Sereno, in *La Mort dans l'âme*, rejoices over the arrival of the German army. In the enemy soldiers he sees angels of hatred come to exterminate his former judges. Although in need of being judged, he dreams of the death of his witnesses because he lived in mortal fear of the mirror they hold up to him. All of Sartre's characters are, to a varying degree, aware of this danger. Boris himself, so curious about his own image, is paralyzed by Lola's side glance ("Boris could not have made the least movement"). Philippe, in *Le Sursis*, feels so permanently "judged" he cannot grow into an adult and turns to self-destruction. Mathieu cannot bring himself to say good-by to Ivich ("So long as he remained with her, he would prevent her from thinking") because he imagines her thoughts of him, and feels himself vulnerable, transparent, annihilated. Significantly, the first time the idea of death becomes a shuddering reality for him is when, just before the battle, he imagines his corpse *seen* by a thousand alien eyes. Nearly religious in intensity, this "*horreur sacrée*" is the awareness that the human being is transformed into an object which no longer can escape or defend itself. The glance of the other thus becomes an instrument of capture and destruction. "Every consciousness seeks the death of another"—this Hegelian pronouncement is the epigraph to Simone de Beauvoir's *L'Invitée*.

No less dangerous, no less destructive is the other temptation of

---

[11] Sartre has always been drawn to *impossible* situations. See the many variations on this theme in *Saint-Genet, comédien et martyr*. Francis Jeanson quite rightly insists on the importance of this text in his *Sartre par lui-même*.

the Sartrean hero: the mirror of his own intelligence, the image-producing distance between his consciousness and himself as object. Sartre in his philosophical writings insists on this ontological distance which makes of man a permanently self-posed problem. That is no doubt the symbolic meaning of the photographs of himself which Hugo, the young intellectual, carries in his suitcase. They represent the shameful burden of his past (Hugo is haunted by his bourgeois childhood that knew no hunger); but they are also a symbol of a narcissistic lucidity and an inability to shake off his bourgeois past. Lucidity is the particular curse of the Sartrean intellectual. The action of *L'Age de raison* takes place at the height of summer. Mathieu walks beneath a "lucid sky." He is "dazzled by the light." He is forced to blink. He suffers from a splitting headache.

This eye of self allows the sufferer no respite. "He thinks everything with his head," is the naïvely ironic comment of one of Mathieu's fellow soldiers. A similarly sarcastic remark is made by Hoederer in *Les Mains sales:* "An intellectual! That's got to think!" Hugo himself bemoans this perpetual cerebration ("There are too many thoughts in my head" . . . "It's chattering in there all the time"). He envies Slick, the tough guy, "because he is strong and does not think." Garcin in *Huis-Clos* also complains of this torture by the mind. "Rather a hundred scorpions, the fire of vitriol, than this mental anguish . . ."

"Except perhaps when asleep, Sartre thinks all the time." This is how a mutual friend at school first described Sartre to Simone de Beauvoir.[12] It would seem that later, in his novels, Sartre generously endowed his intellectuals with this mania of permanent cerebration. They not only think all the time, they watch themselves think. Their thoughts are mirrors, too, in a game of infinitely multiplied reflections which turns into an exercise in torture. "I do not want to think. I think that I do not want to think. I must not think that I do not want to think. That too is a thought." Roquentin is trapped by himself, by a built-in infernal machine with infinitely mobile refractions. One of the meanings of *nausée* is no doubt the sickening lassitude which invades the consciousness as it becomes aware that there is no escape from itself. One never reaches the end of the impasse, and one can never return. The cruel game goes on. (*"On n'en finira donc jamais?"*) Sicklied o'er with the pale cast of thought . . . The

12 *Mémoires d'une jeune fille rangée*, p. 337.

shadow of Hamlet still hovers over the Sartrean *mal du siècle*. Mathieu reminds himself ironically that he is a "thinking reed." But there is nothing noble, nothing Pascalian about this reed. There is only a feeling of fear, disgust and horror. He sees himself think: "He was horrified by himself." "I must always think about everything that happens to me." No abandon, no letting-oneself-go—but always this compulsive, quasi-automatic throbbing of the brain which leads to a feeling of *rottenness* and obscene self-exposure:

> . . . all his thoughts were contaminated from their very birth. Suddenly, Mathieu opened himself like a wound; he saw all of himself wide open: thoughts, thoughts on thoughts, thoughts on thoughts of thoughts, he was transparent and rotten ad infinitum.

This obsession with the self, this hellish game with consciousness explain in part why Sartre so insistently calls for the death of a literature of analysis. He and his characters know from experience that analysis is a form of separatism, a form of self-imprisonment from which there is no escape. Even suicide is but a histrionic pose, an *attempted* suicide. As a boy, Mathieu "played at making himself cease to exist." In the novel, he contemplates his own death in the murky waters of the Seine, and toys with suicide the way all of Europe toys with its own destruction. But he postpones the absolute gesture, as Europe also prefers to postpone its fate, preferring to live in shame.

The other attempt at evasion is self-punishment. The judgment by the witness, preferably the cruelest possible, is prized as an instrument of self-condemnation. But this thirst after expiation remains doomed to frustration. The "other" is not so pliable to our needs. Daniel Sereno, unquestionably a caricature of this type of duplicity, seeks to make another human being the unknowing accomplice of an essentially onanistic moral flagellation. But ironically, Daniel never succeeds in being loathed as he longs to be loathed. Nor does he succeed in the more active form of self-punishment: castration. He cannot drown his cats (an act which would have the full value of self-mutilation) any more than he can use his razor blade for anything but a fastidious morning shave.

Other characters in Sartre's novels appear on the surface to be more successful in inflicting a wound on themselves. Roquentin, Mathieu, Ivich, Goetz, at one time or another, all pierce their hands in a painful, symbolic gesture. Theirs is, however, not a simple, dandyish self-discipline à la Lafcadio or a form of Stendhalian *"morale de soi à soi."* Kenneth Douglas, in an article on the self-inflicted stigmata in Sartre's work, very rightly insists on the metaphysical implications of this knife-thrust into the palm.[13] Roquentin, in *La Nausée*, with his search for "adventure," first of all in his own life and then in the life of an historical personage, obviously attempts to achieve self-identity by *nihilizing* his own contingency. He wants, godlike, to owe himself to no one but himself. But he can neither stop "existence" (which is contingency), nor alter objects and the relations between them. His quest is in advance doomed to failure. As for Ivich and Mathieu, who indulge in the hand-piercing game as a form of mutual defiance during a drunken moment in a night club, they may be in quest of the "perfect moment," a sort of ecstatic solitary death *à deux*, but they too are left frustrated. The ecstasy is short-lived. In spite of the mirror they provide each other, they are both thrown back on themselves. Mathieu later even feels shame at the memory of this gashing of his hand. The self-inflicted wounds, as Douglas puts it, remain "sterile and childish simulacra of union with another or with oneself. . . ." Mirror and knife provide no salvation from paralyzing ambiguities.

¶ VI. *The "impossible" tragedy*

MAN, ACCORDING TO MALRAUX, must rediscover the harmony between the thinker and his thought. No such hope seems held forth by the work of Sartre. All points instead to irremediable inner discord. The attack by the intellectual turns out to be an attack *against* the intellectual. The fascination becomes a revulsion. The reader himself is caught in dialectical ambiguities, where love and the desire to be hated, self-accusation and self-indulgence are strangely interdependent, and even interchangeable. In his relations with the "others," the Sartrean hero finds himself imprisoned in a vicious circle. The need for a witness is bound up with the terror of the judging eye. But part of the witness' prestige is that he is guilty also. Eager to be absolved, yet equally eager to participate in a community of shame, the Sartrean intellectual remains a prisoner surrounded by mirrors he himself uses as welcome instruments of

[13] Sartre and the Self-inflicted Wound," *op. cit.*

self-torture. (One is reminded of Baudelaire's biting lucidity, as expressed in the poem "L'Héautontimorouménos.") Thought and action remain irreducibly at odds. Hugo must choose between the typewriter or the revolver. These are crude symbols, but they adequately represent some of the equivocal aspects of Sartre's art. The very resolution to discard a worn-out literature of analysis for a new literature of "situations" is fraught with ironic contradictions. For what are these "situations" if not, as Sartre himself puts it, "freedoms caught in a trap" ("each situation is a mousetrap, there are walls everywhere" [14])—in other words, each individual's imprisonment in his inalienable subjectivity? Thus Sartrean *freedom* remains thoroughly ambivalent. "The folk of Argos are my folk. I must open their eyes," is Orestes' proclamation of his responsibility to the "others." Yet only a few minutes later, his primary responsibility, it would appear, is toward himself. "Beyond the rivers and the mountains are an Orestes and an Electra waiting for us. We must set out in patient search of them." Sartre's hero is a king without a kingdom.

He is also, in a sense, an actor in search of a role. Hugo's Resistance pseudonym "Raskolnikov" symbolizes this wish for impersonation (The name "Raskolnikov" points moreover, in Russian, to a divided personality.) His fellow party members consider him an undisciplined anarchist intent on "assuming poses." His wife (their very marriage is an exercise in play-acting) accuses him of play-acting the part of "revolutionary." Whether he types or plans to kill, Hugo seems—against his own will—to be indulging in a game. "To be or not to be"—his drunken words as he nearly betrays his mission further complicate the play-acting, creating the illusion of a play within the play ("All I tell you is play-acting. . . . And this too is play-acting"). Hugo, like all the adolescent characters in Sartre's work, is living in what Sartre calls the "age of fakery," the age of artifice, of inauthenticity—an age of sinister levity.[15] But evidently the notion of *adolescence* in the Sartrean context refers not so much to a chronological period of life as to a permanent state of factitiousness.

In contrast to this histrionic lightness of adolescence, the Sartrean

---

[14] "Qu'est-ce que la littérature?," *Situations II*, pp. 55-330.
[15] For a discussion of the adolescent love for play-acting, see Sartre's review of *La Conspiration* by Paul Nizan (*Nouvelle Revue Française*, November 1, 1938, pp. 842-845).

intellectual feels the urge to take on weight, density—to become *solid*. Hugo and Jessica admire the dense "reality" of Hoederer. Brunet appears to Mathieu "enormous" and "solid." This search for solidity is one of the main themes of *Les Mouches*. Orestes wishes to say farewell to the *lightness* that was his. He envies the "solid passions" of the guilty city. He explains to Electra that he must take on his shoulders the burden of a "heavy crime." Weight and solidity are for him a means of freeing himself from the facti- tiousness of his false culture, just as for Mathieu they are a means of outgrowing his false notions of freedom.

Francis Jeanson, who wrote some of the most penetrating pages on this motif of solidity, implies that the Sartrean quest for mas- siveness marks a reaction against the corrosive power of thought. Lightness would thus be symbolic of reflection. Such an interpre- tation seems debatable: it would make of Sartre's work a nearly exclusive critique of intelligence. But Jeanson is certainly right in suggesting that the primary problem for an Orestes is not how to liberate other men, but how to force them to take him seriously —and, to begin with, how to take himself seriously, how to cease being an adolescent and become a man. Hoederer's and Brunet's solidity is that of full manhood. The adolescent admiration for such solidity outside their family is clearly a substitute for the father image against which they have rebelled.

But this rebellion against the father once more closes the circle of ambiguities. "I am not my father's son," proclaims Hugo. But this proud affirmation of bastardy (are there echoes here of Sten- dhal and Gide?) condemns the Sartrean hero to renewed play- acting in search of authenticity. The "bastard" in search of solid passions remains a histrion at heart. On this curious identity between the "bastard," the "play-actor" and the "intellectual," Francis Jean- son has penned some of the most challenging pages in all of Sartre criticism. His *Sartre par lui-même* should be in every reader's hands. It is not only an exciting commentary, but a living example of the Existentialist method in criticism (with its qualities and flaws), and as such deserves to be analyzed in its own right. One may question the over-ingeniousness of some of Jeanson's remarks (he sees Sartre simultaneously as a *philosophe de la comédie* and a *comédien de la philosophie*), but it is impossible not to admire his masterful dialectical exposition. The "bastard," an eternal pariah, is indeed condemned to lucidity just as the intellectual is, by nature as well as by his function, condemned to alienation. *"La bâtardise rend lucide. . . ."* Conversely, lucidity makes the "bastard": intelligence betrays action. "The bastard-intellectual is a traitor: he betrays action in the name of thought." [16]

It is not surprising that these paralyzing ambiguities carry over into the realm of political commitment. Here too, Sartre and his heroes live out a perpetual contradiction, a basic *impossibility*. "Sartre proposes nothing; he plays," complains Pierre Naville who accuses Sartre of exploiting politics as an emotional and intellectual aphrodisiac, as a pretext to philosophize.[17] The game Naville denounces—the literary exploitation of Marxism—has been denounced at great length by Raymond Aron in *L'Opium des intellectuels*. But there is more to this game than parasitism. The game or "play-acting" of politics involves the basic urge to *become another*. "By means of action one becomes another, one tears oneself away from oneself, one changes oneself by changing the world." [18] Sartre's sympathy for the intellectual pariah is not simply the desire "not to miss anything of his own time" which he describes in the introductory manifesto of *Les Temps Modernes;* it is a symptom of his solipsistic malady which goads him on to seek political action (or dream of it!) as an ethical therapy. In his "Matérialisme et Révolution," he diagnoses the intellectual's conversion to Marxism in this very light: "One enters it like Holy Orders: I would define it as the subjectivity of those ashamed of their subjectivity." [19]

But there is a price to pay for such lucidity. While throwing himself generously into a given camp, the Sartrean intellectual is never permitted to forget that it is *himself* he is out to save, that the game of becoming another remains a self-centered enterprise, that the "hero" (an artist in quest of "privileged moments") is preoccupied with his own future funerals. He knows that action, for him, is an end in itself. He *uses* the tragedy of others.

This, more than any other single reason, explains why the Sartrean intellectuals (and for that matter, all the intellectuals in the Existentialist novel) are so permanently haunted by their futility in

---

[16] *Sartre par lui-même*, p. 61.
[17] Pierre Naville, "Les nouvelles mésaventures de J.-P. Sartre," *France-Observateur*, April 19, 1955, pp. 12-13.
[18] Preface to *Portrait de l'aventurier* by Roger Stéphane, p. 15.
[19] *Situations III*, p. 163.

politics. The political tragedy of their time finds them awake and aware, but secretly convinced that they have no mandate whatsoever. "An intellectual has no role to play," sadly concludes Dubreuilh in *Les Mandarins*. He and Perron are made "lucidly aware of their uselessness." "The French intellectuals are in an impasse," observes Scriassine. Sartre himself sums up the hopeless nature of the intellectual's commitment to political action: "I am forced to assume a mandate which no one assigned me. It is in this contradiction that I must live." [20] A voice without a mandate—we are back to the accusation hurled at the intellectual at the time of the Dreyfus Affair. Only this time, it is not invective coming from the enemy camp, but painful self-appraisal. Even in his function as militant writer, Sartre cannot escape a sense of impending failure. The surface optimism and the call for *praxis* in "Qu'est-ce que la littérature?," only thinly disguise the incipient awareness that the writer of good will is faced with an unavailable public—a *"public introuvable."*

Lucid as to the futility of his mandate, the Sartrean intellectual thus feels doomed, on the political plane also, to remain alone. The desire to transcend the barriers of his consciousness remains a *personal problem*. He must agree in advance, with those who are bound to reject him, that his eagerness to join them is a mere caprice, a luxury. In the midst of dedicated commitment, he is after "the exquisite possession of himself." [21] Yet, even though he knows that he, the intellectual-adventurer, is guilty of the "bourgeois" vices of egoism, pride and above all the cardinal sin of *mauvaise foi;* even though he knows that the intellectual-adventurer is wrong all along the line, the Sartrean hero enters the impasse with tragic honesty. "It's the adventurer I will follow into his solitude. He has lived until the end an *impossible* condition."

This *impossible* condition no doubt also marks the limits of Sartre's tragic vision. In this fictional world where guilt is all pervasive and no situation is fully honorable, there seems to be no room for the poetic exaltation of despair. Mathieu dreams of beautiful disasters, rebellion, suicide. But what he experiences in reality is a "modest and peaceful little misery" as reliable as his habits and his income. "There was no question of despair. On the contrary,

[20] *Sartre par lui-même*, p. 187.
[21] Preface to Roger Stéphane's *Portrait de l'aventurier*, p. 18.

it was rather comfortable." He cannot suffer for others, perhaps he cannot even suffer for himself. At best, he knows the anguish of *not being able to suffer*. His is the tragedy of a world in which traditional tragic values seem to have been exhausted, as the intellectual becomes a victim of his ascetic lucidity.

But on the other hand, this peculiar form of anguish is, according to Sartre, the only authentic tragic experience available to the intellectual. The *impossible* condition of his heroes points also to their incipient grandeur. Sartre would agree with Merleau-Ponty that the modern hero can no longer be Lucifer or Prometheus, that he must be "Man" who has intellectually and politically tasted of the fruit of confusion and failure.[22] Sartre's literary achievement is that he has apprehended, more keenly than has ever been done before, the difficulty of man's freedom and man's frailty in the face of this freedom. When Mathieu accepts death on the symbolic church tower, he seems to confirm the tragic nature of his *impossible* situation. "I decide that death was the secret meaning of my life, that I have lived to die. I die to bear witness to the impossibility of living. . . ."

In this peculiar tragic impasse (where life seems to carry its own condemnation), the Sartrean hero searches for no subterfuges, not even the escape through art so characteristic of the pessimistic works of the preceding generation. All illusions are banished as a form of dishonesty. Above all the illusion of happiness, the refuge of the smug. "I am not happy," says one of the characters in *La Mort dans l'âme*, "and I would be a swine if I tried to be happy while all my buddies are in prison or shot." This ascetic allegiance with the suffering of others ultimately leads to an ascetic self-denial that is not without dignity.

[22] *Sens et non-sens*, pp. 379-380.

11

The Fifties: The Anti-Intellectual Reaction

*Je donnerais tous les intellectuels de la fic-
tion contemporaine pour un seul grand personnage d'imbécile.*

—JEAN-LOUIS CURTIS

¶ 1. *The attacks*

Pourquoi des philosophes?—THE VERY INSOLENCE of this book title
is symptomatic of the anti-philosophical mood that prevailed among
young writers during the fifties. It is significant that Jean-François
Revel, the author of this aggressive essay, is himself an *agrégé* of
philosophy. France has experienced in the last ten years a metaphysical tedium, a growing impatience with abstract systems and
doctrinaire involvement. The much discussed *roman nouveau* is the
result, in part, of a widespread reaction against the intellectualist
attitudes that pervaded the novel during the thirties and forties.

This offensive against the philosophical and political novel is often
carried out in the best traditions of irreverent irony à la Stendhal.
"Here at last is a superficial writer!" proclaims Jean Grenier wel-
coming a new edition of Dumas' *Les Trois Mousquetaires*. Characters in contemporary fiction, he declares, can no longer drink a
glass of whisky or vodka without making definitive pronouncements
on life, death, destiny, freedom, Man and Nature.[1] Michel Déon,
in an imaginary letter of advice to a young writer on the make,
urges him to concoct a novel that will question the existence of God
and provoke in his reader a sense of metaphysical *nausea*.[2] In his
Baba, ou l'Existence, a parody of Voltaire's *Candide*, Jean Dutourd
mocks Existentialist literary fads: Monsieur Mélass, the philosophy

---

[1] Jean Grenier, "Alexandre Dumas," *Nouvelle Nouvelle Revue Française*,
August 1, 1957, pp. 330-332.
[2] Michel Déon, *Lettre à un jeune Rastignac*, pp. 18-19.

professor who teaches that man defines himself by existing, is the author of a novel entitled *La Colique*. But more violent reactions are also heard. Roger Ikor, himself a gifted novelist, demands that the writer purge himself of all "philosophical ideas." "What the devil! A novel is not a dissertation!" His *Mise au net* is a call to arms against the *"maniaques de la philosophie"* who have invaded and betrayed literature.

These are not isolated outbursts. The political disillusionment of the years that followed the Liberation, intestinal quarrels among the militant intellectuals, the resurgence of a dynamic group of young "rightist" literati, as well as an increasingly muddled world situation in which "taking sides" became more and more difficult —all account for the growing discredit of *engaged* literature and the return to a notion of "pure" fiction dedicated to telling a story with *brio* or to experimenting with new forms and new techniques. The death of Emmanuel Mounier[3] in 1950, followed in 1952 by the rupture of relations between Sartre and Camus after the publication of *L'Homme révolté*, truly marks the end of an era.

The anti-intellectual reaction of the fifties is of course not limited to the area of the novel. The success of a book such as Marcel Aymé's *Le Confort intellectuel* (1949) was due largely to the public's rejection of a whole generation of literati who posed as the indispensable "witnesses" of their tormented epoch and who, in the wake of Malraux's heroes, sought to convert the widest possible range of experience into conscious thought. But there are other reasons for this widespread hostility: the steady weakening of the non-Communist Left to which the intellectuals were traditionally loyal; the emergence of a group of writers whose intellectual, if not political, affinities are with the Right. This new "Rightist" intelligentsia resents the very word "intellectual," since in their view it conjures up an image of man as unvirile, atrophied, unartistic, and even unintelligent.[4] Dandyish and apolitical—frequently disciples of Laclos, Rétif and Stendhal seen in their own distorting mirror

---

[3] One of the most prominent Leftist Catholic intellectuals, Emmanuel Mounier was the main theoretician of *"Personnalisme."*

[4] Thierry-Maulnier for instance defines the intellectuals as vain men *"qui font profession d'intelligence."* In an article for *Le Figaro Littéraire* (November 26, 1955), he writes: *"On fait appel aux intellectuels pour se dispenser d'avoir affaire à l'intelligence."* ("The intellectuals are in demand so that one may avoid any contact with intelligence.")

—they are committed to the more elegant and individualistic notion of the "*homme de lettres.*"

But there are also more sober and more far-reaching critiques of the intellectuals. Many and varied are the voices that denounce with a genuine bitterness the intellectual leaders' inadequacy in the face of a menacing political situation. Although they avoid the kind of vituperation current at the time of the Dreyfus crisis, French intellectuals themselves show deep concern over their own function and destiny. Discussing the intellectuals' ambition to assume leadership in revolutionary politics, Henri Lefebvre concludes that it has been a complete fiasco. The intellectuals' true mission, according to him, is not direct political involvement, but the creation of cultural values.[5]

E. M. Cioran, as usual, is more somber. With prophetic gloom, he not only dismisses European intellectuals as thoroughly ineffectual cultural histrions (he compares them to the *Graeculi* of the Roman Empire), but sees them as a tired, frustrated group hesitating between the myth of Tolerance and the myth of Terror, and secretly in love with their own ruin.[6] There seems to be a common agreement that this mentality is symptomatic of a civilization now devitalized by its very intelligence, paralyzed by its lucidity and self-consciousness, and sapped by skepticism in spite of political "faiths." Even the intellectuals' liaison activities with different cultures are viewed as a form of moral abdication.[7]

The cultural historian might well be struck by the astonishing recurrence of typical anti-intellectual attitudes. Suspicion and hatred of the professional thinker would seem to be among the chronic diseases of the Western mind, one which, at regular intervals, flares up into an acute crisis. The Dreyfus case unquestionably brought

---

[5] Henri Lefebvre, "Vers un Romantisme révolutionnaire," *Nouvelle Nouvelle Revue Française*, October 1, 1957, pp. 644-672.

[6] "Sur une civilisation essoufflée," *Nouvelle Nouvelle Revue Française*, May 1, 1956, pp. 799-816.

[7] See Roger Ikor, *Mise au net*, pp. 63-64. It is interesting to note that in this liaison activity, particularly prevalent in periods of transition, Arnold Toynbee sees the true function of the intelligentsia. According to Toynbee (*A Study of History*, V, pp. 145-156) the intellectuals of a given country are the counterpart of the "transformer" that changes an electric current from one voltage to another; they are the "liaison officers" who have already learned the tricks of the impinging civilization. The essence of the intelligentsia's profession is thus mimesis.

about one of the most virulent attacks in recent history—at least until the advent of Fascism. But it is easy to see that the accusations (lack of proper authority, atrophied instincts, a poisonous arrogance and subversiveness) are routine charges which, most often, are repeated and embroidered upon by intellectuals themselves. Some of these betray deep misgivings about the scholar's potential threat to his own culture. Even Nietzsche warned that the man of learning, one of the most costly instruments that exists, must remain an *instrument*, that he is not an end in himself, but only a mirror, a reflection, which is powerless to offer dynamic values.[8] Similarly Paul Valéry—in *Monsieur Teste* he had compared Parisian intellectual circles to an inferno of demons frantically staring into paper mirrors—repeatedly deplored the disappearance of the Renaissance ideal of the complete man.[9]

¶ II. *New directions—new "theories"*

THE LITERARY HISTORIAN also is faced with a recurrent phenomenon: the oscillation of successive generations of writers between a literature of ideas and social responsibility, and a literature dedicated to its own autonomy. 1830 and 1850; 1880 and 1910; 1930 and 1950 —it would be tempting to write a history of French literature centered around these pivotal years. After the socially conscious Romantics, the art-for-art's-sakers; after the moral diagnosticians of France's ills, the seekers of aesthetic salvation; after the anguished "meta-practitioners" bent on not merely inheriting, but on changing the world, the pioneers of the non-figurative novel apparently determined to displace "Man" and his problems. This chronic swing of the pendulum is not limited to France. Thus R. W. B. Lewis, while fully aware that the two generations overlap, distinguishes, in *The Picaresque Saint*, the "artistic" generation of Joyce, Mann and Proust from the "human" generation of Silone, Camus, Faulkner, Moravia, Greene and Malraux.

There is no doubt that from a strictly literary point of view, 1950

---

[8] See in particular chapter VI ("We Scholars") in *Beyond Good and Evil*.

[9] See the rather muddled essay *Propos sur l'Intelligence* (1926), in which Valéry suggests that the notion of an *intelligentsia* is a foreign import, incompatible with the classical notion of the *honnête homme*. He recognizes its existence, but grudgingly, with a twist of the Cartesian formula: *"Cette espèce se plaint; donc elle existe."*

marks a reaction against the style, the tone and the preoccupations of this "human" generation. "Our search . . . brings us closer to the artist than to the traditional writer," observes Claude Mauriac, one of the practitioners of the *roman nouveau*.[10] "We try to convey a vision—both inner and outer—which resembles no other." The word "vision" must here be taken quite literally. Alain Robbe-Grillet, probably the most vociferous spokesman for this new generation of novelists, insists that the cinema has demonstrated the priority of the image over psychology and "meaning," and that the art of fiction, in order to renew itself, must also rely heavily on the "optical" adjective—the word that describes, measures, situates and defines.[11]

The excessively *experimental* nature of Robbe-Grillet's art, so markedly characterized by geometric patterns and by the solid presence of objects, is due perhaps to his scientific training (he is an agronomic engineer who also did research in biology and statistics). But this tendency to objectify the world, this avoidance of the godlike psychological, moral and metaphysical omniscience of the traditional novelist, also characterizes an entire generation of writers bent on evoking man's direct experience of a world that is bounded by his own horizon. *L'Ecole du Regard*—the School of the Glance—is the expression some critics have adopted. The extent to which these novelists diverge from their immediate forerunners becomes plain if one recalls that Malraux, for instance, considered the lack of emphasis on objects to be a crucial aspect of modern fiction. Recent literature, fiction as well as poetry (with Francis Ponge's *Le Parti pris des choses*), has on the other hand reaffirmed the prerogative of objects.

Despite this insistence on *thingification* and the "thusness" of experience, despite an avowed repudiation of what Robbe-Grillet scornfully calls "*les vieux mythes de la profondeur*" (the worn-out myths of "depth"), it is only fair to add that the *roman nouveau* is not altogether anti-intellectual. The practice and the theoretical

---

[10] "The 'New Novel' in France," *New York Times Book Review*, June 19, 1960. Claude Mauriac, who has analyzed new trends in fiction in *L'Alittérature contemporaine* (1958), is the author of the prize-winning *Le Dîner en ville* (1959).

[11] See in particular Robbe-Grillet's "manifesto," "Une voie pour le roman futur," *Nouvelle Nouvelle Revue Française*, July, 1956, pp. 77-84. For a general view of the new trends in fiction, see the special issues of *Esprit*, July-August, 1958, and *Yale French Studies*, No. 24, Summer, 1959.

pronouncements of these so-called "midnight novelists" show ascetic tendencies and cerebral preoccupations. Thus Nathalie Sarraute, in *L'Ere du soupçon* (1956), denounces the conventional protagonist as a concession to the reader's laziness, to his fear of estrangement. In fact, most of the practitioners of the anti-novel (Robbe-Grillet, Sarraute, Michel Butor, Samuel Beckett) are deeply concerned not only with experimentation (an undertaking comparable to scientific research), but with an adventurous inquiry into the very essence of the Novel. The "new" novel thus seeks its purpose within its own elaboration, calls itself into question and becomes a subversive speculation upon its own protean nature.

For yet another reason, it would be a mistake to view these new experiments in fiction as entirely non-philosophical. Even though, in subject matter, they sharply depart from the sometimes didactic "metaphysical" content of Existentialist literature, they also quite clearly carry Existentialist themes and techniques to their logical extreme. These fictional anti-fictions negate philosophy in a philosophical manner. The vision they try to convey is probably more purely phenomenological and ontological than anything Sartre and Simone de Beauvoir have succeeded in creating. Sartre's *La Nausée* is, in a way, the unacknowledged model. Its direct influence (together with that of Simenon's detective novels) is very marked—on Robbe-Grillet's *Les Gommes*, for instance, whose hero, the prisoner of a perpetual present, also perambulates through a succession of fragmentary moments and feels himself to be totally devoid of any hidden dimensions. These characters (how many of them seem to drift through gloomy towns as though in quest of a yet undiscovered meaning!) cannot experience any adventures: they move through a time-space totally devoid of tragic omens. This *absence of adventure* —which Roquentin already describes—implies a philosophical point of view: the absence of pre-existent values in the world. Robbe-Grillet himself has affirmed that "essentialist" conceptions lie in ruins, that man cannot simply look on the world as a private possession set up to serve his needs. His insistence on the world of objects and of surfaces goes hand in hand with a deep-rooted suspicion of all anthropomorphic interpretations. Like Sartre's work—but more radically still—the fictional world of Robbe-Grillet testifies to the bankruptcy of optimistic Humanism.

The *roman nouveau* is thus clearly not a return to an ivory-tower, art-for-art's sake aestheticism, and even less to a literature of pure entertainment. All points, however, to an almost surgical attempt to cleanse the novel of all "impure" elements: psychological analysis, social and political "problems," moral predication, the clumsy burden of a philosophical message.[12] This cathartic effort is not confined to the novel. The avant-garde theater of the fifties, particularly the work of Ionesco, Adamov and Beckett, also reacts against the tyranny of ideas, ideologies and abstract systems.

¶ III. *Assessments*

It is too early, no doubt, to call down the judgment of posterity. How justified are these outcries against the "intellectual" novel? Every generation owes it to itself to rebel against its immediate predecessors. But what about the future? Will the political and metaphysical novel of the first half of the twentieth century be judged as harshly as the edifying thesis-literature of the nineteenth century? Is the *roman d'agrégés*, the "professorial novel," doomed to gather dust on forgotten shelves? How right was Sophroniska, in Gide's *Les Faux-Monnayeurs*, when she warned the novelist Edouard that intellectuals in fiction were bound to bore the reader to death?

Gide's oblique, self-directed warning points to a double danger: intellectuals as protagonists not only threaten to devitalize the novel by transforming everything into an abstraction, they remain the prisoners of the author's private preoccupations. There is little doubt that some of the representative novels discussed in this study have incurred this double jeopardy. Some of them, on occasion, seem to come closer to the essay form or the philosophical dissertation than to the traditional novel with its dense, and apparently autonomous, dramatic and poetic texture. When *La Nausée* appeared in 1938, critics did not quite know how to label the work. Marcel Arland refused to call it a novel, preferring instead to use words such as "essay," "satire," "philosophical meditation." Another reviewer, André Thérive, complained that one could never forget that Sartre was a professor of philosophy, and that it was impossible to predict whether Sartre would be a novelist or an essayist. Such hesi-

---

[12] These attempts to "purify" the novel have been discussed by Raymond Giraud in his forceful article "Unrevolt among the Unwriters in France Today," *Yale French Studies*, No. 24, Summer, 1959, pp. 11-17.

tations and qualifications obviously are unjustified. *La Nausée* is not fundamentally aimed at developing an abstract thesis, but is a metaphorically and symbolically textured account of a *lived* experience. If anything, it comes much closer to poetry than to a philosophical dissertation.

But not all the novels of Sartre and Simone de Beauvoir avoid the pitfall of didacticism. The philosophical "voice" of the author can often be heard—even in *La Nausée*. Sometimes, in *Le Sang des autres* for instance, or in certain parts of *Les Chemins de la liberté*, this "voice" indulges in almost theological hairsplitting concerning "freedom," "engagement," the "shame of being," the "crime of existing," the presence of "Others." The very style of the modern novel has been strongly colored by Existentialist clichés, Marxist dialectics and a pompous philosophical jargon about anguish, absurdity and man's "condition." Malraux has been one of the principal offenders. His novels are studded with lapidary formulas that sound like irrevocable answers to man's dilemma. ("One possesses of a being only what one changes in him" . . . "To be loved without seducing is one of the beautiful destinies of man" . . .) These snatches of apocalyptic meditation and fulgurating philosophical insights in the midst of violent revolutionary action will perhaps appear to future generations no less unbearable, and no less dated, than some of the more excessive Romantic poses.

In fairness, however, it must be granted that the philosophical *presence* of the author is not at all the invention of Malraux and the Existentialist generation who, in spite of their metaphysical bent, are much less guilty of philosophical digressions than some of their greatest predecessors. Rousseau's *La Nouvelle Héloïse* is not merely a love story, but also—and in its most original parts—a series of treatises on ethics, politics, agriculture, pedagogy, marriage, pastoral life and religion. Balzac's endless digressions are well known. He himself has defended them, invoking the sociological and historical interest of his novels that were meant to be more than public entertainment. "The digressions were so to speak the main subject of the author," he explains in a brief note at the end of the first episode of *L'Histoire des Treize*.[13] Emile Zola—in spite of his naturalistic doctrine—also indulges in occasional dissertations. *L'Œuvre* is filled with

[13] "Notes de la première édition de *Ferragus, Chef des Dévorants*, Première partie de l'Histoire des Treize," *Oeuvres complètes*, XXII, p. 393.

theoretical digressions on painting, literature and music. As for Anatole France and Romain Rolland, it is notorious that their novels at times depart completely from a basic plot line. The "Monsieur Bergeret" series most often reads like a collection on unrelated, controversial essays, and *Jean-Christophe* at times like a treatise on comparative music or a study in cultural history. In the preface to *Dans la maison*, Romain Rolland even warns his reader that he will find none of the traditional *"aventures de roman,"* that the author was less concerned with his "hero" than with the world and problems around him.

"What the devil! A novel is not a dissertation!" Roger Ikor's ire is obviously aroused not so much by the traditional ambling intrusion of the author (often quite noncommittal and not at all incompatible with the world of fictional make-believe), as by the all-consuming, militant concern with "problems" so characteristic of many recent novels. Ethics and Politics seem indeed to have invaded twentieth-century fiction to the point of crowding out all other interests, including that of creating a work of art. It is as though some of the more gifted novelists of our time felt a pang of guilt every time they surrendered to the sheer joy of creating. Some of them found it almost impossible to reconcile their ethical and political preoccupations with the yearned-for pleasure of writing. Their very style betrays this inner tension. Yet it is not sure that this inner tension did not also provide a sense of drama. Many admirers of Sartre have been disturbed by the nebulousness of his social metaphysics and appalled by the increasing tedium which emanates from the thickly cluttered, indigestible pages of his monthly publication, *Les Temps Modernes*. How much of this aesthetic abdication is a painful self-mutilation has been suggested by Simone de Beauvoir's fictional portrait of Sartre in *Les Mandarins*. But even the novels of Sartre—especially *Les Chemins de la liberté*—reveal an anguished hesitation between literature as an art form (sometimes even as technical prowess) and literature as a means of ethical communication.

Politics in a novel, said Stendhal, are as incongruous as a pistol shot in a concert hall. The incongruity can, however, lend the work of fiction an unexpected intensity. Irving Howe, in *Politics and the Novel*, remarks that while "ideology" is likely to be recalcitrant to the novel's concrete texture, the very difficulty of assimilating it, the frequent conflicts that ensue, create a valuable challenge for the writer and may add an "aura of high drama." In fact, Stendhal fired the political pistol repeatedly, and others did so with even greater relish. Balzac's *Le Médecin de campagne*, partly an instrument of electoral propaganda filled with social, political and religious theories (it was one of Lenin's favorite books!), is no doubt an extreme example. But what important novelist in France has not been tempted by the political tragedy of his time? Even Flaubert, whom our period likes to blame for his aloof and pessimistic aestheticism, was fully aware that in the modern world it was no longer possible to cut off an individual destiny from the events and the currents that victimize him. Frédéric Moreau's failure, in *L'Education sentimentale*, is also the failure of an entire generation. Most novelists—even those determined to affirm themselves primarily as craftsmen and artificers—have sensed that any alexandrian attitude would mean an abdication of the writer's "global" vision, and could lead swiftly to artistic sterility.

Hence it is difficult to agree with those critics who, out of purism or ill-temper, feel that the novel of ideas is bound to be lifeless. It is true that when Ortega y Gasset affirmed that every novel laden with transcendental intentions was doomed to be stillborn, he had in mind a particularly militant form of writing: satire or political propaganda.[14] But even such "engaged" writing need not automatically fall from aesthetic grace. Some of Dante's most successful passages are those in which his personal involvement—his bitterness, his political views—lend added tenseness to his more strictly "poetic" vision.

"Without women and without love there can be no novel," a critic was still pontificating a few decades ago.[15] Few critics today would express their misgivings in such simple terms. But the more sober reservations concerning the "intellectuals'" novel are not altogether unjustified. A certain drying up of sheer creative power and fantasy, artificially contrived problems, disregard for basic "human" passions, an almost morbid delight in distant, impersonal, collective catastrophes—these are some of the obvious defects most often encountered in the novel of ideas. The danger of extreme disincarnation paradoxically goes hand in hand with the danger of oversimplification. The ideological novel frequently sacrifices complexity

---

[14] See *The Dehumanization of Art and Notes on the Novel*, pp. 92-94.
[15] Pierre Mille, *Le Roman français*, p. 14.

to the clear-cut agon of ideas. In the preface to *Le Temps du mépris* —one of his most revealing critical texts—Malraux sets forth the belief that the modern novel, like ancient tragedy, should no longer concern itself with subtly analyzed individual antagonisms, but with the basic struggle between Man and the meaning of life. The risk involved is obvious: conceptualization often precedes the dramatic development. In the hand of less gifted novelists (a Vercors for instance) this may result in a schematic work whose characters seem to be *deduced* as perambulating thoughts rather than living fictional creatures. A literature of lucidity can also be a deadly unimaginative literature, relinquishing in vision and vigor what it acquires in intelligence. "This generation is terribly intelligent," quipped François Mauriac, one of the most authentic novelists in France since Proust.[16] The quip was meant as serious criticism of the sterilizing self-awareness and lack of abandon on the part of writers who seem to have lost the most precious gift of the novelist: the ability to people their fictional world with sympathetically treated *human* beings.

This sterilizing self-awareness is obviously the greatest single danger that Gide had in mind when he exposed Edouard to his indirect sarcasm in *Les Faux-Monnayeurs*. "I know what is going to happen," says Laura; "you won't be able to do anything but describe yourself." Intellectual narcissism, as the novelist himself becomes increasingly and obsessively his own hero, can indeed be nefarious to the art of the novel. The toying with one's own existence and dreams ultimately leads to the creation of a fictional character who is no longer even the substantial novelist, but his shadow, the autobiographer. Totally unsettled works such as Jean-Charles Pichon's *L'Autobiographe* (1956) thus mark the logical consequence of the *roman de l'écrivain* which, after Proust and Gide, was destined to degenerate. But what is true of the "writer's novel" applies perhaps even more to the "novel of the intellectual." Wavering between self-indulgent soul-searchings and an almost Byronic view of himself as the "outlaw of his own dark mind," [17] the intellectual hero at times appears as the victim of a mirror-disease of thought that exhausts him and his very thinking. The most damning criticism leveled at the intellectual hero is that he marks the apogee of the

---

16 Interview in *L'Express*, April 5, 1957.
17 R. M. Albérès points to the danger of this neo-Romantic pose in *Portrait de notre héros*, pp. 202-208.

hero of inaction—the untragic, unheroic hero. Few of them, in all fairness, are as clumsy a caricature of the philosopher as Bourget's Adrien Sixte or cut as pathetic a figure as Guilloux's Cripure, whose very deformity seems to testify to the torment of doing and of living. But most often they are either detached and lonely vagabonds such as Marat in Vailland's *Drôle de jeu*, who reads the *Anabasis* in the midst of Resistance fighting; or lucid victims of paralyzing guilt and spasmodic urges to take action. It is significant that the last volume of *Les Chemins de la liberté*, which according to Sartre himself was to describe a redemption through *real* suffering, has never been written. Mathieu's very ability to suffer seems atrophied by excessive lucidity. His irremediable inner discord, his tendency to self-torture and self-destruction, his sense of futility as he penetrates further and further into a blind alley where thought and action never join, make of Sartre's hero—despite dreams of freedom—the seeming prototype of the modern hero of inaction.[18]

JUDGMENTS SUCH AS THESE may, however, prove excessively harsh and short-sighted. Wholesale condemnation of the intellectual hero also implies the inability to recognize some of the modern novel's serious claims to greatness. When Balzac, in *Illusions perdues*, had one of his characters define the novel as "the most immense modern creation" ("it embraces the *fact* and the *idea*"), he was heralding those works of our time which are not content with revealing a private sensibility by means of introspection and the casuistry of love, but which propose to shake the reader out of his ethical coziness and force upon him a dramatic awareness of his generation's pressing intellectual and moral dilemmas. The figure of the intellectual, refusing to acquiesce, capable of generous revolt and of reaffirming man's potential dignity, stands at the center of this tragic literature.

The scope of this kind of novel is due in part to the stature with which novelists have endowed their intellectual heroes. If originally

---

[18] "Intelligence only leads to inaction," observes one of Martin du Gard's characters. This disease is clearly not the monopoly of any single writer or any single literary group. In an article on "Swann and Hamlet" (*Partisan Review*, May-June, 1942, pp. 195-202), Wallace Fowlie speaks of the emergence in the twentieth century of the "modern hero of inaction." But Flaubert already felt, while writing *L'Education sentimentale*, that the only passion possible in the modern world was "inactive passion" (*Correspondance*, V, p. 158).

the perspective seemed often one of comedy and satire, caricature soon gave way to a tragic vision. Jules Vallès' biting treatment already reveals typical ambiguities. Bourget, in spite of his ideological bias, displays a permanent tendency to create noble intellectual figures. His Adrien Sixte is a "poet of ideas," one of the "princes of modern thought." Even Barrès, so hostile to the politically conscious and opportunistic French intelligentsia, attempted to immortalize the moral beauty of a philosopher such as Hippolyte Taine, and fired his young heroes Sturel and Roemerspacher with a real enthusiasm for ideas. Anatole France's heroes are often erudite ironists who survey their world with a sad lucidity that but thinly disguises a latent though somewhat tired idealism. But it is no doubt with Roger Martin du Gard that the intellectual emerges as the authentic modern hero in the French novel. Jean Barois, but perhaps even more so the nobly virtuous figure of Luce, represent a type destined to occupy the center of the novel's stage for several decades.

The essential *nobility* of this literary type is derived in part from a prevalent notion of intellectual courage. "A beautiful thought is worth a noble deed," Renan asserted in *L'Avenir de la Science*. The Dreyfus Affair did much to confirm a belief that thinking need not be incompatible with doing (or inferior to it), and that courage of the mind was a rarer and more precious virtue than physical courage. Anatole France, speaking of such intellectual bravery, affirmed the "inalienable rights" of Thought. But these "rights" go hand in hand with the gratuitous love of ideas. "You and I, we are two beings passionately in love with ideas," Bourget's Monneron proudly states to his son. Once again, it is Balzac who, much earlier, had set the tone. Few writers have sung with greater exaltation the beauty of man's mental energies and the ineffable pleasure of cerebration.

The intellectual hero, as he emerges toward the end of the nineteenth century, is endowed, furthermore, with a moving faith in his spiritual mission. The word optimism seems hardly to apply to writers who painfully sensed the deep-rooted moral ills of a society that takes itself for granted. Yet behind their surface gloom, one can easily perceive a faith in the future which sometimes, as in the case of Zola, is expressed with lyrical naïveté, and which carries on the Rationalists' dream of Progress. This belief in the power of the Word to change the world is shared by nearly all the writers and their "heroes" considered in this study. It finds its ultimate expression in Sartre's oft-stated claim that he and his generation are not out to possess, but to change, the world.

Was du ererbt von deinen Vätern hast,
Erwirb es, um es zu besitzen.

The words of Faust well illustrate this dynamic intellectual attitude on the part of writers who refuse merely to inherit values, but strive instead to conquer them through a bold confrontation with the problems and the needs of their time.

Such a belief in the power of ideas would not be possible, of course, were it not bound up with a dramatic awareness of the *life of ideas*. This belief that ideas have a life of their own accounts for the dialectical density of some of the best novels of our time. "Ideas . . . live; they fight, they suffer and die like human beings," says Edouard in *Les Faux-Monnayeurs*. The most outstanding achievement of the novel of the intellectual is probably its ability to incarnate ideas to the point where ideas themselves become autonomous dramatic forces. As early as 1929 (his great novels were as yet unwritten), André Malraux prophetically stated that an increasingly powerful "dramatic conception of philosophy" might well lead to a transformation in depth of the art of fiction.[19] His own novels contributed of course greatly to this transformation, but they are also representative of some of the deeper needs of a generation reared on Unamuno's *The Tragic Sense of Life* and keenly aware that philosophy, far from being an abstraction, can be dramatically and even tragically alive. This philosophical sense of tragedy, or better, this tragically *experienced* philosophy, invaded the novel. Albérès, in a pivotal study of contemporary trends, perceptively remarks that although Existentialism fulfilled a need to reincarnate thought, this need for incarnation, for rooting ideas in a living soil, did not spring up suddenly.[20] Nietzsche, whose influence on French letters became noteworthy at the turn of the century, and whose pressing voice was later joined by that of a Kierkegaard, was indeed largely

[19] "Journal de voyage d'un philosophe, par Hermann Keyserling," *Nouvelle Revue Française*, June, 1929, p. 886.

[20] See *Portrait de notre héros*, pp. 73-134. Irving Howe, according to whom the supreme challenge of the political novelis. is to make ideas and ideologies come to life, quotes George Eliot who was also concerned with "the severe effort of trying to make certain ideas incarnate" (*Politics and the Novel*, p. 21).

responsible for this new mystical marriage between literature and philosophy which directed fiction toward ethical speculation.[21]

"One cannot prevent ideas from leading us where they themselves move," says a character in a Bourget novel. Aware that ideas not only live, but can clash (Unamuno liked to speak of the agon of ideas), the modern "metaphysical" novelists have been passionately dedicated to this struggle with the angel of ideas, to the high drama of the Mind. With bold seriousness, at times with almost puritanical gravity, they remain convinced of the writer's mission as a *witness* whose duty it is to set himself, together with his generation, on severe trial. *L'Homme en procès, Procès du héros, Les Témoins de l'homme*—the very titles of these studies by Pierre-Henri Simon reflect the spirit of an age which, as Simon himself reminds us, appropriately begins with the Dreyfus Affair.[22] The novel of the intellectual has thus been in close contact with all the major events and issues of our time: the problems of democracy, the conflict between the individual and society, between science and religion, the horror of world wars, the threats to justice, the totalitarian menace, the Marxist dream, the Spanish apocalypse of the thirties, the reality of torture and concentration camps, the Occupation and the Resistance, the postwar hopes and disillusionments. On the more philosophical level, it has challenged our humanistic tradition with its inherited values, probed into the question of "freedom," and generally communicated to literature modern man's sense of metaphysical anguish. But above all perhaps, this literature, immersed in the present and attracted to extreme situations, has taught us with shocking power that the price for human responsibility in a Godless universe is that evil becomes unredeemable and every silence an act for which we can be held to account.[23]

Such stern, almost intransigent demands on the individual's responsibility imply of course the belief that man does not live and die alone, that he is part of a collective tragedy and that he partakes of a collective guilt. Solidarity thus shines forth as a major theme

[21] The importance of Nietzsche as a symbol of this loss of identity has recently been stressed again by Everett W. Knight in *Literature Considered as Philosophy* (1957).

[22] *Histoire de la littérature française au XXè siècle*, II, p. 199.

[23] Sartre has this to say of his own generation: "We thus came, in spite of ourselves, to this conclusion which seems shocking to sensitive souls: Evil is not redeemable" (*Situations II*, p. 248).

in a literature obsessed with the feeling of isolation and estrangement. The intellectual hero, painfully aware of his alienation, shows himself unwilling to sentimentalize this personal exile, and seeks to overcome his private grief through a concern for the suffering that exists in the world. There lies of course a great deal of courage in this vocation of moral responsibility, in this unselfish desire to reach out to the problems and the anguish of others. These ethics of guilt and responsibility have in fact helped create a new type of hero and a new type of tragedy. For a Martin du Gard, as well as for a Camus and a Sartre, writing is in a sense an exercise in generosity, a means of embracing the human condition from within.

In many cases, the motif of solidarity is primarily an emotional fact. A Zola, staring into the spectacle of misery, develops a religion of human solidarity that helps explain the evolution of his fiction from naturalism to utopia. Others, like Louis Guilloux, Brice Parain or Sartre, consider private happiness an indecency and seem to be driven on by a compelling need to find and save their lost brothers. André Malraux admired Guilloux's ability "to pose the drama outside of the individual," which to him was a sign of Guilloux's "deep and tragic fraternity." [24] The remark could apply to many writers of the tragic decades of the thirties and the forties. "It can be shameful to be happy alone," says one of Camus' characters in *La Peste*. But behind all these dynamics of shame, behind this pious respect for the suffering of others, there also exists a sense of history, or rather a philosophy of history, which implies collective tragedy. "There no longer existed any individual destinies, but only a collective history . . . ," observes the narrator in *La Peste*. Even for Martin du Gard, man was a being-in-situation, immersed, not as a witness, but as a responsible participant in the drama of history. Sartre and his generation have further developed this non-archeological, non-theological view of history. Pierre-Henri Simon's *L'Esprit et l'Histoire* (1954), an essay on the historical sense of our times, clearly reveals how the word "history" (few words, he notes, are used with greater reverence by contemporary philosophers, essayists and novelists) has come to mean a movement of adhesion, of solidarity with the present, a question posed to destiny, our modern fatum.

The vocation of moral responsibility, the specific role of witness and denouncer into which he has deliberately cast himself, places the

---

[24] "En marge d' 'Hyménée,'" *Europe*, June 15, 1932, pp. 304-307.

intellectual at the very center of the historic current of his time. His prophetic calling is, however, not that of the Romantic writers who viewed themselves as the unacknowledged legislators of humanity, peering into the future with the visionary powers of a *vates*. The modern prophet is an ailing prophet, himself caught in the compromises and turpitudes of his epoch. But of the traditional prophet he possesses the major characteristics. His message is a permanent accusation. Silence in the face of social injustice or political tyranny is for him a shameful *act*, a manner of collaborating with evil. To give society a "bad conscience" is, according to Sartre, the writer's first duty.[25] The "anguish" which such a literature attempts to provoke is thus not exclusively metaphysical. To be sure, not all intellectuals, even in fiction, quite resemble the philosopher Gracch, in Vercors' *Les Yeux et la lumière*, who lets himself be killed in order to tell the truth and not compromise with the dictator. Moreover, even Vercors' philosopher knows that it is the curse of the writer to be read but not followed, that ironically the tyrant often finds in his works an encouragement for his crimes. But that precisely is the unceasing fate of the prophet: to be in the wrong even when he is right, to have a public but not a true following, to be a moral pariah in a society ever ready to see him stoned. The enmity he provokes only confirms the tragic nature of his calling.

Solitude in a hostile community, the permanent divorce between the philosopher and Caliban, are part of the intellectual's tragic burden. But it is the inner tragedy, the inner torment so movingly evoked by many philosophical novels, which confer upon the intellectual hero nobility and stature. For these inner tensions—erosive doubt, torturing lucidity, the self-denial of intelligence, the death-wish of the thinker—are infinitely more anguishing experiences than open war with society. As Max Scheler put it in *Philosophische Weltanschauung* (1929), man, in our times, has become so completely a *problem* to himself that he no longer knows *what* he is. Assailed by doubts, hesitations, scruples; undermined and paralyzed by his own lucidity and passion for honesty—the intellectual hero, better than any other literary type, exemplifies this fundamental self-questioning which is man's pride and man's misery. His suffering, no matter what the other circumstances, remains ultimately a suffering of the mind. "To think is to suffer," flatly stated Flaubert, who

[25] *Situations II*, p. 129.

also suspected early in life that man's greatest claim to greatness was the "heroism of the mind." [26]

But unlike the artist-hero, who can transmute his despair into a lasting work of art, the intellectual remains alone with his own desolate image, staring into the unmasked face of his destiny, cruelly aware of the walled-in quality of human existence. Perhaps he comes closer to a real hand-to-hand struggle with the *meaning* of suffering? "Every great novel," writes Albérès, "has become a struggle with the Angel." This struggle has done much to endow the novel with renewed dignity. In a sense, the true importance and originality of the intellectual hero in the novel of ideas is that he appeared on the literary horizon at a time when the image of man in literature was constantly shrinking under the impact of psychological and sociological investigation. The novelists discussed in this study obviously refused to consider man in a narrowing perspective. Faithful once again to a tragic view of life, they preferred to project the image of man against the broad backdrop of a difficult world, and confront man with the highest, and often conflicting, exigencies of his own mind.

[26] *Correspondance*, I, 456.

A. *Appendix to Chapter 6*

Joseph Malègue: The Dialogue with *Jean Barois*

Dieu a besoin d'agrégés.

Augustin ou le maître est là (1933), a moving presentation of the life-long religious crisis that besets a university professor, stands as a unique work among Catholic novels. Bernanos and Mauriac display more creative flashes of insight into man's capacity for evil and into the somber regions of sin. But Malègue, writing about the spiritual tragedy of a scholar, has set himself a more difficult and more original task. The interest of this book is largely due to the scholarly thoroughness with which this scholar's tragedy is developed. For Malègue deals not merely with the religious crisis of one intellectual. He poses the religious problem in intellectual terms, patiently explores a religious temperament in an intellectual context and from an intellectual point of view— and succeeds in doing so without loss of either dramatic or psychological intensity.[1] "Unbelievers who happen to be intellectuals are the most difficult to convert," says one of the priests in the novel. The author, one imagines, was fully aware that such a conversion was also a double challenge for the novelist; it required him both to vindicate religious belief and to redeem the intellect.

Like *Jean Barois*, Malègue's novel is also a story of faith lost and regained. Augustin Méridier is the son of a provincial lycée teacher. His mother is profoundly religious. His education is thus from the start exposed to a double influence. From his father he learns that

[1] Intellectuals and the drama of intelligence usually appear in a different light in Catholic novels. Bernanos, for instance, shows the ravages of intellectualism on a "bad priest." The Abbé Cénabre, in *L'Imposture* (1927), discovers that intellectual life is the opposite of charity, that it is "a limpid and icy solitude." "Yes, intelligence can penetrate everything, just as light can penetrate everything, just as light can go through the thickness of crystal, but it is incapable of moving, of embracing. It is a sterile contemplation."

learning can be a joy; his mother inspires him with Christian faith and Christian humility.[2] Soon, however, outside influences prevail. In school he discovers the excitement of speculative philosophy and develops a thirst for scholarship. At the university, in Paris, he bites into the tempting but bitter fruit of Biblical exegesis. His faith begins to crumble, corroded by doubts. One morning, he discovers that he can no longer pray.

Up to this point, the novel seems to confirm the corrosive effect of scholarship on the religious sensibility. Intelligence is seen as a poison to the spirit. Young Augustin is literally *seduced* by philosophy. The disappearance of dogmatic points of reference, the sudden opening of horizons without visible boundaries, give him a drunken sensation of intellectual mountain-climbing. In a letter to Paul Claudel, Malègue refers to the "inebriation of an intellectual youth nourished on the substance of contemporary historical methods."[3] Later in the novel there is talk about the "indocility of the Intellect." Augustin, clearly the victim of the *libido sciendi*, sins through a haughty pride in his own mental achievements. As a young boy, when initiated by his father into intellectual methods and satisfactions, he experiences not only an "acute pleasure" in solving problems, but a feeling of "intellectual domination" and "pride." Yet Malègue insists less on this pride than on the seductions of the mind. To his friend Jacques Chevalier, who blamed Augustin's loss of faith on "hardness" and "haughtiness," Malègue replied that Augustin's fault lay in "the aesthetic taste for manipulating ideas."[4]

Jean Barois also experiences the intoxication of ideas in an almost lyrical fashion. But the parallelism between the two destinies holds

[2] The novel appears incidentally also as a corrective to Vallès' *Jacques Vingtras*. Augustin's family shares many traits with Vingtras' family (peasant background; atmosphere of provincial schools and petty functionaries; pathetically clumsy father, persecuted by cruel, undisciplined students; vicarious suffering of the son). Yet the differences are even more striking. Here the family atmosphere signifies not hate and rebellion, but love, tenderness, warmth. The relation between father and son is particularly moving. They live and study in close communion with each other. After his father's death, Augustin, out of filial piety, publishes under his own name fragments from his father's unfinished and inadequate thesis.

[3] Quoted by Elizabeth Michael in *Joseph Malègue*, p. 172.

[4] See Jacques Chevalier, "Mon souvenir de Joseph Malègue," *La Table Ronde*, July-August, 1958, pp. 72-81.

true only up to a point. From there on, they provide a study in contrasts. Love, disease and tragedy bring Augustin back to faith. But his is not a submissive return to the fold; it is a reconquest hard won through pain and lucidity. His struggle with the Angel does not lead to an abdication of intelligence. He only gains in stature as his mind, purified by pain, rises above the boundaries set by cold reason. Even disease, which in both novels plays such a crucial role (both Martin du Gard and Malègue seem haunted by it), is shown in a different perspective. Whereas Martin du Gard gives an almost pathological account of conversion (Barois, sapped by illness and terrified by death, searches for peace and consolation), Malègue presents disease as a unique opportunity for heroic renunciation, and as allowing profound insights into man's noble nature.

On three points, in particular, Malègue appears to challenge the rationalistic perspective of Martin du Gard. The first is the very experience of loss of faith. For Barois, this loss is synonymous with liberation, and leads to a nearly fanatical anti-religious proselytizing. But there is also repressed bitterness in this militant atheism. Augustin, on the other hand, is from the outset inconsolable. The discovery that he can no longer pray results not in joy but in tears. He makes no attempt to find a substitute faith. And the religious practices of his family, far from nettling him, only increase his deep nostalgia for a lost beauty in his life.

The second major point of difference is the relationship between faith and intelligence. It is significant that Augustin is converted *in extremis* not by a priest who no longer believes, but by his closest friend who is a scientist. There is no sense of shame in his conversion, no suggestion of defeat. Augustin may not regain his faith by dint of intellectual effort, but certainly his mind and his religious beliefs are ultimately not at odds. He learns that every instrument of knowledge is limited to the realities of its own sphere and consequently not attuned to the truths of a higher order. But this hierarchical concept of the various "orders" of perception in no way discredits intelligence. Malègue repeatedly insists on the high function of the cultured mind. *"Dieu a besoin de haute culture,"* maintains one of the priests in the novel. In all his works,

Malègue underlines the capital role of intelligence and "man's strict duty to make use of it" in his search for truth.[5]

Finally, *Augustin ou le maître est là* sharply departs from *Jean Barois* in the dramatic and moral functions attributed to suffering. Barois' physical and mental anguish provokes a state of moral depression and a yearning for childhood coziness. Barois chooses to die in his native village, surrounded by familiar faces and familiar objects. But for Augustin suffering is an exalting experience which elevates him to the "icy zones" of spiritual meditation. It is no coincidence that, unlike Barois, he chooses to die in a quintessential solitude, in the impersonal sickroom of a Swiss mountain sanatorium. The very altitude symbolizes a spiritual state capable of transmuting suffering into beauty.

[5] See Yvonne Malègue's judgment of her husband's work, quoted by Elizabeth Michael, *op. cit.*, p. 193.

B. Appendix to Chapter 8

Camus' "Le Renégat" or the Terror of the Absolute

FUTURE GENERATIONS may well admire, above all the rest of Camus' work, the nightmarish perfection of this parable, with its incantatory rhythms and blinding images of pain. It is, however, a disturbing text. Brutality assumes hysterical proportions. Feverish, convulsive images build up to an apocalypse of cruelty.

"*Quelle bouillie, quelle bouillie!*" The opening words refer to the pulplike state of the narrator's mind.[1] But it is his body which was first literally beaten to a pulp. In an unlivable, "maddening" landscape, under the rays of a savage sun, the human flesh is exposed to the worst indignities. In the white heat of an African summer, the victim is whipped and salt is lavishly sprinkled on his wounds. Beaten about the head with wet ropes until his ears bleed, he is left moaning under the eyes of a bloodthirsty Fetish. Sadistic women assist his torturers, while he in turn is forced to witness the torture and rape of others. Inhuman cries, bestial matings, orgiastic rituals culminate in scenes of mutilation. His tongue is cut out, his mouth filled with salt. But nothing seems to satisfy this lust for pain. The victim himself—willing collaborator of his tormentors—yearns for more punishment.

Punctuated by onomatopoeic effects (the submissive interjection *ô*, the guttural *râ, râ*, the haunting rattle of thirst, hate and death), this frenzied tale offers no respite. But what is all this violence about? Why does the narrator accept it with gratitude, even with relish? On the surface, the story appears simple enough. A student in a theological seminary is consumed with the desire to convert heathens, to force upon others the truth of his faith. He decides

---

[1] "L'Esprit confus" was the original title of this story when it appeared in *La Nouvelle Nouvelle Revue Française*, June 1, 1956. Camus changed the title when he included it in *L'Exil et le Royaume* (1957).

227

to set out as a missionary to the African "city of salt," Taghâza—a "closed city" which few have entered, and from which even fewer have returned. Having heard of the spectacular cruelty of its inhabitants, he feels attracted by the glorious possibility of converting them to the God of Love. Although warned by his superiors that he is not ready, not "ripe," he dreams of penetrating into the very sanctuary of the Fetish, of subjugating the savages through the sheer power of the Word.

Events take, however, an unexpected turn. He discovers that evil is stronger than he thought, and soon accepts this strength as the only truth. The tortured missionary is thus, ironically, converted by the very Fetish he set out to destroy. He discovers the joy and the power of hatred. His new masters teach him how to despise love. He adores, as he has never adored before, the axlike face of the Fetish who "possesses" him. At the end of the story, as though to outdo his new masters and to avenge himself on his old ones, he savagely kills the new missionary, while calling for the eternal Reign of Hatred.

The virtuosity of these pages is remarkable. Nowhere else has Camus revealed himself so accomplished a master of images, sounds and rhythms. The fulgurating whiteness of the landscape, the piercing sun-fire of this white hell, the liquefaction of time under the burning refraction of a thousand mirrors—all this is suggested in the hallucinating interior monologue which presses forward as though indeed the only speech left the tongueless narrator were the metaphorical "tongue" of his feverish brain. In this "cold torrid city" Taghâza, with its iron name and the steel-like ridges of its landscape, a defiant race has built a surrealistic city of salt.

The salt and the sun—these are indeed the basic images in "Le Renégat." The word "sun," in itself symbol of absolute violence, appears up to four times in the same paragraph. "Savage" and "irresistible," it is the sun of death and of flies. It "beats," it "pierces," making holes in the overheated metal of the sky. Visual images, as well as images of sound and touch, are relentless reminders of the theme of hardness. The narrator hears in his own mouth the sound of rough pebbles. He fondles the barrel of his gun, while the stones and rocks all around him crackle from the heat. There is hardly a transition between the ice-coldness of the night and the crystal-like dazzlement of the day. But it is the very rhythm of the speech

—panting, harsh, elliptical yet smooth—which marks the greatest achievement of this text. Audacious, yet pure in a Racinian manner, the language and the syntax swiftly glide from affirmation to negation.

Virtuosity is, however, not Camus' purpose. Even when originally inspired by vivid personal impulses and sensations (surrender to air, sun, water; love of nature; pagan sensuality), most of Camus' writing seems irresistibly drawn toward an allegorical meaning. The very titles of his work which so often suggest a loss, a fall, an exile or a spiritual disease, point to a parabolic tendency and at times even seem to come close to Christian theological concerns. He may be, like Jean-Baptiste Clamence in *La Chute*, an *ailing* prophet, sick with the very illusions and weakness he feels compelled to denounce. But this solidarity with illness only makes the diagnosis more urgent.

The missionary in "Le Renégat," who discovers that only guns have souls, is very sick indeed. His sickness, a particularly dangerous one: the obsessive quest for the absolute. His superiors at the seminary are perfectly right: he does not know "who he is." This ignorance of his true self sets the stage for the most shocking discoveries. But, on the symbolic level, it also points to the transcendental urges which bring about self-negation and self-destruction.

Who, indeed, is the narrator? Who is this missionary-renegade with his desire for "order" and his dream of absolute power? "Dirty slave," he calls himself with characteristic self-hatred. Intelligent, but hard-headed (*"mulet," "tête de vache"*), he is from his youth on attracted to cruelty, finding the very idea of barbarians exciting. A hunter of pain, he imagines that the very girls in the street will strike at him and spit in his face. He dreams of teeth that tear, and enjoys the voluptuous image of his imagined pain.

This masochistic eroticism which instinctively leads him to Taghâza is clearly of a symbolic nature. The rape by the evil Fetish is perpetrated not so much on his body as on his mind. The missionary surrenders to the Fetish in a quasi-sexual ecstasy of pain. But this surrender is of an intellectual nature: the allegory deals with the drama of the mind. In a climate whose extreme heat precludes contact between human beings, his new masters, these "lords" of the salt mines, succeed in brainwashing the absolutist, or rather in converting him. *Absolute* dedication to good is transmuted into *absolute* dedication to evil.

The allegorical identity of the Renegade thus emerges. He is the modern intellectual, heir to a Humanist culture, but now impatient with the "seminary" coziness of his tradition and with its sham, and who, in search of systems and ideologies, espouses totalitarian values that have long ago declared war (and he knows it!) on the thinker and his thought. Thus amorous hate and amorous surrender are the logical consequence of a denial of life in favor of abstraction. The missionary-intellectual believes he is out to convert the barbarians; in fact he seeks tyranny in order to submit to it.

This betrayal, however, remains ambivalent. On the one hand, it shows up the poison of ideological absolutes; on the other, it reveals the deep-rooted suicidal impulses of the intelligentsia. The missionary-renegade, bitter against his former teachers and ashamed of his cultural heritage, seeks not only the destruction of what he is, but of what he represents. He has "an account to settle" with his entire culture. That is, one must assume, the meaning of his murdering the missionary. By killing him, he attempts to kill what he himself stands for, as well as the spiritual guild to which he belongs. The betrayal is a vengeance, but this vengeance is also self-punishment!

The terror of the absolute, so powerfully conveyed by this story, is one of Camus' permanent themes. The missionary who reneges his mission does so because his thirst for a despotic ideal can only find satisfaction in evil. For evil, unlike good, can be absolute in human terms. The Renegade, seeing that good is a constantly postponed and tiring project, refuses to pursue any further an ever receding boundary. He knows that the Reign of Goodness is impossible. So he turns to the Reign of Evil as to the only abstraction that can be translated into a flawless truth. For only the square truth, the "heavy" and "dense" truth, can be acceptable to the seeker of the absolute. "Only evil can go to its own limit and reign absolutely." The conversion, to be sure, leads to a denial of all values. "Down with Europe, down with reason, honor and the cross." But this is the price to pay: the militant need for absolute affirmation implies absolute negation. Ideology replaces life. The missionary-intellectual becomes a grave-digger who prepares his own burial. No problem of our time has preoccupied Camus more than this disastrous temptation of the absolute and the death-wish of the modern intellectual.

C. Appendix to Chapter 10

Simone de Beauvoir and Le Sang des Autres

Je tourne en rond au milieu de mes remords.
—Jean Blomart

"A SUICIDE is always more or less a murder," comments one of Simone de Beauvoir's characters. *Le Sang des autres* (1945) is no doubt, of all the Existentialist novels, the one to focus most sharply on the problem of involvement, giving it its neatest artistic formulation. The epigraph from *The Brothers Karamazov* sets the tone: "Everyone is responsible to everybody for everything." The novel, on the surface at least, appears to illustrate this dictum.

It also queries it. *Le Sang des autres* is far from a simple demonstration. Concerned with the dense and shifting texture of existence, Simone de Beauvoir is aware that no situation can ever be entirely limpid or entirely imperative. The interest of the book stems in part from an implicit dialectical movement. The author develops an ethic of *engagement*, while concerned, on the psychological level, with the intertwined and often paralyzing strands of guilt, solidarity and alienation. Similarly the hero, in quest of a guiding truth, discovers that he has penetrated into a blind alley. If on the one hand the novel is a clear formulation of Existentialist ethics, it also presents in dramatic terms the most characteristic Existentialist ambiguities.[1]

Superimposed on the tension between the hero's "complexes" and the ethics he is to evolve, are the additional complexities inherent in the doctrine of solidarity. It is one thing to involve oneself, but does one have the right to involve others? "It is easy to pay with the blood of others," remarks one of the protagonists.[2] *Le Sang des*

---

[1] Simone de Beauvoir significantly entitles one of her important essays *Pour une morale de l'ambiguïté* (1947).

[2] Similarly Mathieu, in *La Mort dans l'âme*, declares that no one has the right to decide for others when to fight.

autres, part of which is concerned with the French Resistance, raises the question in concrete historical terms. Does one have the right to risk other people's lives in what may be a "just war"? How "just" is it to provoke the enemy to execute hostages, who may not approve of the meaning thus bestowed on their death? The answer, in a sense, appears to be negative. "I can pay with my body, with my blood; but other human beings are not currency for my usage." But this answer is found to be unsatisfactory. The novel clearly establishes that one can also be guilty for the lives one spares, that the blood one did not spill can also be inexpiable.

The "plot" of the novel, reduced to an outline, is fairly simple. Jean Blomart, sitting by the bedside of his dying mistress, recalls the succession of events that led to her receiving a mortal wound, as she was taking part in Underground activity. He also, in retrospect, lives through the stages of his own life. The novel thus makes its way across an undying *present*. Son of a wealthy printer, Jean Blomart rebels against his bourgeois father, leaves his home, becomes a typesetter, befriends his fellow workers, agitates for Communism —until the day he feels he is directly to blame for the violent death of a younger friend at a political rally. At once he decides to withdraw from political action, and to devote himself exclusively to trade-union activities. This negative, noncommittal, abstentionist attitude is further revealed by his refusal of Hélène's love, and above all by his uncompromising pacifism at the time of the political tragedies of Spain, Austria and Czechoslovakia. He soon finds out, however, that no one can shirk his responsibilities; that not to choose is a choice, and that this choice of passivity can be the most brutal. He learns that he is ultimately responsible for Hélène's abortion and that he cannot refuse her love. He learns that he is answerable for the victories of Fascism (just as France as a country is answerable), and that he cannot refuse to fight. Similarly Hélène, who at first believed that only their love had meaning, witnesses the deportation of Jewish children and understands that she too is responsible for this crime. So she accepts the hard struggle in the Underground and faces death without a murmur.

An outline such as this fails to suggest the complexity and the artistic validity of the novel. *Le Sang des autres* is not an easy book. The point of view, largely retrospective, implies a steady reassessment of past events and past attitudes. The language is often abstract. The fundamental outlook, when love is being considered, is remarkably austere. The characters, as well as the author, seem permanently afflicted with a Jansenist pessimism ("Do you believe there are any just situations?"). Yet the difficulty of the technique (the frequent unheralded switches of point of view), as well as the intransigent moral tone of the book, also prevent the main themes from degenerating into pedestrian thesis-literature. Moreover, the novel deals not merely with abstractions. *Le Sang des autres* is among the few excellent books about the Occupation and the Resistance. Simone de Beauvoir succeeded not only in creating a number of touching scenes (Blomart's departure for the army and Hélène's frustrating visit to him at the front masterfully convey the pathos and clumsiness that invest important moments), but in dramatizing in a sustained manner the difficulty of living.

The moral and intellectual density of the novel may discourage some readers. Written with didactic fervor, *Le Sang des autres* at times resembles a breviary of Existentialist beliefs. Themes, attitudes and language could easily be interchanged with those of Sartre. About existence:

> I am alone. I am that anguish which exists alone, in spite of myself; I become one with this blind existence. . . . Refuse to exist: I exist. Decide to exist: I exist. Refuse. Decide. I exist.

Or about the relations between the consciousness and the object (man has not created the world, but he recreates it every moment through his presence):

> . . . my eyes are all that is needed for this street to exist. My voice is all that is needed for the world to have a voice. Whenever it is silent, I am to blame.

This logically leads to a belief in the irrevocable nature of our acts, and to an ethic of *choice*. Our reasons for living do not fall like manna from heaven; it is up to us to create our values. Each heartbeat thrusts into the world a decision never to be recalled. Choice cannot be eluded. Even the vocabulary of the novel, with its metaphorical variations around the image of *stickiness*, are characteristic Existentialist clichés. In the glutinous, viscid quality of existence, Simone de Beauvoir, no less than Sartre, finds true poetic inspiration. The hero agrees to bog down (*"s'embourber"*) in the *"glu terrestre."* The sex act leads to *"ténèbres gluantes."* The soul itself seems caught in its own gluey mire (*"tout engluée en elle-même"*). Suffering is nauseatingly sweetish: one sinks into it as into a lukewarm glue. The basic image of slime or glue even lends itself to lyrical developments: "Stuck fast in this world by gummy roots which, together with a thousand borrowed saps, made up my own sap . . ."

The notion of *remorse* (one of the leitmotifs of the novel) also inspires Simone de Beauvoir to metaphorical developments. Remorse appears throughout the book as a physical reality, insidious, filling the atmosphere, penetrating through the eyes, the ears, the nostrils, through the very pores of the protagonists. It can almost be beautiful: "Remorse stretched itself out in silky threads." Or it prowls like a criminal waiting for the propitious moment. Like a filterable virus, it is the specific morbid principle which invades and poisons the organism. It can even have an odor (Blomart can smell remorse in the subway); "intimate and tenacious," it can stick to the skin.

It is appropriate that both the stickiness of existence and the physical reality of remorse should be invested with poetic density. *Existence* and *remorse* are the hard basic facts of what Simone de Beauvoir might call the "human condition." Remorse or shame is everywhere. Early in his life, Blomart learns that he must live with it. "One could chase it from one corner of life, cleanse it, polish it, make it all nice and pretty. But immediately it was hidden in another corner. It was always somewhere."

Specifically, it is his comfortable bourgeois background that fills him with guilt. He imagines that his fellow workers can guess that, under his stained overalls, he wears an elegant tweed suit. He remembers the smugness with which his father talks about his "rights," and the voluptuous pleasure with which he seems to inhale the "corrupt odor of the world." But these are, so to speak, only external, contingent phenomena. In reality, the feeling of shame, guilt and remorse are ingrained as a fixed idea or an age-old curse. Guilt and remorse assume, in *Le Sang des autres*, an almost metaphysical reality. "I was at fault forever, since my birth and beyond my death." Blomart lives with this permanent shame as one lives with the tragic awareness of an original sin. Like the theological notion of the fall, it implies a constant re-enactment of a past deed. "Because of me . . ." "Because I exist . . ." "Because I was there . . ." —the very first pages suggest the shame of *being*, the *crime of existing* ("Crime is everywhere, irremediable, inexpiable"). Blomart knows that he is guilty no matter what he does—guilty for what he says as well as for what he does not say. "No matter what one does, one is always responsible," sadly comments his mother. This feeling of guilt and shame, this permanent remorse is inextricably bound up with the basic fact of existence, and more precisely with the solipsistic obsession. *"La faute d'être un autre"*: the fault of being another. Like Sartre's heroes, Blomart feels trapped by his own consciousness, turning in circles within his "remorse" and his "scruples."

Le Sang des autres does, however, seem to propose a solution. Given this global guilt, a means of salvation is available that may transform it into a *felix culpa*. Communion through group action, the acceptance of a common responsibility, the exalted awareness of human solidarity—all these could conceivably cure man of his sense of "otherness" and cleanse him of his guilt. After the first mass meeting, Blomart loses the "smell of remorse" as he breathes in the smell of dust, sweat and work. The Dostoevski epigraph thus points not only to a fact, but to a possible therapy. Hélène at first appears as the embodiment of irresponsibility, the negative proof of moral liability. Her life has no meaning. She stagnates in her own self without knowing what to "become." She also has to learn that the endeavor not to be trapped in the universal absurdity is the most absurd, and the most impossible, of all attitudes. Man must choose a destiny for himself, and the destiny he chooses must be a common destiny. That is the meaning of the mass meeting and the exhilaration which follows. The singing crowd communicates to Blomart, together with the smell of sweat, a feeling of joy and pride. "It was in pride that he communed with them, as he thought: I am one of them." It feels like the rebirth of the world.

Or so it seems. For the note of hope is almost immediately neutralized by contrapuntal notes of dejection. Virile fraternity, the brotherhood of militant commitment, can only provide sporadic elations. Nothing can cleanse Blomart of his sense of guilt or cure him of his chronic remorse. The "fault of being another" becomes the unmedicable wound—the fatality, the curse of humanity. Man remains essentially an alien. ("You are not in your own home," Sartre's Jupiter explains to Orestes in *Les Mouches*, "you are in the world like a splinter in the flesh, like a poacher in his lordship's forest.") Simone de Beauvoir's contrapuntal effects are worked out through effective symbols. Blomart's modest room in the workers' quarter of Clichy is a symbol of his rebellion against parental comfort, but also of a taste for monastic living. The dingy room which represents his emancipation from the bourgeois *beaux quartiers,* is also the cell that protects and isolates him. "I was pleased that my lodgings were reduced to the exact measure of a man: the six surfaces necessary for the construction of a cube. . . ." Similarly, the very setting of the novel remains symbolically ambivalent. The meditation at the bedside of a dying woman represents, on one level, the sacrifices accepted in a common cause. But it also serves to remind us that one human being is dying and that another remains helplessly alive; that one cannot die or suffer for another. "Avidly, he bends over this agony. But he cannot share it."

This walled-in quality of human experience is brought out explicitly in a socio-political context. Blomart is constantly reminded, by his friends or by himself, that his solidarity with the workers is an abstraction, an impossibility. One cannot *make* oneself underprivileged. "*Nous ne sommes pas dans le coup.*" Between Blomart, the bourgeois intellectual, and an authentic proletarian there will always remain the wide gap separating choice from necessity. "You cannot undo your past. . . . There will always be an abyss between a worker and yourself. You choose freely a condition which was inflicted on him." It is the eternal distance between the hero and the victim. Despite his professed love for the workers, Blomart feels an obscure hatred for what is different in them. But the hatred is not directed against them. It is the hatred of his own dilemma. He knows, with a full measure of bitterness, that he must remain alone ("I have never been one of them"), that he is condemned to be left, undecided and unwanted, in the no-man's-land of the modern intellectual. "I was neither a bourgeois nor a worker because I could never be anything: neither bourgeois, nor worker, nor warmonger, nor pacifist, nor a lover, nor indifferent." The social and political situation points in explicit terms to man's permanent "condition" as seen by Simone de Beauvoir. Jean Blomart and Hélène may have come to be dissatisfied with their imprisonment, but has the lesson of moral accountability really led to freedom? At the beginning of the novel, Hélène is living inside a shell:

> There was no one facing her. She was all locked up in herself. She could pretend to love; but this love was only a tiny lukewarm

palpitation at the center of her shell. And this boredom, this insipid sourness of curdled milk, was the very flesh of which she was made.

But has common action freed Hélène from her own "shell"? Is it not the irony of the novel, that behind the apparent solidarity established in war or political action, man always rediscovers the frontiers of his own consciousness? Caught in their own dialectics, the characters of Simone de Beauvoir—no less than those of Sartre—live out to its tragic conclusion an *impossible* condition. It is this irony which, despite the didactic flavor of the novel, lends it intellectual as well as poetic density. Even the last pages remain ambiguous. As Hélène dies, Blomart understands that his only possible freedom lies in the courage with which he meets his own loneliness. But the reader can hear another voice, hardly perceptible, and much less heroic, which breathes a note of sadness, perhaps even of despair.

Bibliography

THE FOLLOWING BIBLIOGRAPHY does not attempt to be all-inclusive. It is strictly limited to the works cited in the text. Dates refer to the editions consulted by me. I have supplied the titles and publishers of available English translations only in the case of contemporary novels, since translations of earlier works are by this time widely known.

Agee, James, "Religion and the Intellectuals: A Symposium," *Partisan Review*, February, 1950, pp. 106-113.

Albérès, René-Marill, *Portrait de notre héros*, Le Portulan, Paris, 1945.

——, "Romanciers italiens 1957," *La Table Ronde*, September, 1957, pp. 9-24.

Aragon, Louis, *Les Communistes*, 6 vols., La Bibliothèque Française, Paris, 1949-1951.

Arland, Marcel, "Essais critiques," *Nouvelle Revue Française*, July, 1938, pp. 129-133.

Aron, Raymond, *L'Opium des intellectuels*, Calmann- Lévy, Paris, 1955.

——, "Postface" in *Le Dieu des ténèbres*, Calmann-Lévy, Paris, 1950.

Auden, W. H., "Talent, Genius and Unhappiness," *The New Yorker*, November 30, 1957, pp. 221-237.

Aux Artistes, Du Passé et de l'avenir des Beaux-Arts, Alex. Mesnier, Paris, 1830. Cited by Bernard Guyon, *La Pensée politique et sociale de Balzac*, pp. 324-325.

Avenel, Henri, *Histoire de la presse française depuis 1789 jusqu'à nos jours*, Flammarion, Paris, 1900.

Aymé, Marcel, *Le Confort intellectuel*, Flammarion, Paris, 1949.

Bakunin, Mikhail (Bakounine, Michel), *La Politique de l'Internationale*, Editions de la Vie Ouvriére, n.d.

Balzac, Honoré de, *Le Chef-d'oeuvre inconnu*, "Bibliothèque de la Pléiade," vol. IX, Gallimard, Paris, 1950.

——, *Correspondance*, 1819-1850, *Oeuvres complètes*, vol. XXIV, Calmann-Lévy, Paris, 1876.

——, *Correspondance inédite avec Zulma Carraud (1829-1850)*, Armand Colin, Paris, 1935.

——, *Correspondance avec Zulma Carraud*, ed. by Marcel Bouteron, Gallimard, Paris, 1951.

——, "Des Artistes," *La Silhouette*, February 25, March 11 and April 22, 1830. Reprinted in *Oeuvres complètes*, vol. XXXVIII, Conard, Paris, 1912-1940.

——, *Etudes philosophiques*, "Bibliothèque de la Pléiade," vols. IX and X, Gallimard, Paris, 1950.

239

———, *Illusions perdues*, "Bibliothèque de la Pléiade," vol. IV, Gallimard, Paris, 1952.
———, *Lettres à l'étrangère*, 4 vols., Calmann-Lévy, Paris, 1899-1950.
———, *Louis Lambert*, "Bibliothèque de la Pléiade," vol. X, Gallimard, Paris, 1950.
———, *Le Médecin de campagne*, "Bibliothèque de la Pléiade," vol. VIII, Gallimard, Paris, 1949.
———, "Notes de la première édition de *Ferragus* . . . ," *Oeuvres complètes*, vol. XXII, Michel Lévy, Paris, 1872, p. 393.
Barrès, Maurice, *L'Appel au soldat*, Charpentier, Paris, 1900.
———, *Mes Cahiers*, vols. I, II, Plon, Paris, 1929-1930.
———, *Les Déracinés*, 2 vols. Plon, Paris, 1954.
———, *Scènes et doctrines du nationalisme*, Félix Juven, Paris, 1902.
———, *Sous l'oeil des Barbares*, Perrin, Paris, 1892.
Barthes, Roland, *Le Degré zéro de l'écriture*, Editions du Seuil, Paris, 1953.
Barzun, Jacques, *The House of Intellect*, Harper, New York, 1959.
Beaunier, André, *Les Dupont-Leterrier*, Société Libre d'Edition des Gens de Lettres, Paris, 1900.
Beauvoir, Simone de, *L'Invitée*, Gallimard, Paris, 1943. (*She Came to Stay*, transl. Roger Senhouse & Yvonne Moyse, World, Cleveland and New York, 1954).
———, *Les Mandarins*, Gallimard, Paris, 1954 (*The Mandarins*, transl. Leonard M. Friedman, World, Cleveland, 1956).
———, *Mémoires d'une jeune fille rangée*, Gallimard, Paris, 1958.
———, *Pour une morale de l'ambiguïté*, Gallimard, Paris, 1947.
———, *Pyrrhus et Cinéas*, Gallimard, Paris, 1944.
———, *Le Sang des autres*, Gallimard, Paris, 1945 (*The Blood of Others*, transl. Roger Senhouse & Yvonne Moyse, Knopf, New York, 1948).
Benda, Julien, *Dialogues à Byzance*, Editions de la Revue Blanche, Paris, 1920.
———, *La Fin de l'éternel*, Gallimard, Paris, 1928.
———, *La Jeunesse d'un clerc*, Gallimard, Paris, 1936.
———, *La Trahison des clercs*, Grasset, Paris, 1927.
Bérenger, Henry, *Les Prolétaires intellectuels en France*, Editions de La Revue, Paris, n.d. (Other collaborators are Paul Pottier, Pierre Marcel, P. Gabillard, Marius-Ary Leblond.)
Bergson, Henri, *Le Rire*, F. Alcan, Paris, 1930.
Berl, Emmanuel, *Mort de la pensée bourgeoise*, Grasset, Paris, 1929.
Bernanos, Georges, *L'Imposture*, Plon, Paris, 1927.
Berth, Edouard, *Les Méfaits des intellectuels*, Marcel Rivière, Paris, 1914.
Blum, Léon, "Les Livres," *La Revue Blanche*, 1897, pp. 389-393.
———, *Souvenirs sur l'Affaire*, Gallimard, Paris, 1935.
Boorsch, Jean, "Primary Education," *Yale French Studies*, No. 22, Winter-Spring, 1958-1959, pp. 17-46.
Borgal, Clément, *Roger Martin du Gard*, Editions Universitaires, Paris, 1957.
Bourget, Paul, *Un Crime d'amour*, Plon, Paris, n.d.
———, *Cruelle énigme*, Plon, Paris, 1907.
———, *Le Démon de midi*, 2 vols., Plon-Nourrit, Paris, 1914.
———, *Le Disciple*, (With an introduction by T. de Wyzewa), Nelson, Paris, n.d.

——, *Essais de psychologie contemporaine*, Alphonse Lemerre, Paris, 1886.

——, *L'Etape*, Plon, Paris, 1902.

——, "Gustave Flaubert," *La Nouvelle Revue*, May-June, 1882, pp. 865-895.

——, "Jules Vallès" in *Portraits d'écrivains et notes d'esthétique* (*Etudes et portraits*, I), Plon, Paris, 1905.

——, *Mensonges*, Arthème Fayard, Paris, 1948.

——, *Nos Actes nous suivent*, 2 vols., Plon, Paris, 1927.

——, *La Terre promise*, Alphonse Lemerre, Paris, 1892.

Brandes, George, *Anatole France*, The McClure Company, New York, 1908.

Brée, Germaine, *Camus*, Rutgers University Press, New Brunswick, N.J., 1959.

Brée, Germaine and Guiton, Margaret, *An Age of Fiction; the French Novel from Gide to Camus*, Rutgers University Press, New Brunswick, N.J., 1957.

Bromfield, Louis, "The Triumph of the Egghead," *The Freeman*, December 1, 1952, pp. 155-158.

Bruckberger, Raymond-Leopold, "An Assignment for Intellectuals," *Harper's Magazine*, February, 1956, pp. 68-72.

Brunetière, Ferdinand, "Après le procès," *Revue des Deux Mondes*, March 15, 1898, pp. 428-446.

——, "Après une visite au Vatican," *Revue des Deux Mondes*, January 1, 1895, pp. 97-118.

——, *Discours de combat*, 1ère série, Perrin et Compagnie, Paris, 1914.

——, *Les Ennemis de l'âme française*, Hetzel et Compagnie, n.d.

——, "Le *Paris* de M. Emile Zola," *Revue des Deux Mondes*, April 15, 1898, pp. 922-934.

Buisson, Ferdinand, *La Foi laïque*, Hachette, Paris, 1913.

Cachin, Marcel, "Préface" to Jules Vallès' *L'Insurgé*, Les Editeurs Réunis, Paris, 1950.

Camus, Albert, *La Chute*, Gallimard, Paris, 1956 (*The Fall*, transl. Justin O'Brien, Knopf, New York, 1957).

——, *La Peste*, Gallimard, Paris, 1947 (*The Plague*, transl. Stuart Gilbert, Knopf, New York, 1948).

——, "Le Renégat," in *L'Exil et le Royaume*, Gallimard, Paris, 1957. Appeared originally as "L'Esprit confus," *Nouvelle Nouvelle Revue Française*, June, 1956, pp. 961-978. (*Exile and the Kingdom*, transl. Justin O'Brien, Knopf, New York, 1958.)

——, "Roger Martin du Gard," *Nouvelle Nouvelle Revue Française*, October, 1955, pp. 641-671.

Casanova, Laurent, *Le Parti communiste, les intellectuels et la nation*, Editions Sociales, Paris, 1949.

Champigny, Robert, *Stages on Sartre's Way*, Indiana University Press, Bloomington, Ind., 1959.

Chamson, André, *La Neige et la fleur*, Gallimard, Paris, 1951.

Charles-Brun, Jean, *Le Roman social en France au XIXème siècle*, V. Giard et E. Brière, Paris, 1910.

Chevalier, Haakon M., *The Ironic Temper; Anatole France and His Time*, Oxford University Press, New York, 1932.

Chevalier, Jacques, "Mon souvenir de Joseph Malègue," *La Table Ronde*, July-August, 1958, pp. 72-81.
Cioran, E.-M., "Sur une civilisation essoufflée," *Nouvelle Nouvelle Revue Française*, May, 1956, pp. 799-816.
Clark, Eleanor, "Death of a Thinker," *Kenyon Review*, Summer, 1941, pp. 322-334.
Clemenceau, Georges, *Le Grand Pan*, G. Charpentier et E. Fasquelle, Paris, 1896.
Cormeau, Nelly, "Révolte contre le temps chez les romanciers d'aujourd'hui," *L'Age Nouveau*, May, 1951, pp. 37-44.
Crossman, Richard, "Introduction," in *The God that Failed*, ed. Richard Crossman, Harper, New York, 1949.
Curtis, Jean-Louis, *Haute-Ecole*, Julliard, Paris, 1950.
——, *Les Justes Causes*, Julliard, Paris, 1954.
David, Jean, *Les Passes du silence*, Editions du Seuil, Paris, 1954.
Delay, Jean, "Dernières rencontres," *Le Figaro Littéraire*, August 30, 1958.
Delhorbe, Cécile, *L'Affaire Dreyfus et les écrivains français*, V. Attinger, Neuchâtel, 1932.
Déon, Michel, *Lettre à un jeune Rastignac*, Fasquelle, Paris, 1956.
Diderot, Denis, *Essai sur les règnes de Claude et de Néron*, Oeuvres complètes, vol. III, Assézat et Tourneux, Garnier, 1875.
Dieckmann, Herbert, *Le Philosophe; Texts and Interpretation*, Washington University Studies, Languages and Literature, No. 18, Saint Louis, Mo., 1948.
Douglas, Kenneth, "The French Intellectuals: Situation and Outlook," in *Modern France*, ed. Edward Mead Earle, Princeton University Press, Princeton, N.J., 1951.
——, "Sartre and the Self-inflicted Wound," *Yale French Studies*, No. 9, pp. 123-131.
Drieu La Rochelle, "Libéraux," *Nouvelle Revue Française*, November, 1942, pp. 600-607.
Duclaux, Émile, *Avant le procès*, P.-V. Stock, Paris, 1898.
Dutourd, Jean, "Baba, ou l'Existence," *Nouvelle Nouvelle Revue Française*, July, 1957, pp. 66-82.
Duveau, Georges, *Les Instituteurs*, Editions du Seuil, Paris, 1957.
Duvignaud, Jean, "Le Marxisme est-il arrêté?" *Les Lettres Nouvelles*, May, 1956, pp. 746-752.
Emmanuel, Pierre, "Réflexions sur la littérature moderne," *La Nef*, December, 1949-January, 1950, pp. 196-202.
Erckmann-Chatrian, *Histoire d'un sous-maître*, J. Hetzel, Paris, 1871.
Feuillerat, Albert, *Paul Bourget*, Plon, Paris, 1937.
Finas, Lucette, *L'Echec*, Editions du Seuil, Paris, 1958.
Fischer, John, "Intellectual with a Gun," *Harper's Magazine*, February, 1956, pp. 10-18.
Flaubert, Gustave, *Bouvard et Pécuchet*, 2 vols., Société Les Belles Lettres, Paris, 1945.
——, *Correspondance*, in *Oeuvres complètes*, 9 vols., Conard, Paris, 1926-1930.
——, *L'Education sentimentale*, Garnier, Paris, 1954.
——, *La Tentation de saint Antoine*, Garnier, Paris, 1936.

Fowlie, Wallace, "Swann and Hamlet: A Note on the Contemporary Hero," *Partisan Review*, May-June, 1942, pp. 195-202.
France, Anatole, *L'Anneau d'améthyste* (*Histoire contemporaine*, III), *Oeuvres complètes*, vol. XII, Calmann-Lévy, Paris, 1927.
——, M. *Bergeret à Paris* (*Histoire contemporaine*, IV), *Oeuvres complètes*, vol. XII, Calmann-Lévy, Paris, 1927.
——, *Crainquebille, Oeuvres complètes*, vol. XIV, Calmann-Lévy, Paris, 1928.
——, *Le Crime de Sylvestre Bonnard, Oeuvres complètes*, vol. II, Calmann-Lévy, Paris, 1925.
——, *Les Dieux ont soif, Oeuvres complètes*, vol. XX, Calmann-Lévy, Paris, 1931.
——, *L'Ile des pingouins, Oeuvres complètes*, vol. XVIII, Calmann-Lévy, Paris, 1929.
——, *Le Mannequin d'osier* (*Histoire contemporaine*, II), *Oeuvres complètes*, vol. XI, Calmann-Lévy, Paris, 1927.
——, "La Morale et la Science. M. Paul Bourget," in *La Vie littéraire*, 3ème série, Calmann-Lévy, Paris, 1905.
——, *Les Opinions de M. Jérôme Coignard*, Calmann-Lévy, Paris, 1920.
——, *L'Orme du mail* (*Histoire contemporaine*, I), *Oeuvres complètes*, vol. XI, Calmann-Lévy, Paris, 1927.
——, *La Révolte des Anges, Oeuvres complètes*, vol. XXII, Calmann-Lévy, Paris, 1930.
——, *La Rôtisserie de la reine Pédauque, Oeuvres complètes*, vol. VIII, Calmann-Lévy, Paris, 1926.
——, *La Vie en fleur*, Calmann-Lévy, Paris, 1922.
——, *La Vie littéraire*, 4 vols. Calmann-Lévy, Paris, 1923-1924.
Frohock, W. M., "André Malraux: The Intellectual as Novelist," *Yale French Studies*, No. 8, 1951, pp. 26-37.
——, *André Malraux and the Tragic Imagination*, Stanford University Press, Stanford, 1952.
Gaulmier, Jean, "Quand Jean-Paul Sartre avait dix-huit ans . . . ," *Le Figaro Littéraire*, July 5, 1958, p. 5.
Guéhenno, Jean, "Le Sens d'un certain honneur," *Nouvelle Revue Française*, December, 1958, pp. 1036-1041.
Gide, André, *Les Faux-Monnayeurs*, Gallimard, Paris, 1925.
——, *L'Immoraliste*, Mercure de France, Paris, 1902.
——, "Worshippers from Afar: André Gide, presented by E. Starkie," in *The God that Failed*, ed. Richard Crossman, Harper, New York, 1949.
Giraud, Raymond, *The Unheroic Hero*, Rutgers University Press, New Brunswick, N.J., 1957.
——, "Unrevolt among the Unwriters in France Today," *Yale French Studies*, No. 24, Summer 1959, pp. 11-17.
Giraud, Victor, *Paul Bourget*, Blond et Gay, Paris, 1934.
Goncourt, Edmond et Jules, *Charles Demailly*, Flammarion-Fasquelle, Paris, 1926.
——, *Manette Salomon*, Flammarion-Fasquelle, Paris, 1925.
——, *Journal des Goncourt—Mémoires de la vie littéraire*, 9 vols., G. Charpentier et Cie, Paris, 1888-1896.
Gorki, Maxim, *On Guard for the Soviet Union* (introduction by Romain Rolland), International Publishers, New York, 1933.

Grenier, Jean, "Alexandre Dumas," *Nouvelle Nouvelle Revue Française,* August, 1957, pp. 330-332.
Guilloux, Louis, *Compagnons,* Grasset, Paris, 1931.
———, *Dossier confidentiel,* Grasset, Paris, 1930.
———, *Hyménée,* Grasset, Paris, 1932.
———, *Jeu de patience,* Gallimard, Paris, 1949.
———, *La Maison du peuple,* Grasset, Paris, 1927.
———, "Notes sur le roman," *Europe,* January 15, 1936, pp. 5-9.
———, "A propos de Jules Vallès," *Nouvelle Revue Française,* October 1, 1930, pp. 437-443.
———, *Le Sang noir,* Gallimard, Paris, 1935 (*Bitter Victory,* transl. Samuel Putnam, McBride and Company, New York, 1936).
Guyon, Bernard, *La Pensée politique et sociale de Balzac,* Armand Colin, Paris, 1947.
Halévy, Daniel, *Apologie pour notre passé,* Cahiers de la Quinzaine, 11th series, Paris, 1910.
Hervé, Pierre, *La Révolution et les fétiches,* La Table Ronde, Paris, 1956.
Hoog, Armand, "André Malraux et la validité du monde," *La Nef,* March, 1947, pp. 121-126.
Howe, Irving, *Politics and the Novel,* Horizon Press, New York, 1957.
Hubert, Renée Riese, *The Dreyfus Affair and the French Novel,* Eagle Enterprises, New York, 1951.
Huszar, George Bernard de, *The Intellectuals; a controversial portrait* (edited with an introduction and overviews), Free Press, Glencoe, Ill., 1960.
Ikor, Roger, *Mise au net,* Albin Michel, Paris, 1957.
Jameson, Frederic, *A Reading of Jean-Paul Sartre,* Yale University Press, New Haven, in press.
Jeanson, Francis, *Sartre par lui-même,* Editions du Seuil, Paris, 1957.
Kanapa, Jean, *Situation de l'intellectuel,* Editions Sociales, Paris, 1957.
Kautsky, Karl, *Le Socialisme et les carrières libérales,* Le Devenir Social, 1895.
Knight, Everett W., *Literature Considered as Philosophy,* Routledge and Kegan Paul, London, 1957.
Koestler, Arthur, *Arrival and Departure,* MacMillan, New York, 1943.
———, "The Initiates," in *The God that Failed,* ed. Richard Crossman, Harper, New York, 1949.
———, "The Intelligentsia," in *The Yogi and the Commissar,* MacMillan, New York, 1945.
La Bruyère, *Les Caractères ou les moeurs de ce siècle,* 2 vols., René Hilsum, Paris, 1931.
Lagardelle, Hubert, *Les Intellectuels devant le socialisme,* Cahiers de la Quinzaine, 2nd series, Paris, 1901.
Lafargue, Paul, *Le Socialisme et les intellectuels,* V. Giard et E. Brière, Paris, 1900.
Lalou, René, *Roger Martin du Gard,* Gallimard, Paris, 1937.
Lanson, Gustave, *Histoire de la littérature française,* Hachette, Paris, 1896.
Lavergne, Antonin, *Jean Coste, ou L'Instituteur de village,* Cahiers de la Quinzaine, 2nd series, Paris, 1901.

Lefebvre, Henri, "Vers un Romantisme révolutionnaire," *Nouvelle Nouvelle Revue Française*, October 1, 1957, pp. 644-672.
Lefèvre, Frédéric, "Une heure avec M. Louis Guilloux," *Les Nouvelles Littéraires*, December 15, 1935.
Levin, Harry, *James Joyce*, New Directions, Norfolk, Connecticut, 1941.
Lewis, R.W.B., *The Picaresque Saint*, Lippincott, Philadelphia and New York, 1959.
L'Hote, Jean, *La Communale*, Editions du Seuil, Paris, 1957.
Magny, Claude-Edmonde, *Histoire du roman français depuis 1918*, vol. I, Editions du Seuil, Paris, 1950.
Malègue, Joseph, *Augustin ou le maître est là*, 2 vols., Editions Spes, Paris, 1933.
Malraux, André, "Adresse aux intellectuels," *Le Cheval de Troie*, July, 1948.
——, *La Condition humaine*, Gallimard, Paris, 1933 (*Man's Fate*, transl. Haakon M. Chevalier, The Modern Library, New York, 1934).
——, *Les Conquérants*, Grasset, Paris, 1928 (*The Conquerors*, transl. Winifred Stephens Whale, Harcourt, Brace, New York, 1929).
——, *L'Espoir*, Gallimard, Paris, 1937 (*Man's Hope*, transl. Stuart Gilbert and Alastair MacDonald, Random House, New York, 1938).
——, "Journal de voyage d'un philosophe, par Hermann Keyserling," *Nouvelle Revue Française*, June, 1929, pp. 884-886.
——, "Laclos," in *Tableaux de la littérature française, XVIIè, XVIIIè siècles*, Gallimard, Paris, 1938, pp. 417-428.
——, "En marge d' 'Hyménée' par Louis Guilloux," *Europe*, June 15, 1932, pp. 304-307.
——, *Les Noyers de l'Altenburg*, Gallimard, Paris, 1948 (*The Walnut Trees of Altenburg*, transl. A. W. Fielding, John Lehmann, London, 1952).
——, *Saturne*, La Galerie de la Pléiade, Paris, 1950.
——, *Le Temps du mépris*, Gallimard, Paris, 1935 (*Days of Wrath*, transl. Haakon M. Chevalier, Random House, New York, 1936).
——, *La Tentation de l'Occident*, Grasset, Paris, 1926.
——, *La Voie royale*, Grasset, Paris, 1930 (*The Royal Way*, transl. Stuart Gilbert, H. Smith and R. Haas, New York, 1935).
Martin du Gard, Roger, "Consultation littéraire.—Lettres à Pierre Margaritis," *Nouvelle Revue Française*, December, 1958, pp. 1117-1135.
——, *Devenir!*, Ollendorff, Paris, 1909.
——, *Jean Barois*, Gallimard, Paris, 1918 (*Jean Barois*, transl. Stuart Gilbert, Viking, New York, 1949).
——, "In Memoriam," in *Oeuvres complètes*, "Bibliothèque de la Pléiade," Paris, 1955, I, pp. 561-576.
——, "Souvenirs autobiographiques et littéraires," in *Oeuvres complètes*, "Bibliothèque de la Pléiade," Paris, 1955, I, pp. xxxix-cxl.
——, *Les Thibault*, 11 vols., Gallimard, Paris, 1922-1940 (*The World of the Thibaults*, transl. Stuart Gilbert, Viking, New York, 1941).
Martinet, Gilles, "La Politique et le roman," *France-Observateur*, April 19, 1956, p. 12.
Martino, Pierre, *Le Roman réaliste sous le Second Empire*, Hachette, Paris, 1913.
Marx, Karl and Friedrich Engels, *Manifesto of the Communist Party*, International Publishers, New York, 1932.

Masson, Loys, *Le Requis civil*, Gallimard, Paris, 1945.

Maupassant, Guy de, "Va t'asseoir," *Le Gaulois*, September 8, 1881.

Mauriac, Claude, *L'Alittérature contemporaine*, Albin Michel, Paris, 1958.

——, *Le Dîner en ville*, Albin Michel, Paris, 1959 (*The Dinner Party*, transl. Merloyd Lawrence, G. Braziller, New York, 1960).

——, *Malraux ou le mal du héros*, Grasset, Paris, 1946.

——, "The 'New Novel' in France," *New York Times Book Review*, June 19, 1960.

Mauriac, François, "Le Métier d'écrivain," *L'Express*, April 5, 1957.

Merleau-Ponty, Maurice, *Sens et non-sens*, Nagel, Paris, 1948.

Michael, Elizabeth, *Joseph Malègue*, Editions Spes, Paris, 1957.

Michelet, Jules, *Le Peuple, Oeuvres complètes*, vol. VIII, Flammarion, Paris, 1893-1899.

"Midnight Novelists," *Yale French Studies*, No. 24, Summer, 1959.

Mille, Pierre, *Le Roman française*, Firmin-Didot, Paris, 1930.

Milosz, Czeslaw, *The Captive Mind*, Knopf, New York, 1953.

Moeller, Charles, "Les Idées," *La Revue Nouvelle*, February 15, 1955, pp. 181-185.

Monod, Gabriel, *Portraits et souvenirs*, C. Lévy, Paris, 1897.

Mounier, Emmanuel, *L'Espoir des désespérés*, Editions du Seuil, Paris, 1953.

Nadeau, Maurice, "Sartre et 'l'Affaire Hervé,' " *Les Lettres Nouvelles*, April, 1956, pp. 591-597.

Naville, Pierre, "L'Intellectuel communiste," *Les Lettres Nouvelles*, June, 1956, pp. 871-886.

——, "Les Mésaventures de Nekrassov," *France-Observateur*, March 8, 1956.

——, "Les Nouvelles mésaventures de J.-P. Sartre," *France-Observateur*, April 19, 1956.

Nietzsche, Friedrich, *The Philosophy of Nietzsche*, The Modern Library, New York, n.d.

Nizan, Paul, *La Conspiration*, Gallimard, Paris, 1938.

Nomad, Max, *Rebels and Renegades*, MacMillan, New York, 1932.

Ortega y Gasset, José, *The Dehumanization of Art and Notes on the Novel*, Princeton University Press, Princeton, N.J., 1948.

Paléologue, Maurice, *Journal de l'Affaire Dreyfus. 1894-1899*, Plon, Paris, 1955.

Parain, Brice, *L'Embarras du choix*, Gallimard, Paris, 1946.

——, *La Mort de Jean Madec*, Grasset, Paris, 1945.

Péguy, Charles, *De la Situation faite au parti intellectuel dans le monde moderne*, Cahiers de la Quinzaine, 8th series, Paris, 1908.

Peyre, Henri, *The Contemporary French Novel*, Oxford University Press, New York, 1955.

Pichon, Jean-Charles, *L'Autobiographe*, Grasset, Paris, 1956.

Picon, Gaëtan, *André Malraux*, Gallimard, Paris, 1945.

——, "Portrait et situation de Roger Martin du Gard," *Mercure de France*, September, 1958, pp. 5-25.

Ponge, Francis, *Le Parti pris des choses*, Gallimard, Paris, 1945.

Quillard, Pierre, "Le Manifeste électoral de M. Ferdinand Brunetière," *La Revue Blanche*, January-April, 1898, pp. 481-485.

Rabain, Jean, "Pourquoi trahissent-ils," *Revue Bleue*, November, 1929, pp. 657-660.

Rahv, Philip, *Image and Idea*, New Directions, New York, 1949.

Remarque, Erich Maria, *All Quiet on the Western Front*, Little, Brown and Co., Boston, 1929.

Renan, Ernest, *L'Avenir de la Science*, Calmann-Lévy, Paris, 1890.

——, *Dialogues et fragments philosophiques*, Calmann-Lévy, Paris, 1876.

——, *Le Prêtre de Némi*, Calmann-Lévy, Paris, 1886.

Revel, J.-F., *Pourquoi des philosophes?*, Julliard, Paris, 1957.

Réville, Albert, *Les Etapes d'un intellectuel*, P.-V. Stock, Paris, 1898.

Richard, Jean-Pierre, *Littérature et sensation*, Editions du Seuil, Paris, 1954.

Robbe-Grillet, Alain, *Les Gommes*, Editions de Minuit, Paris, 1953.

——, "Une Voie pour le roman futur," *Nouvelle Nouvelle Revue Française*, July, 1956, pp. 77-84.

Rolland, Romain, *Clerambault*, Ollendorff, Paris, 1920.

——, *Jean-Christophe*, 10 vols., Ollendorff, Paris, 1909-1912.

Romains, Jules, *Les Hommes de bonne volonté*, 27 vols., Flammarion, Paris, 1932-1952.

Sainte Beuve, "Espoir et voeu du mouvement littéraire et poétique après la révolution de 1830," in *Premiers Lundis*, "Bibliothèque de la Pléiade," vol. I, Gallimard, Paris, 1949.

Sarraute, Nathalie, *L'Ere du soupçon*, Gallimard, Paris, 1956.

Sartre, Jean-Paul, *L'Age de raison* (*Les Chemins de la liberté*, vol. I), Gallimard, Paris, 1945 (*The Age of Reason*, transl. Eric Sutton, Knopf, New York, 1947).

——, "Après Budapest," *L'Express*, November 9, 1956, pp. 13-16.

——, "Avant-propos à *Aden Arabie* de Paul Nizan," in *Aden Arabie*, François Maspero, Paris, 1960.

——, " 'La Conspiration' par Paul Nizan," *Nouvelle Revue Française*, November, 1938, pp. 842-845.

——, *Le Diable et le Bon Dieu*, Gallimard, Paris, 1951.

——, *L'Etre et le Néant*, Gallimard, Paris, 1943.

——, *Huis-clos*, Gallimard, Paris, 1945.

——, *Les Mains sales*, Gallimard, Paris, 1948.

——, "Matérialisme et révolution," in *Situations III*, Gallimard, Paris, 1949, pp. 135-225.

——, *La Mort dans l'âme* (*Les Chemins de la liberté*, vol. III), Gallimard, Paris, 1949 (*Troubled Sleep*, transl. Gerard Hopkins, Knopf, New York, 1951).

——, *Morts sans sépulture*, Marguerat, Lausanne, 1946.

——, *Le Mur* (including also: *La Chambre, Erostrate, Intimité, L'Enfance d'un chef*), Gallimard, Paris, 1939 (*Intimacy and Other Stories*, transl. Lloyd Alexander, New Directions, New York, 1948).

——, *La Nausée*, Gallimard, Paris, 1938 (*Nausea*, transl. Lloyd Alexander, New Directions, New York, 1949).

——, Introductory "Etude" to Roger Stéphane's *Portrait de l'aventurier*, Sagittaire, Paris, 1950.

——, "Présentation des *Temps Modernes*," in *Situations II*, Gallimard, Paris, 1948, pp. 9-30.

——, "Qu'est-ce qu'un collaborateur?" in *Situations III*, Gallimard, Paris, 1949, pp. 43-61.

——, "Qu'est-ce que la littérature?" in *Situations II*, Gallimard, Paris, 1948, pp. 55-330.
——, "Questions de méthode," *Les Temps Modernes*, September, 1957, pp. 338-417.
——, "Le Réformisme et les fétiches," *Les Temps Modernes*, February, 1956, pp. 1153-1164.
——, "Réponse à Albert Camus," *Les Temps Modernes*, August, 1952, pp. 334-353.
——, *Saint Genet, comédien et martyr* (vol. I of the *Oeuvres complètes* of Jean Genet), Gallimard, Paris, 1952.
——, *Les Séquestrés d'Altona*, Gallimard, Paris, 1960.
——, *Le Sursis* (*Les Chemins de la liberté*, vol. II), Gallimard, Paris, 1945 (*The Reprieve*, transl. Eric Sutton, Knopf, New York, 1947).
——, *Théâtre* (*Les Mouches, Huis-clos, Morts sans sépulture, La Putain respectueuse*), Gallimard, Paris, 1947.
Scheler, Max, *Philosophische Weltanschauung*, F. Cohen, Bonn, 1929 (*Philosophical Perspectives*, transl. Oscar A. Haac, Beacon Press, Boston, 1958).
Seillère, Ernest Antoine, *Anatole France, critique de son temps*, Editions de la Nouvelle Revue Critique, Paris, 1934.
Silone, Ignazio, "The Initiates," in *The God that Failed*, ed. Richard Crossman, Harper, New York, 1949.
Simon, Pierre-Henri, *Histoire de la littérature française au XXè siècle*, 2 vols., Armand Colin, Paris, 1956.
——, *L'Homme en procès*, La Braconnière, Neuchâtel, 1950.
——, *L'Esprit et l'Histoire*, Armand Colin, Paris, 1954.
——, *Procès du héros*, Editions du Seuil, Paris, 1950.
——, *Les Témoins de l'homme: De Proust à Camus*, Armand Colin, Paris, 1951.
Spender, Stephen, "Worshippers from afar," in *The God that Failed*, ed. Richard Crossman, Harper, New York, 1949.
Stéphane, Roger, *Portrait de l'aventurier*, Sagittaire, Paris, 1950.
Sue, Eugène, *Martin l'enfant trouvé*, F. Gaillardet, New York, 1846.
Taine, Hippolyte, *Sa Vie et sa correspondance*, 4 vols., Hachette, Paris, 1905-1914.
Tardieu, Jean, *Théâtre de Chambre I*, Gallimard, Paris, 1955.
Tieghem, Philippe van, "Jean Barois et nous," *Nouvelle Revue Française*, December, 1958, pp. 1064-1067.
Thérive, André, "Note sur La Nausée," *Le Temps*, July 14-15, 1938.
Thibaudet, Albert, "Pour l'Histoire du parti intellectuel," *Nouvelle Revue Française*, August, 1932, pp. 265-272.
——, "Réflexions—Péguy et Bergson," *Nouvelle Revue Française*, April, 1931, pp. 580-592.
——, *La République des Professeurs*, Grasset, Paris, 1927.
Thierry-Maulnier, "Les Intellectuels avec nous," *Le Figaro Littéraire*, November 26, 1955.
Tison-Braun, Micheline, *La Crise de l'Humanisme, I, 1890-1914*, Nizet, Paris, 1958.
Toynbee, Arnold, A Study of History, 2nd ed., 6 vols., Oxford University Press, London, 1939.
Trilling, Lionel, *The Liberal Imagination*, Viking, New York, 1951.

Unamuno y Jugo, Miguel de, *Amor y pedagogía*, Henrich, Barcelona, 1902.
——, *The Tragic Sense of Life*, Macmillan, London, 1926.
Vailland, Roger, *Drôle de jeu*, Corrêa, Paris, 1945.
Vaillant-Couturier, Paul, *Au Service de l'Esprit*, Éditions Sociales Internationales, Paris, 1936.
Valéry, Paul, *Monsieur Teste*, Gallimard, Paris, 1927 (*Monsieur Teste*, transl. Jackson Mathews, Knopf, New York, 1947).
——, *Propos sur l'Intelligence*, A l'Enseigne de la Porte Etroite, Paris, 1926.
Vallès, Jules, *Le Bachelier* (*Jacques Vingtras*, vol. II), Les Editeurs Français Réunis, Paris, 1950.
——, *L'Enfant* (*Jacques Vingtras*, vol. I), Les Editeurs Français Réunis, Paris, 1950.
——, *L'Insurgé* (*Jacques Vingtras*, vol. III), Les Editeurs Français Réunis, Paris, 1950.
Vercors, *Colères*, Albin Michel, Paris, 1956 (*The Insurgents*, transl. Rita Barisse, Harcourt, Brace, New York, 1956).
——, *Les Yeux et la lumière*, Paris, 1948.
Vigny, Alfred de, *Oeuvres complètes*, "Bibliothèque de la Pléiade," 2 vols., Gallimard, Paris, 1948.
Villefosse, Louis de, *Le Tocsin*, Julliard, Paris, 1955.
Villiers de l'Isle-Adam, Jean-Marie, *L'Eve future*, Mercure de France, Paris, 1914.
Wright, Richard, "The Initiates," in *The God that Failed*, ed. Richard Crossman, Harper, New York, 1949.
Wyzewa, Theodor de, "Introduction" to Paul Bourget, *Le Disciple*, Nelson, Paris, n.d.
Yvetot, Georges, *Les Intellectuels et la C.G.T.*, La Publication Sociale, Paris, n.d.
Zola, Emile, *L'Assommoir*, Fasquelle, Paris, 1958.
——, *Nos Auteurs dramatiques*, Bibliothèque Charpentier, Paris, 1896.
——, *Le Bête humaine*, Les Oeuvres complètes, vol. XX, François Bernouard, Paris, 1928 (*The Human Beast*, transl. Louis Colman, Julian Press, New York, 1932).
——, *Correspondance*, Les Oeuvres complètes, vol. XLIX (1858-1871) and vol. L (1872-1902), François Bernouard, Paris, 1928-1929.
——, *La Débâcle*, Les Oeuvres complètes, vols. XXII-XXIII, François Bernouard, Paris, 1927-1928.
——, *Le Docteur Pascal*, François Bernouard, Paris, 1928.
——, *Fécondité* (*Les Quatre Évangiles*, vol. I), Les Oeuvres complètes, vols. XXIX-XXX, François Bernouard, Paris, 1928.
——, *Germinal*, Les Oeuvres complètes, vol. XVI, François Bernouard, Paris, 1928.
——, *Lourdes* (*Les Trois Villes*, vol. I), Les Oeuvres complètes, vol. XXV, François Bernouard, Paris, 1929.
——, *L'Œuvre*, 2 vols., Fasquelle, "Bibliothèque Charpentier," Paris, 1952.
——, *Paris* (*Les Trois Villes*, vol. III), Les Oeuvres complètes, vol. XXVIII, François Bernouard, Paris, 1929.
——, *Le Roman expérimental*, Fasquelle, Paris, 1909.

——, *Rome* (*Les Trois Villes*, vol. II), *Les Oeuvres complètes*, vols. XXVI-XXVII, François Bernouard, Paris, 1929.

——, *La Terre*, *Les Oeuvres complètes*, vol. XVIII, François Bernouard, Paris, 1928 (*Earth*, transl. Ann Lindsay, Elek, London, New York, 1954).

——, *Travail* (*Les Quatre Evangiles*, vol. II), *Les Oeuvres complètes*, vols. XXXI-XXXII, François Bernouard, Paris, 1928.

——, *Vérité* (*Les Quatre Evangiles*, vol. III), François Bernouard, Paris, 1928.

——, *La Vérité en marche* (and *Nouvelle campagne*), François Bernouard, Paris, 1928.

Index

251